Dream Derby

Dream Derby

The Myth and Legend of Black Gold

AVALYN HUNTER

UNIVERSITY PRESS OF KENTUCKY

A note to the reader: Some of the quotations printed in this volume contain racially insensitive language. The author has chosen to document the original terminology to provide full historical context for the events under discussion. Discretion is advised.

Scholarly publisher for the Commonwealth,
serving Bellarmine University, Berea College, Centre
College of Kentucky, Eastern Kentucky University,
The Filson Historical Society, Georgetown College,
Kentucky Historical Society, Kentucky State University,
Morehead State University, Murray State University,
Northern Kentucky University, Spalding University,
Transylvania University, University of Kentucky,
University of Louisville, University of Pikeville,
and Western Kentucky University.
All rights reserved.

Editorial and Sales Offices: The University Press of Kentucky
663 South Limestone Street, Lexington, Kentucky 40508-4008
www.kentuckypress.com

Library of Congress Cataloging-in-Publication Data

Names: Hunter, Avalyn, author.
Title: Dream derby : the myth and legend of Black Gold / Avalyn Hunter.
Description: Lexington, Kentucky : The University Press of Kentucky, [2023] | Series:
    Horses in history | Includes index.
Identifiers: LCCN 2023005967 | ISBN 9780813198040 (hardcover) | ISBN
    9780813199191 (pbk.) | ISBN 9780813198064 (pdf) | ISBN 9780813198057
    (epub)
Subjects: LCSH: Black Gold (Race horse) | Race horses—Oklahoma—Biography. |
    Horse-racing—United States—History—20th century. | Kentucky Derby.
Classification: LCC SF355.B55 H86 2023 | DDC 798.4—dc23/eng/20230324
LC record available at https://lccn.loc.gov/2023005967

This book is printed on acid-free paper meeting
the requirements of the American National Standard
for Permanence in Paper for Printed Library Materials.

Manufactured in the United States of America.

Member of the Association
of University Presses

To Tab, the love of my life

Contents

Introduction
The Legend

There were no fancy grandstands, no bands providing music, and none of the trappings of wealth around the dusty fairgrounds strip near Chickasha, Oklahoma—just two mares kicking up clouds of dust as they charged down the lane that divided a whooping, shouting crowd of Chickasaws, Cherokees, and whites. The one in front was a chunky little two-year-old, Useeit, and she was flying; the other was a bigger, older mare, Belle Thompson, and she was coming hard. Amid the crowd's frenzied yells, Belle Thompson stuck her head in front right at the finish. Money changed hands as bets were paid off, and the crowd slowly dispersed.

Among the spectators was an Oklahoma rancher named Al Hoots. Some said he was Indian, others that he was part Indian or just married to an Indian, but everyone agreed he had an eye for a horse. He walked over to where one of the owners was standing about; words and a handshake were exchanged; and then Hoots went over to collect the horse he had just traded eighty acres of land for—not the victorious Belle Thompson, but the defeated Useeit.

For the next seven years, Hoots raced Useeit in match races and at little tracks all over the West. She kept food on his table and a roof over his head wherever he went, but she was much more than a breadwinner to him; she was his pet, and everyone else around the races knew how Hoots felt about her. Then the day came when Hoots entered Useeit in a selling race at Juarez, Mexico. She lost, and he was consoling his favorite when another man came to the stable with a halter and lead rope. He had put in a claim for Useeit, he said, and the mare was now his; he had come to take her away.

Hoots was shocked. He had not known this could happen, not understanding the terms of the race, or perhaps he understood them but believed that everyone would honor a gentlemen's agreement about not taking his beloved Useeit. It didn't matter. When the man tried to put his halter on the mare, shock became rage, and Hoots hauled out a shotgun. The man took off, and that night Hoots got on a train with Useeit and headed back for Oklahoma.

By the time Hoots got back to his home in Tulsa, the news was out: he and Useeit were outlawed and could never race again. Hoots didn't care. He still had Useeit, and he was sure that someday Useeit would have a foal that would grow up into a great racehorse. And if he couldn't race the foal, his Osage wife, Rosa, could.

That was Al Hoots's dream, but before it could happen, he became sick. Soon it became clear that he was dying. He called Rosa to his side.

"Promise me you will never sell Useeit," he said. "I have had a vision. Send her to Kentucky and breed her to Black Toney. She will have a colt, and the colt will win the Kentucky Derby for you."

Rosa promised, and Hoots died, leaving her with the promise and not much else. She could not afford to send Useeit far away to Kentucky, but the discovery of oil on the reservation lands the Hootses had ranched changed that a few years later. The "black gold" made Rosa Hoots rich, and with some of that money, she fulfilled her husband's last request and sent Useeit to Black Toney. When a colt arrived—as Al Hoots said it would—Rosa named it "Black Gold" for the oil that had made the mating possible.

No one except Rosa believed that the colt would amount to much. He was too small and scrawny; his trainer was a hard-drinking ranch hand who overworked him and ignored his frequent lameness; and the jockey he got along best with was a bush-league kid barely out of his teens. But Black Gold had speed and heart, and those with a bent for the mystical said he had something else going for him; he had the spirit of Al Hoots looking after him and urging him on. He kept winning races, and more and more people starting believing in him. And on May 17, 1924, Hoots's prophecy was fulfilled as Black Gold won the "Golden Jubilee," the fiftieth Kentucky Derby.

That is the legend behind Black Gold, whose story is one of the best-known and most romantic in Kentucky Derby lore. The truth is less known but perhaps even stranger, for in real-life history, Black Gold's tale is still the story of a dead man's dream and a woman's determination to make that dream a reality.

Black Gold in 1923. Photograph by H. C. Ashby. Courtesy of the Keeneland Library
Meadors Collection.

1

A Man and a Mare

Legend and history agree that Black Gold's story began with a man and a mare. The details of exactly when and where have been blurred by time, but sometime in 1910, Alfred Worth Hoots bought a little bay filly named Useeit for a price most commonly reported as eighty acres of good grazing land near Skiatook, Oklahoma.

From there, the tale becomes a matter of sorting out facts from myth—a task akin to piecing together a broken mosaic from a heap of fragments containing both its lost tesserae and random bits of glass and pottery. From time to time a tantalizing picture may emerge, but it is always incomplete and perhaps altered significantly by the inclusion of mistakenly introduced material or the telescoping of events that took place over a period of months or even years. So it is with the legend's picture of the first meeting between Hoots and Useeit: a match race somewhere in the grasslands of northeastern Oklahoma or at the half-mile track of a county fair, a narrow defeat for the fleet but inexperienced filly, and an impulse purchase of the loser by a man of Indian heritage who saw a horse that spoke to his soul.

The truth is both more complex and more prosaic, but many elements of the legend do correspond with reality, beginning with Useeit herself. Foaled before Oklahoma had officially become a state, she was born on the ranch of Charles B. Campbell near the town of Minco, sometime in the spring of 1907. John Riddle had worked for Campbell as a ranch hand, and when he got too old to continue the work he left, taking Useeit with him either as a partial payment on his back wages or as an outright purchase. Either way, the future dam of a Kentucky Derby winner cost him about $200.[1]

It was a high price for an "Indian pony" or an ordinary saddle horse at the time, but then Useeit was neither. Although some racing writers insisted that she was an Arizona range mare, a quarter horse, or even a mustang, she was in fact a registered Thoroughbred, if not from particularly blue-blooded lines. Bred from Campbell's Thoroughbred mare Effie M., she was sired by Bonnie Joe, a Thoroughbred stallion who stood at the nearby ranch of long-time owner-trainer Jim "Uncle Jimmie" Gray. Bonnie Joe had never raced after injuring himself as a yearling, but after being installed as a stallion on Gray's spread, the horse rapidly developed a reputation with horsemen all over the Southwest as a reliable sire of fast runners. Having been around Useeit since the time she was foaled, Riddle undoubtedly had a pretty good idea of what he was getting for his money, and sometime in 1909, he started getting that money back by racing her.

Organized race meets with stewards, judges, and rulebooks that were patterned after the rules of racing long used farther east existed at Oklahoma City and Tulsa, but much of the racing that took place in the newborn state of Oklahoma was in what was colloquially called "the bush," without formal sanction. That was where Useeit began her racing career, running against a motley assortment of Thoroughbreds, half-breds, and who-knew-what in more or less impromptu match races—the kind of events where the starting line was scratched in the dirt and a dropped blanket or hat by the side of the path served to mark the finish a quarter mile or so away, and where the only rules were those the participants agreed on beforehand. Varying degrees of chicanery were not uncommon, especially when some local champion was meeting an opponent from outside the area.

Bush races invariably drew a crowd of Cherokees, Chickasaws, Creeks, or Osages along with the local whites. The onlookers lined both sides of whatever dusty strip was serving as the track, whooping, yelling, and tossing their hats into the air as the horses charged through the lane between them. Betting between the owners of the participants and among the spectators was heavy and often offered more profit than the tiny purses involved. In one such match, Useeit may have crossed paths with another legend in the making, as she was said to have been narrowly defeated by a mare trained by Ben Jones, then racing in the Southwest and later to gain fame as the trainer of six Kentucky Derby winners.[2]

Exactly how many of these unsanctioned races Useeit competed in will probably never be known, but she had apparently done well enough that when the Tulsa Racing Association held a sanctioned meeting in the fall of 1909, Riddle took her there to try her luck. After finishing dead last in a field of six on October 21 and running third in a field of four on October 25, she won her first official race by three lengths on October 26, going four and one-half furlongs against other two-year-olds. For her effort, she earned a purse of seventy-five dollars.

Among the horsemen attending the Tulsa races was Al Hoots, whose Firecatcher (a gelding he co-owned with his son, Alfred) was also racing at the meet. Firecatcher was not having a great deal of success that October, but that was not a problem for Hoots, a successful rancher and farmer who could well afford to race a horse for the fun of it. The tall, lean Illinois native had been one of the area's more prominent cattlemen and had at one point controlled the grazing rights to tens of thousands of acres in the area. He and his wife, Rosa, held multiple properties in Tulsa and its environs, and both were active in the real estate market. He was also a son-in-law of Jane Appleby, the wealthiest woman in Tulsa, and he and Rosa were established members of Tulsa society, with mention of their activities regularly seen in the local newspapers' social columns.

At fifty, Hoots was largely out of the cattle business and was spending more time in town than on his ranch near Skiatook. His health was not what it had once been after a severe case of pneumonia a few years earlier, and he had hired hands to run the day-to-day agricultural operations at the farm, leaving him free to stay in his Tulsa house on South Detroit Avenue with his wife and children. Nonetheless, he was used to outdoor activity, a need that town life could not entirely satisfy. Having a racehorse or two provided a compromise, a way that, as Rosa Hoots later said, he could "loaf around and take things easy" while enjoying a link back to more vigorous days.[3]

Whether or not Al Hoots took notice of Useeit at the Tulsa meeting is a moot point, as Riddle had no intent of selling at that time. That changed by the time the man and the mare crossed paths again in June 1910. At that time, the Hootses were in town for the seventeen-day summer race meeting at the Oklahoma City fairgrounds, bringing Firecatcher with them.

The Hootses won one race with Firecatcher and finished third with him in another, but Al Hoots was keeping an eye out for a chance to acquire another racehorse. As it happened, Useeit was on the market. The fifth race on the June 25 card was a three-furlong race intended as a spot for horses that had been racing out in the bush during the spring, and that was where John Riddle entered Useeit.

Even by the standards of a minor track such as Oklahoma City, it was a cheap race, with a purse of just one hundred dollars. It was also a selling race, one in which the rules of racing called for the winner to be put up for auction after the race at a fixed initial price. If no one put in a bid for the horse, the original owner kept the animal. If someone else chose to make a claim by filing the required paperwork and putting up the minimum allowed bid, the auction was on and continued until all but one person dropped out of the bidding. In most such races, losing horses could also be bid on, provided that the claimant also had a horse in the same race and was willing to meet a minimum price that equaled the price tag placed at entry plus the value of the winner's purse.

The selling race system had its abuses; sometimes a rival owner would bid up a horse out of spite, forcing the original owner to pay an inflated price to keep the animal, and sometimes "selling-race wars" developed in which one owner or trainer deliberately targeted another's horses, usually leading to an escalation of hostilities as the targeted owner reciprocated. There were also cases in which an owner deliberately dropped a horse into lesser company than its ability warranted to pull off a betting coup, counting on being able to repurchase the animal out of gambling winnings even if someone else tried to claim it. Still, selling races served a purpose in encouraging owners to race their horses at the true level of their ability, since a horse raced above its level was unlikely to win, and a horse raced below its level was almost certain to draw a claim. At tracks where virtually all the owners and trainers knew one another, gentlemen's agreements against claiming animals that were properly placed were often in force, and under such circumstances, a horse might race dozens of times without changing owners.

Useeit was assigned only 106 pounds for her race against a minimum of 119 pounds on all her opponents. Even with a big weight advantage, she was the fifth choice out of a field of seven at odds of 5–1, suggesting that she had not fared well in her most recent matches. She cleaned up at Oklahoma City, though. Four lengths in front at the stretch call, she had six lengths on her nearest pursuer at the finish, and her time of 0:33¼ was said to have been the fastest ever seen at the track.[4]

The filly did not change hands following the race, but when Riddle moved on with her to the summer Tulsa meeting, he let it be known that he was willing to sell if the price was right.[5] She remained in his ownership throughout the meeting, but Hoots, who had returned to Tulsa at the conclusion of the state fair, was keeping an eye on her with increasing interest. When the filly easily whipped his Firecatcher and four others in a race on July 16—the closing day of the Tulsa meeting—he was ready to start negotiating with Riddle about the purchase of a mare he knew he had to have.

Why Hoots had become so enamored of Useeit is anyone's guess. Later descriptions of her agree that she was small, chunky, and unimpressive in appearance. She had raw speed, though. Hoots had seen her scorching three-furlong win for himself, and there were reports that unofficial timers had caught the filly reeling off the first eighth-mile of a half-mile race in 0:10⅕, an opening split seldom equaled even by championship-class sprinters a century later.[6] She had learned her lessons well from the bush races of her youth: get off fast, get out front, and make the opposition chase you until you or they cracked. She was intelligent and had plenty of competitive spirit.[7] And perhaps Hoots saw something else in her, something that sparked a born horseman's intuition that could not be learned or explained. Whatever he saw, it was worth trading a tract of good land for, a transaction apparently finalized in late August 1910.[8] For Riddle, the trade probably represented a measure of security for an aging man. For Hoots, it was the beginning of a love affair that would last for the rest for his life.

2

Useeit's Odyssey

Prices for undeveloped farmland in the neighborhood of Skiatook were running at seventeen to eighteen dollars per acre in 1910 according to advertisements in the *Skiatook Sentinel,* so Useeit was not cheap by Oklahoma standards, especially given that she may have suffered some illness or injury that threatened to curtail her racing career. When the Hootses went to the Oklahoma State Fair and its race meeting in September, they brought Firecatcher with them but not Useeit; in fact, Rosa Hoots recalled that Useeit had been bought as a prospective broodmare.[1] Nonetheless, once it became obvious that Useeit was healthy enough to race, Al Hoots was not immune to the itch to see more of what she could do, especially with the Hootses' friends and neighbors encouraging them. As Rosa later related, "Everyone thought it was a pity that she was not raced, so we started out with her."[2]

Thus, after six months away from the races, Useeit's name came up in the entries at Jacksonville's Moncrief Park,[3] where the Hootses were enjoying a Florida getaway from the Oklahoma winter. They were accompanied by Riddle, who served as Useeit's trainer,[4] and they were probably acquainted with another Oklahoman who made the trip east: Guy Gray, a son of Uncle Jimmie Gray, who trained and raced horses all over western North America and had been active at the Oklahoma State Fair in 1910. Buying horses out of selling races was a large part of Gray's business, and he was busy at Moncrief Park, picking up a number of horses there.

Useeit was not one of them, but Gray could probably have bought her had he cared to. Along with her stablemate Firecatcher, Useeit raced at Moncrief

Park beginning in mid-December 1910, but she was hampered by a lung infec-tion—possibly a recurrence of earlier illness, given her long layoff.[5] Repeated attempts at winning a purse race or handicap with her fell short, and by mid-February 1911, Al Hoots was apparently ready to risk losing her, for Useeit was entered in a six-furlong selling race on February 18. She ran up the track yet again but was put in another selling race on February 27, this one at five and a half furlongs. This time she got the job done, scoring her first win in Hoots's colors at 8–1 odds.

After that, the filly went into another losing streak, which lasted until the meeting closed at the end of March. She next appeared in newspaper accounts in September 1911, when Guy Gray (who may have been lessee as well as trainer) took her up to the Lake City track near Coeur d'Alene, Idaho. From there, she moved over to Spokane, Washington, where she won a couple of races and set a track record before the season closed out in Octo-ber. On her reemergence in June 1912, she won three races at Oklahoma City for Al Hoots before returning to the Northwest in Gray's care, winning races at Minoru Park near Vancouver and at Spokane. She then returned to Oklahoma for the winter.

Useeit's odyssey was not unique among western racehorses of her time. Most venues held racing for only two or three weeks at a time, so of necessity horses and their trainers and owners spent long days on trains, traveling from race meet to race meet. Close quarters, stress, poor ventilation, and a lack of modern sanitation practices meant that "shipping fever" (a catch-all term that could cover everything from mild viral infections to pneumonia) was a con-stant risk for stakes horses and selling platers alike. Boxcars were the common mode of transportation; only wealthy owners could afford a luxurious private horse car to minimize their animals' discomfort and exposure to infection, and owners with that kind of money weren't frequenting the kind of minor-league tracks where Useeit was running.

If a horse managed to avoid getting sick while riding the rails, that didn't mean its hardships were over. There was a reason why horsemen commonly referred to the minor tracks as being on the "leaky roof circuit," and fights between trainers or grooms over those stalls that actually stayed dry during a rainy stretch were commonplace—the more so since horsemen were often sleeping in the barn alongside their charges. Rodent control was a constant problem, as was finding a reliable source for clean bedding and good feed. At that, the horses as often as not ate better-quality food than the people, who usually lived on coffee and greasy-spoon fare from the track kitchens when they had a little money and on whatever they could scrounge up when they didn't. Purses were small, and horses were raced hard and often to make ends meet until the winter closed down the season at all but a few southern tracks.

Tulsa ran a race meeting in the spring of 1913, and that was where Useeit emerged from winter quarters, winning the Inaugural Handicap on opening day. Hoots and Gray had parted ways, with the latter heading back up to Idaho, and under ordinary circumstances Useeit might well have stayed in Oklahoma, where she was popular and a consistent winner.

What changed things was Al Hoots's physical condition, which was continuing to go downhill. Sometime that same spring he visited his physician, who advised him to travel to cooler climes for his health's sake. Deciding he could combine medical necessity with his favorite pastime, Hoots headed up to Quebec, Canada, and took his wife and Useeit with him. He also took along one other person: Hanley Webb, who was now Useeit's trainer and would become a central figure in Black Gold's story.

Webb was as unlikely a figure to become involved with a top racehorse as any in racing history. Born about 1870 in Missouri to farming folk from Kentucky, he had drifted farther west as a young man. As other western figures did, he seems to have bumped about on both sides of the law; his first mention in newspapers of the time was following an arrest in Topeka, Kansas, for having obtained six hundred dollars "under false pretenses" with some mortgaged cattle.[6] He later lived the life of an itinerant cowboy before becoming a small-town lawman in the Indian Territory.[7] Along the way, he acquired the nickname "Three-Fingered Webb" (thanks to an accident) and a drinking habit.[8] His use of alcohol was perhaps an anodyne for chronic loneliness; he had neither wife nor family, and over the course of his lifetime could probably count his close friends on the fingers of his injured hand. He had no experience with training racehorses or caring for Thoroughbreds prior to his making Al Hoots's acquaintance, and only friendship seems to explain why Hoots would have placed his prize mare in Webb's care.

Webb was never at ease in a suit and tie. No matter how formal the surroundings, he routinely wore a soft shirt with an open collar, a battered broad-brimmed hat that hid a balding pate, and an old rain slicker that draped comfortably over his short, round, bowlegged figure. His clothing was one with his personality. A living stereotype of the old-time westerner, he could be gregarious enough with those he knew well, but to those outside that circle he was taciturn, self-contained, and slow to admit any need for help or change.

On taking over Useeit's training, Webb began sending the mare through a series of long daily gallops to increase her fitness. Perhaps he hoped to build her stamina as well, but if such was his aim, he was to be disappointed. She remained a pure sprinter, and though he did get her to stretch out as far as six furlongs, that was her absolute limit. Nonetheless, Useeit thrived on the work, and she was probably in the best condition of her life when she got onto the train for Canada.

In the pre–World War I era and during the decade after the war, racing in Ontario and Quebec tended to be where wealthy eastern horsemen sent the second or third strings from their stables in June through September, horses that were not worthy of Saratoga or Belmont Park but were too good just to let go. It was also one of the summer stops for decent horses from Kentucky and Chicago that were not quite up to standard for a trip to the elite New York circuit, and it drew in the best southwestern horses as well. Compared to the cheap tracks where Useeit had been racing, it was a marked step up in class—in Canadian bettors' opinion, too big a step for an unknown mare whose previous form was highly suspect, especially in view of her previous undistinguished foray against eastern competition.

Useeit first appeared in Montreal, and she had not fully recovered from the long train ride to Quebec when she was entered in a selling race to be run on June 7 at Blue Bonnets over five and one-half furlongs. Sent off at 12–1, she ran up the track and appeared to confirm that she was in over her head. She was out of action for a month after that as Webb patiently got her back into shape. By the time she made her first start at Windsor, Ontario, on July 19, she was apparently in top form again. Made a co-favorite at 4–1 by a contingent of horsemen up from Texas—men who knew something about her true ability—she skipped home a winner. She next raced at Hamilton, where she was hailed as the "Oklahoma Flyer" after setting a track record for five and one-half furlongs on July 26.

Useeit's next outing resulted in an upset by Calgary at Fort Erie on August 6, but her second in that race may have been an even bigger feather in her cap than her victories, for the horse immediately behind her was Leochares, a top eastern sprinter who won several stakes races in New York and Maryland during his career. His fame would not outlast his lifetime, but the horse that finished fourth was another story; she was Pan Zareta, who was building a legend of her own. "Panzy" was still only a three-year-old, but she was already widely considered the fastest filly in the West, and Useeit was to see plenty more of her later on.

Returning from Fort Erie to Windsor, Useeit finished her Canadian tour with another win on August 16. The Windsor meeting still had a week to go at that point, but for Al Hoots, it was time to go home. He had business to attend to in Tulsa, and perhaps he was pleasantly anticipating a bit of bragging regarding his favorite when the Tulsa Jockey Club's race meeting came around in September. Vindicating the promise he had seen in her when she was a three-year-old, Useeit had faced the toughest competition she had yet encountered and had more than held her own. Her Canadian performances were also a vindication of Hoots's decision to engage Webb as her trainer, for the mare had never run better in her life.

The journey home was uneventful and pleasant. Allowed to stretch her legs at the Mineral Springs track near Porter, Indiana, on the way home, Useeit upheld her growing reputation with an easy win in the feature race on August 21 before rejoining the stream of horses headed down from Canada, Mineral Springs, and western venues as far away as Butte, Montana, for what promised to be the biggest and most competitive Tulsa race meeting yet. She was joined in her journey by a new stablemate, Husky Lad, a horse that Hoots bought at Mineral Springs from Captain W. F. Cisco.[9]

Webb had apparently learned a lesson about throwing Useeit into action too soon after a long trip, for Useeit did not appear immediately when the racing started on September 1. Instead, she was reserved for the first big feature of the meeting, a handicap on September 11—a rather ambitious spot, perhaps, as the race was carded at seven furlongs, farther than she had ever raced. Local fans awaited her appearance eagerly, but on race day, Useeit and five other entrants scratched out of the eleven-horse field. Ostensibly the reason was a muddy track, something that Useeit had never handled well, and Husky Lad salvaged matters for the Hoots stable by winning in her absence. But when the meeting closed on September 18, Useeit still had not made an appearance—and though neither Hoots nor anyone else knew it yet, it was a harbinger of the future, for Useeit would never race again on the tracks of her native state.

3

The Queen of Juarez

Whatever the cause of her inaction, Useeit did not return to the races until late in November 1913. In seasons past, she would have been well into a winter break at the ranch by then, but that year, Hoots and Webb took Useeit and Husky Lad south to Ciudad Juarez, Mexico, where Terrazas Park was operating just across the border from El Paso, Texas.

Usually referred to simply as "Juarez," Terrazas Park had a short but colorful history lasting from its opening in December 1909 until it shut down in 1917. Much of that color came from Mexican politics, for about six months after the track's opening, Ciudad Juarez had been captured by forces led by Pascual Orozco and Pancho Villa in one of the major early battles of the Mexican Revolution. A second battle in 1913 left Villa as the primary power-holder in the area, and he became the provisional governor of the state of Chihuahua (in which Juarez lay), a post he held into 1914. Extremely popular for a time and with a widespread reputation as a Robin Hood figure, he had fallen from official power and lost most of his army by late 1915, though he continued guerrilla activities in Chihuahua until granted amnesty and a large hacienda in 1920 by interim Mexican president Adolfo de la Huerta in exchange for his cessation of hostilities against the Mexican government. Villa was assassinated three years later, most likely by political enemies.

Villa was partial to an occasional day at the races when he was not off fighting or starring as himself in Hollywood films, and Terrazas Park officials took care not to give him offense, to the extent that they would dip into track operating funds to give him a "winner" when a horse he backed failed to come through. The track's relationships with the other revolutionaries and guerrillas who came rampaging through the area while race meets were in progress were more variable. It was a running joke among horsemen that track officials sent someone into town every morning to ensure that they knew who was in power on any given day, and it was also rumored that races took place between gunfights, with bullets sometimes zipping across the track. For the most part, this was simply a bit of exaggeration in keeping with the "Wild West" reputation of the place. Although the racing plant was Mexican property, most of the horses were not, and even the wildest and most high-handed of the revolutionary commanders generally thought better of molesting *yanquis* or seizing their property while they were at Terrazas Park. The track and the gamblers it attracted to Juarez were a golden goose they were reluctant to kill, and besides, one never knew when one might need to duck across the Texas border for sanctuary.

Opening day at Juarez fell on November 27 in 1913, and neither Americans nor Mexicans were letting a little thing like a civil war dampen their spirits. Although Villa had secured control of the area only two weeks earlier, accommodations in both Juarez and El Paso were full to the bursting point, as were the stables and the stands at the track, and eight bookies were on hand to accommodate those desiring a bit of betting action. Adding to the festive atmosphere, it had been announced that Villa himself would be in attendance as the track's guest of honor, and two military bands were present to provide suitable music for the occasion.

Villa got a hero's welcome when he and his staff showed up after the fifth race, but he was too late for the real fireworks down on the track. Those took place in the fourth race, the Juarez Handicap. Carded at six furlongs and carrying a purse of $1,500 in American dollars, the race had drawn an excellent group of nominees by anyone's standards, headed by the great sprinter Iron Mask, Pan Zareta, and future Hall of Fame member Roamer. The nominees also included Useeit, who had been assigned 110 pounds for the event.

It was an ambitious placing, even after Iron Mask was declared out as not quite fit enough to carry his 136-pound weight assignment against such a field. Roamer, still only a two-year-old, also declined the issue and apparently did not even ship to Juarez, but that left Useeit still facing Pan Zareta, Juarez track record–setter Upright, and other proven speedsters at six furlongs rather than her favored five. Still, Hoots and Webb apparently thought her up to the task and not without reason, considering that Useeit was carrying eight pounds less than Pan Zareta. Given that Useeit had conceded Pan Zareta ten pounds over the same distance and beaten her home by a length and a half in August, their confidence was not unreasonable.

Nonetheless, it was misplaced, for Pan Zareta in November at Juarez was not the same filly she had been in Canada more than three months earlier. She had grown and matured and was now far more formidable than when Useeit had faced her in Ontario. Further, she was racing on her favorite track, where she had won her first races and where she had been the unquestioned queen of the 1912–1913 winter meeting. In the Juarez Handicap, Pan Zareta proved that she had no intention of relinquishing her crown to Useeit or anyone else. She simply outbroke and outran her older rival, and Useeit had to settle for third behind the Texas-bred filly after being overhauled by the fast-closing Mimorioso in the stretch.

That evened the score between the "Texas Whirlwind" and the "Oklahoma Flyer," and state pride heightened the interest in the mares' next meeting, which took place on December 2 in another six-furlong handicap. It wasn't even close. Although Pan Zareta was not quite able to concede twenty-two pounds to longshot Vested Right, she carried her 124-pound impost well enough to beat everything else. That included Useeit, who broke first but never looked like a winner during the running and ended up next to last after being shut off entering the stretch. She had carried 110 pounds.

Useeit atoned for her humiliating defeat on December 11, when she led all the way under future Hall of Fame jockey Johnny Loftus to win another six-furlong sprint. Again carrying 110 pounds, she stopped the timer's watch in 1:11, which (according to the *El Paso Times*) was only a fifth of a second off the world record for the distance, and her victims included future record holder Dorothy Dean. But when wheeled back in two days to face Pan Zareta at five and one-half furlongs, she was once again outrun and outclassed. Making nothing of a 126-pound impost, Pan Zareta took the track from the start and equaled her own American record of 1:04⅗ for the distance without apparent effort. Useeit, carrying only 105 pounds, was two lengths behind her in second.

After that, Hoots and Webb sensibly kept Useeit out of Pan Zareta's way, and the only other time that winter that the two mares were entered in the same race was in the third race on January 4. That race was intended as a match between Iron Mask and Pan Zareta, and, with the connivance of the other owners involved, Useeit was entered and then withdrawn to circumvent track regulations that specifically forbade match races. Even at her best, her chances of victory had she remained in the race may be measured by the fact that Iron Mask outran Pan Zareta by six lengths in 1:09⅗, setting a new world mark for six furlongs.

Useeit, though, was not at her best. Up to that point, she had shown very good form in three of her four races at Juarez. That form deserted her as 1913 gave way to 1914. In four starts in January and February, she could not even finish in the money, and Hoots took her home to rest and await the spring Tulsa meeting—a meeting that passed without her participation, suggesting that something more was wrong than simple exhaustion.

Perhaps hoping that returning to the scene of her earlier triumphs would have the desired effect, Hoots took Useeit with him when he and Rosa revisited Ontario in 1914. It did not. While Useeit was at least able to resume racing in July at Hamilton, the one race in which she showed her best form was also the one in which she ran right back into Pan Zareta. This time, Pan Zareta had 126 pounds to Useeit's 100, but it made no difference; despite a "bold effort" on Useeit's part, Pan Zareta won eased up by three lengths.[1] Four weeks later, the mares met for the last time in the Eclipse Handicap at Connaught Park, and though Pan Zareta may have been going off form—she had to struggle to beat Back Bay by three-quarters of a length—it did not matter to Useeit, who finished another seven lengths back.

The rivalry—if one can call it that—between Useeit and Pan Zareta ended with a decidedly lopsided scorecard; in six encounters, Useeit finished ahead of the pride of Texas only once. Still, Useeit was hardly disgraced. By the time Pan Zareta was done, she had won 76 times from 151 starts, setting or equaling eleven track records along the way including a world record of 0:57⅕ for five furlongs. Her feats earned her entry to the National Museum of Racing Hall of Fame in 1972, and her American record for total races won by a female Thoroughbred is still unbroken. And in 1914, she did not rule only Juarez; though there was no official voting for championships in those days, the consensus of racing historians is that Pan Zareta was North America's champion handicap mare for that year.

Pan Zareta was again at Juarez during the winter of 1914–1915 and continued her domination of racing at Terrazas Park with six wins and a second from seven starts during the meeting. But when the meeting closed, the queen of Juarez left, never to return to either Mexico or the plains of her birth.

Continuing to race through 1917, Pan Zareta expanded her realm far and wide. She became a great popular favorite during the 1916–1917 winter season at the Fair Grounds in New Orleans and then at Oaklawn Park in Arkansas, and in the summer of 1917, she reached the peak of her career. Racing in New York, she earned the title of "Queen of the Turf" from the *New York Times* after packing up to 140 pounds to victories against the best speedsters in the East and setting a track record at Jamaica.[2] It was a sad anticlimax to the career of the great mare when, after losing her form in the fall, she returned to the Fair Grounds late in 1917. Perhaps her owner hoped that she would rekindle her speed and energy there, but it was not to be. Pan Zareta died of pneumonia in her stall on January 19, 1918, and was buried in the track infield.

4

A Month in New Orleans

Late September and the end of the Canadian racing season found Useeit still mired in futility, without a win since December 11 at Juarez. The Hootses were apparently in no hurry to return home, however, for Useeit's name next appeared among the entries at Bowie, part of the Maryland circuit.

Like the racing in Canada, Maryland racing tended to be a cut or two below the standard set at the major New York tracks. Nonetheless, it attracted some good horses, particularly during the fall, and it was no soft spot for a seven-year-old mare going through the worst season of her life.[1] Useeit went from Bowie to Laurel to Pimlico without success, and it was not until November 25 at Havre de Grace that she finally found a race she could win—a five-and-one-half-furlong selling race with a purse of four hundred dollars. Five days later, she won a similar event over the same distance and then moved to Palmetto Park near Charleston, South Carolina, where she won a five-furlong purse race on December 8.[2]

As quickly as Useeit had turned things around, she regressed, though perhaps not as far as she had earlier sunk. She ran unplaced in two more December starts at Palmetto Park to finish 1914 with a record of twenty-three starts, three wins, and five seconds, but she must have been showing something in training after her December losses as she ran second as the 3–2 favorite in another selling race on January 2, Palmetto Park's closing day. Then it was back on the rails, but not home to Tulsa. Her destination was the Fair Grounds, where a chance encounter would play its part in creating the legend that was Black Gold.

A French grande dame with a Spanish veneer, New Orleans was already an old city by the standards of the United States when Yelverton Oliver opened its first public racetrack in 1837. Surprisingly, it had little prior history with horse racing; although François Livaudais had laid out a private racetrack on his plantation in 1820, for the most part the local aristocracy had sniffed disdainfully at the enjoyments favored by the Americans and other newcomers.

Oliver's new Eclipse Course changed that attitude. Opulent and catering particularly to the ladies, it made Thoroughbred racing fashionable virtually overnight. Within the next fifteen years, the Metairie Race Course, the Union Course, and the Bingaman Course were founded in and around New Orleans, which became the racing capital of the South during the 1850s.

None of the city's antebellum tracks survived the Civil War in its original form except Metairie, which reopened in 1866 following a wartime hiatus but went bankrupt in 1872. Perhaps appropriately, its heir was the old Union Course, which—probably bowing to local antipathy for anything "Union" in the postwar years—was conducting racing as the Creole Race Track. Taken over by the reorganized Louisiana Jockey Club the same year that the Metairie track went bust, it became the Fair Grounds, one of the few American racetracks with a history dating to the antebellum period or the Civil War era that are still conducting Thoroughbred racing today.

Though popular with the sporting citizens of New Orleans, the Fair Grounds and its management passed in and out of favor with Louisiana politicians—more out than in after a wave of antigambling legislation swept the entire United States as part of the reforms sponsored by the Progressive political movement. Along with other legislation targeting alcohol use, prostitution, and other real or perceived social ills, antigambling bills had particularly strong support among women of the middle and upper classes, who were flexing an increasing amount of political muscle despite not being granted suffrage until 1920. Popular revivalists such as Sam Jones and Billy Sunday also wielded considerable influence that was not to the racetrackers' advantage.

Supporters of racing fought back, but to no avail. The Fair Grounds went dark in 1908 after the June passing of the so-called "Locke Law" effectively banned both bookmaking and pari-mutuel gambling at racetracks in Louisiana, shutting down the track's financial lifeblood. It stayed closed until the Business Men's Racing Association (BMRA) cautiously made preparations throughout December 1914 for the traditional winter meeting, hoping that the system of oral betting they had devised would pass through a loophole in the Locke Law that left "individual betting" as permissible. Knowing that they could not offer large enough purses to attract the best racers then running, the BMRA made the decision to forgo stall fees and licensing fees for trainers and valets for the duration of the meeting in order to make the meeting more attractive to owners and trainers. Likewise, the licensing fee for jockeys was set at just five dollars, and this money was to be set aside to pay for the services of an on-track physician for the jockey colony. In addition, the BMRA scheduled regular "ladies' days" when women would be admitted free of charge, hoping to attract a relatively genteel crowd of horsemen and racegoers that would boost tourism to the city without offending remaining moralist sentiments.[3]

New Year's Day marked the opening of the forty-day meeting, and it was everything that the track's promoters could have hoped for, with a close to record crowd in attendance. There were some opening-day glitches with patrons who had difficulty in navigating the wagering system, which was modeled after the antebellum practice of wagers "between gentlemen" being held by a stakeholder, but by the time Useeit stepped off the train from Charleston, the meet was running smoothly and a carnival atmosphere prevailed.

Useeit must have shown something when she first stretched her legs at the Fair Grounds, for the bettors made her the 0.70–1 favorite for a five-and-one-half-furlong selling race on January 5. She did not disappoint her backers as she broke in front and stayed there all the way to win by an easy three lengths.

That was the start of a wonderful month in New Orleans for the Hootses, who had plenty of time to take in the sights and sounds of "The City That Care Forgot" before Useeit's next race on January 15. Why she was sent off at 8–1 in the six-furlong selling event is not apparent from the available accounts, but she paid off in style for those who had kept faith in her, again leading from start to finish to score by a length and a half.

Local heroine Bayberry Candle won the feature race on the same card, a mile handicap, and the two mares hooked up when Useeit stepped up in class for a six-furlong overnight handicap on January 22. Dismissed at 10–1—the longest shot among five entries—Useeit came flying away from the barrier and led for all but the final stride after a ding-dong battle in the final furlong. Bayberry Candle got the win by a nose on superior stamina and a three-pound weight advantage, but Useeit gained more respect than she lost, especially since another well-regarded local runner, favored Lady Moon'et, finished well beaten behind her.

Far from being knocked out by the hard race, the tough little mare was ready to go again just five days later in the C. J. Mitchel Handicap, another six-furlong overnight race. This time she was not disregarded, going off as the 1.40–1 choice. She was not left to cruise unmolested on the lead as she had been in her earlier races, either. After getting mild pressure from Sir Blaise through the first quarter, she hit the half-mile mark with Richwood at her saddle girth. From there, it was a desperate battle to the finish, with Richwood—who had a two-pound advantage in the weights—gaining inch by inch as Useeit ran to the limits of her tether. With the crowd's cheers rising to a frenzied level, Useeit found just enough left to cross the finish line with her head still in front. The third-place horse, Transportation, was another four lengths back.

No one in the stands paid much attention as Brick and Mortar trailed in last, beaten by about eleven lengths, but he was the reason that a tall, dignified gentleman with keen eyes and a face lined by life waited among the small group of fellow owners offering Al Hoots their congratulations on his mare's performance. When his turn came, he expressed his own admiration for Useeit's race, then added, "If you are ever in Kentucky, look me up. I would like you to consider breeding Useeit to one of my stallions."[4]

That was all; with a few concluding pleasantries, the man moved on. But Al and Rosa Hoots had reason to remember that brief conversation years later, for the Kentucky gentleman was already a rising name in racing circles. His name was Edward Riley Bradley, the master of Idle Hour Stock Farm and the owner of Useeit's future mate, Black Toney, and the day would come when Al Hoots would have reason to be grateful that Useeit had come to Bradley's notice in so favorable a manner.

Two days later, Useeit brought Al Hoots his highest moment as a racehorse owner. While the feature race on January 29 was not a stakes event, the six-furlong handicap was touted as boasting the best field of sprinters seen during the entire Fair Grounds meeting.[5] That assertion was supported by the fact that Useeit went off as the fourth choice at 5–1 in spite of her three-for-four record since her arrival in New Orleans. Perhaps she was insulted, for she ran like a hot favorite instead. Getting the jump on her seven rivals at the start, Useeit ripped off an opening quarter in 0:23 to open a three-length lead. From there on out, it was a matter of how much she would win by. She was getting leg-weary in the final sixteenth of a mile, but she still had one and one half lengths on Lady Moon'et when she crossed the line in 1:12, setting a new track record.

Useeit was never a great horse by any stretch of the imagination. At her best, she was just above the selling-race class at tracks that were generally considered second-tier or worse by the standards of the time, and she made no pretense of ever staying more than six furlongs. In looking back over her career, many later historians dismissed her as merely "cheap speed," and in terms of raw ability, that was a fair assessment. Nonetheless, what she did have she gave generously, again and again, and in January 1915, that quality was enough to make her the darling of New Orleans.

5

Ruled Off

After racing six times in January as well as making a rail trip of close to eight hundred miles early in the month, Useeit had a right to be tired. Apparently, she was, for the Useeit that came out for another six-furlong race on February 3 was not the Useeit of just five days earlier. Cofavorite with Lady Moon'et at odds of 2–1 but carrying six more pounds than that rival, the Hoots mare got away well but was pressured early by Judge Wright and was never able to relax on an open lead. When Lady Moon'et sailed up on the turn into the stretch, Useeit was clearly tiring and was unable to put up more than a token battle. Not only did Lady Moon'et pull away readily to win the race by a length in 1:12⅖, but Useeit was overhauled for the place by Resign, who had just 96 pounds aboard to 110 on Useeit. The weary Oklahoman finished third, beaten two and one-half lengths all told.

Seven days later, Useeit made her final start of the Fair Grounds meeting in the feature race of February 12, another six-furlong handicap. Only four were entered, and the race was expected to be essentially a rematch between Useeit and Lady Moon'et. Instead, both were upset by Yenghee. A former track record holder at the distance, the gelding dawdled along at the back of the small field while Useeit set the pace in her usual fashion through the first half mile. Then he launched his bid. Useeit still had the lead by half a length at the stretch call, but Yenghee had her well measured and drew off to win by two lengths. The tiring Useeit held second, but it was a disappointing finish to a meeting that had seen her show what was probably the best form of her life.

After that, Useeit got a break until the April meeting at the old Lexington Association track in Kentucky. She was a winner there, but the eight-year-old mare may have been starting to feel the wear and tear of years of long campaigning. Through the rest of the year, the wins came only sporadically while Useeit raced at the various Kentucky tracks and in Canada.

Al Hoots may already have started thinking about his mare's long-range future, for that summer he turned away several breeders' offers to buy Useeit as a prospective broodmare.[1] Nonetheless, he was still out to make money with her on the track, and on September 10, he allowed Webb to drop her into the third race on the card at Lexington, a selling race over six furlongs. It proved a bad mistake. Useeit got second money after tiring in the stretch, but owner-trainer J. W. "Bub" May saw an opportunity and put in a bid for her during the postrace auction. Apparently, Hoots was short on ready cash, for May ended up walking away with the mare for $810.[2] In contrast to his later actions regarding Useeit, there are no indications that Hoots made any protest about the claim or the sale; if he bemoaned what had happened, he did so privately before settling back to bide his time.[3]

Useeit continued racing on the Kentucky circuit that fall as May's property, and after she won a six-furlong selling race at Douglas Park on September 24, Hoots tried to buy her back but was outbid by May, who gave $1,000 to keep her.[4] May perhaps regretted his victory in that auction, for afterward, Useeit went into a tailspin. By the time the Latonia meeting closed in late October, she had run unplaced four straight times. She had flashed early speed here and there but invariably tired in the late going, and Kentucky horsemen had written her off as a fainthearted quitter, unable to win against even the cheaper selling horses. It was a sad tumble from the reputation she had gained in New Orleans.

At that point, Al Hoots reentered her life. Hoping that May might be ready to listen, he approached the man at the close of the Latonia meeting and asked if he would sell Useeit back to him. Touched by the affection Hoots showed for the mare—and perhaps willing to cut his losses on an aging racer who appeared to be past her best days—May agreed to let Hoots have her back at the same price May had paid for her.[5]

Hoots was ecstatic about regaining possession of his favorite, proclaiming, "I will never part with her again or race her where there is any danger of her being claimed."[6] But then he made a fateful decision. Instead of going home to Oklahoma, he and Webb put Useeit on a train bound for Juarez, along with her younger full brother Utelus and her old stablemate Husky Lad.

Utelus and Husky Lad were soon winners at the meeting, but even before Useeit got to Juarez, things began going wrong for her as she got sick on the way down.[7] She soon recovered but endured a seven-race losing streak that spanned more than two months before she got back into winning form again in late January, taking two selling races in succession. Then, just as she seemed to be getting into a hot streak, misfortune intervened.

Starting a race of hot-blooded, excitable Thoroughbreds is no easy thing even in the modern era, when smooth-functioning mechanical gates and well-drilled gate crews are the norm at major racetracks. What Useeit faced as she approached the starting line for the fifth race on February 12, 1916, was far more primitive. Starting gates, an Australian innovation, had not yet crossed the Pacific Ocean; instead, the Juarez runners faced a barrier that was nothing more than a wide strip of webbing stretched between two mechanical arms. The idea was that once the horses were all standing just behind the barrier with their noses pointed down the track, the starter would pull a lever that caused the webbing to fly up and out of the way.

The web barrier was supposed to guarantee a fair, even start. It didn't always work out that way. Horses wheeled out of their assigned places and back as jockeys struggled with fractious mounts or tried to maneuver for advantage. Sometimes a horse plunged entirely through the barrier, and then the starter had to call the false start back while someone scurried out to knot the strands of webbing back together. Often an animal lost all chance at the break, either because it had been facing the wrong way or because it had been slammed or kicked by another horse. Sometimes flighty or inexperienced horses flinched or reared when the barrier flew up, again compromising their chances. If there were assistant starters, they could be as much a hindrance as a help. A badly timed pull on reins or bridle could turn a horse sideways while its rivals were breaking, and rough handling made dangerous rogues of many horses.

Useeit was an old hand at starting from the barrier, and she was all business as she lined up. But another starter, Carrie Orme, had her mind on trouble rather than racing. The unruly mare skittered about, reared, and generally played havoc with one attempt after another to get the field lined up and away. Useeit, apparently distracted by her rival's antics, wheeled sharply forward and to one side—and that was the same instant in which the barrier flew up, catching and entangling the startled mare. Adding to the confusion, another horse, Kid Nelson, also became caught in the webbing.[8]

It was only a second or two before Useeit broke free, but the damage was done. From the stands, Hoots watched helplessly as Useeit plunged down the track with the broken strands of material flogging her about her neck and getting entangled in her stirrup straps. Her jockey's frantic efforts to claw the stuff away kept throwing her off-balance, and though he finally succeeded, she had lost too much ground to have any chance. Remarkably, she managed to finish third anyway, but although she seemed physically all right when Webb brought her back to her stable, the memory of her bad experience stayed with her. The barrier was now something to be afraid of, and in her next race, Useeit seemed distracted at the post and was well beaten after starting poorly.

Hoots's luck with Useeit hit its nadir on February 22, 1916, when she lined up for a five-furlong selling race. Once again, she lacked her usual dash and eagerness at the post; she was off slowly and was never in the hunt. That was bad enough, but this time, something worse happened: E. J. "Tobe" Ramsey, whose horse Moller had finished third in the same race, put in a claim for the nine-year-old mare, bidding her in for $525.[9] Hoots, short of cash but unwilling to surrender Useeit, approached Ramsey with an offer to trade one hundred acres of "the finest land in Texas" for the mare.[10] He was turned down but still refused to give up Useeit, instead turning in his owner's badge to the Juarez stewards.

Why Hoots had risked Useeit when he clearly did not want to lose her remains a mystery. Although later writers portrayed him as an ignorant "Indian" who had not understood what it meant when he put his mare in a selling race, Useeit's record shows that Hoots was in fact thoroughly familiar with the selling-race system. He had not only run Useeit in selling races at various tracks since her four-year-old season but had run Useeit in at least seven such events earlier in the 1915–1916 Juarez meeting. If he believed Useeit would not be taken, it obviously was not because he did not understand the conditions of a selling race. Further, on the one previous occasion when Useeit was claimed away from him, he had made no protest and simply waited until he could legally recover the mare. So, what was the difference this time?

His final words to track officials offer a clue: "I have come to surrender my badges, knowing that I am going to be ruled off. . . . I am not going to give up Useeit, however, because she was not beaten on the square. Had she been beaten on her merits I would not have a word to say, but when the turf becomes a place where an honest man is placed at a disadvantage then I am willing to retire. Jockey Ormes would not allow my mare to run, and I claim that a conspiracy existed to bring about the defeat of Useeit so that she could be claimed."[11] In a report to the *Louisville Courier-Journal*, sportswriter Walter Pearce added further details, reporting that Hoots accused Ramsey of having had a claim for Useeit written out early in the day in the knowledge that Ormes would not put forth his best efforts.[12] Ramsey, of course, denied this allegation, stating he had simply been looking for a useful Thoroughbred to take to Kentucky and thought Useeit was cheap at her asking price.[13]

Hoots's statements suggest that he had been under the impression that had Useeit won, she would not have been liable to being sold, perhaps due to his misunderstanding of a temporary ban on claiming horses out of selling races that had been placed earlier in the Juarez meeting after a selling-race war developed.[14] It is also possible that Hoots believed he had a gentlemen's agreement with the other owners and trainers at the meeting to the effect that they would not claim Useeit and that Ramsey violated his expectation.[15] An additional factor in his actions after the claim may have been the fear that Ramsey intended to depart Juarez with his racing string as other trainers had recently done, leaving Hoots with no opportunity to repurchase Useeit later.

Whatever his reasoning, Hoots was not about to surrender his favorite, though the exact actions he took are up for dispute. By the time the story finished evolving, Hoots supposedly stood Ramsey off with a shotgun when the latter came for Useeit and then absconded with the mare on the next train out of Juarez. This tale may have had its genesis in a February 25, 1916, story by Frank Teahan, which reported a secondhand allegation that Hoots had "threatened" Ramsey when the latter came to get the mare but did not mention a gun.[16] That detail does not seem to have been added until the publication of a story told by starter Marshall Cassidy (who was officiating at the 1915–1916 Juarez meeting) that initially appeared in 1924.[17] According to Cassidy's tale, Hoots had a helper in the barn named "One Arm" Kelly who threatened Ramsey or his representative with a shotgun when the man came to get the mare, and Hoots followed up by threatening the Juarez stewards with a pair of .44 revolvers when they called him on the carpet to answer for his subordinate's action.

It made for a colorful story, but as reported by the *El Paso Morning Times* of February 24, 1916, the truth was more prosaic: Hoots had refused to surrender Useeit to a valid claim by Ramsey, and in accordance with the rules of racing, the Juarez stewards had ruled him off, along with the mare.[18] For the rest of their lives, neither Hoots nor Useeit would be permitted to enter a race at any sanctioned meeting anywhere in North America. The ban also extended to Useeit as a broodmare and would have prevented her foals from being registered, in turn barring them from sanctioned races, but an acquaintance made a year earlier came to her rescue. On hearing of the action against Hoots and Useeit and remembering his admiration for the mare, Colonel Bradley used his considerable influence in racing circles to get Useeit reinstated for breeding purposes, perhaps hoping that Hoots would return the favor by booking Useeit to one of his stallions.[19]

For unknown reasons, that did not happen immediately. What did happen is that Hoots quickly sold Utelus and Husky Lad and another horse he had acquired at the Juarez meeting, Gallant Boy—apparently to Webb, who later raced all three as owner and trainer. As for Useeit, Hoots loaded her into a boxcar. She was going to Kentucky for a breeding to Ivan the Terrible, a stakes-winning stallion who was considered a good sire of useful winners. If Hoots could no longer hope to own a good racehorse, he would pursue a new dream. He would breed one, one that could be raced by his wife or perhaps his son.[20]

After returning to Oklahoma, Hoots soon received the good news that Useeit was safely in foal at H. B. Headley's farm in Kentucky, where she was being boarded until she could be shipped west. Hoots had been in declining health since coming home, however, and by mid-January 1917 was reported to be seriously ill with pneumonia at his Tulsa home.[21] Nursed by his devoted wife, he recovered, but not completely; he was frailer than before and had visibly aged beyond his fifty-seven years.

That spring, Useeit delivered a healthy colt (later named Tulsa) before being bred to the excellent sprinter Jack Atkin, but whether Hoots ever saw the firstborn of his beloved mare is unknown. Sometime during the fall, Hoots traveled to Eureka Springs, Arkansas, a town in the Ozark Mountains that had become a fashionable spa and retirement center. The spring waters were reputedly of medicinal value, and Hoots was one of thousands of people who visited in the hope of relief from some malady.

He did well at first, enough so that Rosa Hoots felt she could leave her husband's side and return to Tulsa to be with her ailing mother; at ninety-two, Jane Appleby had been in poor health for some time, and Rosa was anticipating the worst. But it was only a few days after her return home that there was a knock at the door, announcing a telegram delivery boy. After the lad had been paid and gone his way, Rosa broke the seal on the envelope and pulled out the message inside. The words struck like a blow: Al Hoots was dead.[22]

It was Tuesday, November 13, 1917. They had been married for thirty-one years.

Later, there were more details: it had been his heart that gave way, and he had died suddenly. It hardly mattered. Somehow, the needed tasks got done: transportation for the body arranged; the funerals scheduled for Al Hoots and then for Jane Appleby, who died four days after her son-in-law; the possessions of the dead inventoried and distributed to the heirs.

One possession was not in dispute. Useeit was now Rosa's, and Rosa would not part with her, for a promise lay between her and her dead husband regarding the mare. "Never sell her," Al Hoots had told his wife before their last parting. "Breed her to the best stallion possible. Someday a colt will arrive that will bring you a fortune."[23]

6

A Woman of Two Worlds

Viewed from a century later, Rosa Hoots can seem more a symbol than a human being who once lived, worked, loved, and died. To some, she may represent the oppression faced by women and indigenous peoples in a culture dominated by males of European descent. To others, she is a figure of either condescension or romance because of her Native American heritage and her place in Black Gold's legend. In truth, like all human beings, she was both unfathomably complex and the product of her heritage and culture—in her case, a heritage and culture that were inextricably mixed between the white man's world and that of the Osage people.

Born Rosa Mognett Captain, the future Mrs. Hoots came into the world on November 20, 1868. Her birthplace was a Jesuit mission station, a settlement in Neosho County, Kansas, that later became the city of St. Paul. Although she proudly identified as Osage all her life, she was actually more European than Native American in ancestry. A generation earlier, a number of French traders and riverboat men had married Osage women, and her father, Augustus Captain (sometimes called Peter Augustus), was the son of one such marriage. He, in turn, married Jane Moore, a white woman who was born in Ohio but had lived among the Osage since childhood and had been raised according to their customs.[1] Their marriage produced fifteen children; of that number, Rosa was the youngest to reach adulthood.

It was not an easy world that Rosa Captain was born into. Her father, who had chosen the ways of his mother's people, had been prominent in Osage affairs during the Civil War. Most of the Osage leaned toward the Union cause, but not Augustus Captain, who felt that the national government had betrayed his people. Fiery in nature, physically imposing, and an eloquent speaker in both English and Osage, he was among the leaders of a faction that was not only sympathetic to the Confederacy but took up arms on the Confederates' behalf. When it became obvious that the Confederate cause was lost, he managed to escape arrest and, through the interventions of his wife and a neighboring couple, was allowed to lay down his arms on his pledge to cease warfare against the Union.[2] Nonetheless, he never forgot his distrust of the federal officials who had failed to protect the Osage from raiding by both sides and who were doing little or nothing about thousands of white squatters who had moved into Osage lands—including Theodore Reynolds, who had squatted on land to which Captain held legal title, and who was only evicted after a strenuous court battle. The prevailing white attitude about the dispute and others like it was expressed by Kansas governor Samuel J. Crawford, a former Union general, who reportedly told Reynolds that, if he shot Captain, Crawford would issue a pardon "before the smoke clears away from the end of your gun."[3]

As Captain probably suspected, the reason behind the inaction on the squatter issue was that the federal government had determined to move the Osage from Kansas to the Indian Territory farther south and therefore considered the squatters to be potential settlers rather than lawbreakers. Previous agreements with the Osage were swept aside with the rationalization that those agreements had been broken when some Osage joined the Confederacy, even though the majority had not. The fact that the Osage had made a treaty with the Confederacy in an attempt to protect their own interests in an unstable situation was merely further excuse for ignoring previous promises. With no redress for their grievances and facing increasing competition for available land and resources from the encroaching whites, the Osage saw that they would be forced to yield.

Nonetheless, the Osage were more fortunate than many other native peoples. In 1868, Augustus Captain was among those present when the Osage initially ratified the Drum Creek Treaty (later modified and finalized in 1870), which provided for their lands to be sold and the proceeds used to relocate the tribe. The sale of their Kansas lands to the federal government permitted them to buy their new reservation lands outright, which meant that they could not be readily displaced yet again if the white man found something he wanted on their new homeland. Nearly 1.5 million acres—what is now Osage County in

Oklahoma—became the legal property of the Osage people, and most of the remaining Osage packed up their goods, moved to the Indian Territory, and began establishing homes, farms, and towns.

The Captains were part of the migration, and in 1873, Augustus Captain and his son-in-law Cyprian Tayrien established a trading post near the falls of Hominy Creek, north of Tulsa and not far from what became the town of Skiatook. There the Captains exchanged coffee, flour, and other dry goods brought in from Independence, Kansas, for buffalo hides; they also raised cattle on nearby lands, where their children—Rosa included—learned to ride and to handle horses and livestock. Augustus Captain—or "Oseege," as he was known among his Osage kin—remained prominent in tribal affairs and often hosted councils among his Osage trading partners, as well as serving as a speaker and interpreter in the Osages' contacts with government representatives. Jane Moore Captain likewise held a respected place with the tribe, becoming one of their foremost oral historians and giving advice regarding their treaties and agreements.[4]

Rosa Captain was not yet nine years old when her father died in 1877. He left his wife the land he had ranched and the fine stone house he had just had built for his family—the first such structure erected in the Indian Territory—but also left $1,180 in debts (equal to about $33,000 in 2022), most likely run up through the Captains' efforts to help the less fortunate among the Osage.[5] As part of the agreement governing their removal to the Indian Territory, the Osage were supposedly guaranteed annuities from the federal government based on the money still remaining from the sale of their Kansas lands. These annuities were intended to help support them as they transitioned from an economy based on hunting, gathering, and small-scale vegetable farming to a fully agricultural economy. Their new land was not suited to raising crops, however, and the annuity agreement allowed for the payments to be made in goods or cash. This latter provision left the Osage vulnerable to unscrupulous middlemen, who either palmed off poor-quality food and goods on the recipients or simply failed to provide enough supplies to equal the value of the cash the Osage should have gotten.

It was not until 1879 that an Osage delegation sent to Washington, DC, managed to persuade government representatives that their annuities should be paid in cash only. By that time, hunger, sickness, and lack of appropriate medical care had reduced the Osage to half or less of their pre–Civil War population. Augustus and Jane Captain lost a married daughter and at least one grandchild during the 1870s, and at the time of Augustus's death, the two were fostering a half-dozen orphans while still caring for two of their own children—Rosa and her seventeen-year-old brother Peter Augustus, who had been left mentally impaired by typhoid when he was five.[6]

Rosa Captain could have had no better example for responding to adversity than her mother, who not only paid off the family's debts but amassed a fortune eventually estimated at a minimum of $200,000 (equivalent to over $6 million in 2022) through astute dealings in cattle and real estate.[7] Sometime during the hard years, however, Rosa was sent back to the Osage Mission in Neosho County, Kansas, where she appears on the 1880 US Census rolls as a boarding student at St. Ann's Academy.

For Jane Captain, sending her daughter to school in Kansas may have been a welcome option while she struggled to get her family back onto a sound financial footing. Illiterate herself (ineligible for education at the mission schools because she was not a Native American, she did not learn to read and write until her grandchildren were in school), she may also have been determined to ensure that her child would not suffer from that handicap in conducting her business, whether it was the business of managing a household as a wife and mother or that of making her own way in a man's world.[8]

Other Osage families were given little choice in the matter of their children's upbringing. Although there were some whites who were sympathetic to the desires of most native peoples to retain their unique identities and at least some of their own ways, official policy was shifting more and more toward encouraging Native Americans on the various reservations to adopt the predominant white culture—and some officials were willing to apply coercion when encouragement did not produce the desired results, forcing children into government-prescribed boarding schools where use of their own language was punished and assimilation into white culture was mandatory.[9] Further pressure toward acculturation came from within the Osage community, as an increasing number of mixed-blood families created by intermarriage with whites began to outnumber the remaining full-blooded Osage on the tribal rolls. Although not all of the mixed-blood Osage favored wholesale adoption of white customs and ways, they were generally more inclined toward assimilation than their full-blooded kin.

Rosa Captain apparently returned to her mother's home in between school terms—she is mentioned as being "of Tulsa" in the newspaper announcement of her marriage—but she was at the mission when she married Al Hoots on

February 11, 1886. Soon afterward, the young couple moved into the house that Augustus Captain had built, and the surrounding spread became known as the Hoots Ranch. In addition to raising cattle and farming, the Hootses leased grazing rights to their own land as well as subleasing grazing rights to land they leased from their Osage neighbors.

Although the Hootses' marriage appears to have been stable and deeply affectionate, it was attended by tragedy. Two of the couple's children died in infancy, and another was killed when his eldest brother—then but eight years old—accidentally shot him in the head with a cowboy's gun.[10] Another child died of measles at the age of six. Only two of the Hoots children survived to adulthood, and both would eventually predecease their mother. In addition to the loss of her children, Rosa Hoots had also suffered the pain of estrangement from her mother, who had remarried to Luther "Lew" Appleby. Appleby, more than twenty years younger than Jane Captain, had been a ranch hand working on her spread, and Rosa and her surviving sisters disapproved because they felt their mother had "lowered her standards."[11] The sisters' opinion may have been substantiated in 1903, when Appleby was sued for damages on the grounds that he had alienated the affections of another man's wife.[12] Small wonder, then, that a surviving photograph of Rosa Hoots with her husband and then-teenage children shows a woman whose strong, square face seems marked by struggles already endured in its shadowed eyes and determined mouth.

Rosa and Al Hoots were affected not only by their personal losses but by turmoil in the larger world as the relationship between the Osage and the federal government continued to evolve. By the late 1800s, the Osage were being pressured to sign an allotment act similar to those that had been forced on other tribes. Under the terms of these acts, reservation lands were parceled out to tribal members in 160-acre allotments, the same amount of land as was given to settlers of public lands under the Homestead Act of 1862. If the reservation had more land than was needed to provide every member an allotment, the remaining land was considered surplus and could be sold to non-natives or opened to homesteaders.

Unlike other peoples, however, the Osage legally owned their lands by purchase, and they held up statehood for Oklahoma while forcing the government to negotiate. In the end, they had to accept allotments, but their surplus lands were not confiscated. Under the terms of the Osage Allotment Act of 1906, these lands were apportioned among the tribal members, so that each Osage on the tribal rolls received 657 acres instead of 160. In addition, the Osage retained communal mineral rights to their lands, which meant that when mineral resources were discovered and extracted, each enrolled member of the tribe would receive a share of the resulting royalties by headright. This was not a mere technicality, for by 1894, it was already known that large reserves of oil and natural gas lay beneath the reservation. Surface rights to the land could be sold or leased as the owner pleased, but the headrights could not be bought, leased, or sold, only inherited.

As the daughter of Augustus Captain, Rosa Hoots was entitled to a headright, which was listed on the tribal rolls as number 1,356. (She would later inherit another half headright.) Development of the oil resources beneath Osage lands proceeded slowly during the 1890s, but by 1907, tribal lands were producing five million barrels of what the Osage called "black gold" annually, and the yields increased rapidly thereafter. Rosa Hoots, therefore, was hardly left destitute when her husband died, as she had an ever-rising amount of oil royalties coming to her as well as the property and livestock that she and Al Hoots had amassed during their marriage—including one Thoroughbred mare and her foal. The following year, Rosa's tiny band of Thoroughbreds expanded to three when Useeit produced the Jack Atkin filly she had been carrying when Al Hoots died.

Honoring her husband's memory, Rosa Hoots named the new arrival "Tuscola" after the Illinois town where Al Hoots had been born. Nonetheless, Useeit did not produce another foal in 1919 or 1920, and the *American Stud Book* records nothing regarding those two years—no report of barrenness and no record of a slipped or dead foal, suggesting that she simply was not bred in 1918 and 1919.

Why this was so is not known, but economics probably played a role. On a national scale, this was the period of the post–World War I recession, which, though brief, hit ranching and farming hard due to lessened demand for beef and grain. Another factor may be that Mrs. Hoots was preoccupied with grieving for her husband and her mother and with legal affairs related to the settling of both estates. Most likely, both reasons were in play. In any event, with one of her major income streams reduced and with funeral expenses and any remaining debts owed by the decedents needing to be paid, there may have been no ready cash to spare for paying transportation and stud fees for Useeit until probate was completed.

Whatever the cause of her previous inaction regarding Useeit, when the spring of 1920 rolled around, Rosa Hoots was apparently ready to turn her mind back to fulfilling her husband's dream of breeding a champion racehorse from his mare. That year, Useeit was sent in the care of Hanley Webb to Colonel Bradley's Idle Hour Stock Farm near Lexington, Kentucky, for a mating with Bradley's young stallion Black Toney.

7

Bradley's Luck

Later legend would insist that Al Hoots told Rosa with his dying breath that a vision given by his Indian ancestors had shown him that a mating between Useeit and Black Toney would give rise to a Kentucky Derby winner.[1] In the spring of 1924, when Black Gold was a leading Kentucky Derby candidate, that story had at least a veneer of plausibility. Black Toney was fashionable at that time, and the unlikely idea of his being bred to an obscure mare owned by an Indian lent itself nicely to the theme of the "impossible dream."

In November 1917, the same story would have been laughable. Aside from the facts that Hoots was not an Indian (as Rosa Hoots herself attested) and that Rosa was not present at Al's deathbed, Black Toney was anything but fashionable or in demand at that time; he was a third-rate racehorse whose first tiny crop of foals had just been weaned.[2] If Hoots actually predicted that he would be the perfect mate for Useeit, he must indeed have had something akin to supernatural insight to see the horse's potential at a time when no one else had much faith in him. In fact, Black Toney's rise to becoming one of Kentucky's top stallions is a study of the twists and turns of fate, leavened with a generous dollop of "Bradley luck."

There is no question that Edward Riley Bradley appreciated luck. Born in 1859 to an Irish American family in Johnstown, Pennsylvania, he worked briefly as a clerk and in the steel mills before striking out on his own at the tender age of fifteen with not much more to his name than a two-headed silver dollar that he carried for luck . . . and, perhaps, for the occasional fast wager, followed by an equally fast departure.[3] Like many another restless and ambitious soul, he headed for the American West. There, Bradley supposedly mined for gold, served as a US Army scout during the Indian Wars, tended bar, worked as a ranch hand and bronco buster, and made money on the side by betting on races between Indian ponies. He was also said to have cultivated a friendly acquaintance with the colorful lawman Wyatt Earp and to have had occasional run-ins with the infamous outlaw Billy the Kid, mostly when "the Kid" wanted to borrow money. (As Bradley wryly observed later, Billy was never turned down because "he'd shoot you if you didn't loan him the money.")[4]

Which (if any) of these stories actually had any truth to them is for the most part unknown. Bradley himself, habitually reticent regarding his past, seldom spoke much of his "Wild West" years, but when he returned to more settled parts of the country, he brought three skills with him that would make his fortune: the ability to assess real estate for its profit potential, the ability to set odds profitably as a bookmaker, and the ability to judge good horseflesh. After having been involved with bookmaking operations in Hot Springs, St. Louis, and Memphis, he reportedly made a killing in gambling at the 1893 world's fair in Chicago, allowing him to move into the real estate market in that city.[5]

Bradley made good use of the opportunity, for by the early 1900s, he was well established in the Windy City. A co-owner in Chicago's posh Hotel Del Prado, he continued to be active in bookmaking, which occasionally led to arrests based on violations of antigambling statutes. With his brother John, he also owned elegant gambling clubs in several cities; these were run with strict integrity other than for the minor detail that most of them were illegal in the states in which they were operating. (Local law enforcement generally turned a blind eye to these establishments, probably because they catered to wealthy visitors rather than locals.) The most famous of these was the Beach Club in Palm Beach, Florida, which remained the place to be for eastern elites on winter vacations until it closed in 1945, a year before Bradley's death.

Bradley's initial interest in horse racing had been as a vehicle for his book-making, but in 1898, his physician, Leonard St. John, advised him that he needed to spend more time outdoors if he wanted to prolong his life. Bradley considered the advice and decided that attending the races regularly as an owner would serve admirably for getting more fresh air and sunshine. With "Dynamite" Jack Thornby as partner, he purchased his first racehorse, a cheap runner named Friar John, at Washington Park for six hundred dollars on July 20, 1898.[6] The horse won its first race in Bradley's colors on July 27 at odds of 8–1, and Bradley was hooked.[7] For the rest of his life, he would own and breed racehorses, becoming one of the best-known figures in the Thoroughbred world of his time.

Friar John was never much of a racer, but Bradley idolized the animal that had brought him his first big thrill as a horse owner. He soon bought out Thornby's share in the gelding and in due time retired Friar John to a life of ease. For years afterward, the horse was Bradley's adored pet, with no expense spared when it came to his care, and when Friar John finally died at the age of twenty-seven, Bradley put up a monument to the memory of his first race-horse.[8] The gesture was typical of the man, who throughout his life reconciled two seemingly contradictory personas: the calculating gambler and businessman with the sentimentalist whose charities and personal loyalties were legendary.

Not long after that first win with Friar John, Bradley bought another horse, Brigade, and landed a big gamble on him as well when he raced the horse at Saratoga. The proceeds from that bet and others allowed Bradley to buy a more promising runner, the gelding Bad News (whose name came from the saying, "bad news travels fast"). Though no champion, Bad News became Bradley's first stakes winner and was a tough, honest racehorse. He ended his racing career with fifty-four wins from 185 starts and was immortalized in Bradley's later habit of giving all his horses names beginning with the letter *B*—a practice that, in Bradley style, combined sentiment with gambling superstition that decreed clinging to anything seen as "lucky."

Having had some success with horses he had bought from others, Bradley next decided that he would try breeding his own winners. In 1906, he and his wife, Agnes, bought the 336-acre Ash Grove Farm on Old Frankfort Pike near Lexington, Kentucky. They renamed their acquisition "Idle Hour Stock Farm" and settled in to pursue their new passion. Over time, Idle Hour grew by another 1,100-plus acres and became one of the showplaces of the Bluegrass region, and Colonel Bradley (whose title was an honorary one, bestowed by Kentucky governor A. O. Stanley) became a fixture in horse racing circles.[9]

Although the Kentucky Derby did not become established as a nationally significant event until decades after its inception, it had been an important regional race for most of its history, and it was rising in prominence during the 1910s. Bradley apparently determined early in his career as a breeder that he would breed and raise Derby winners, and to that end, he modeled his breeding program on that of James R. Keene, who had enjoyed great success by crossing American sire lines—particularly the one stemming from his great speedster Domino—on European-bred mares.

There was just one hitch: most of the proven sires from Domino's male line were in the hands of either Keene or Harry Payne Whitney, and none was available for sale. Nonetheless, Bradley's luck came to his aid. He had already managed to secure Helmet, a son of Domino's good son Disguise; one of the best two-year-olds of 1908, Helmet won the important Hopeful Stakes at Saratoga as well as the Champagne Stakes and the Matron Stakes at Belmont Park before becoming a stallion at Idle Hour. Then, in 1912, Bradley's friend William Prime bought eighteen yearling colts from Keene's Castleton Stud just before losing his shirt in the cotton market. Needing help, he turned to Bradley, who (depending on the source) either bought the lot of young horses outright for $25,000 to bail Prime out or extended Prime a loan of similar amount to tide him over until the yearlings could be sold. In any event, the Keene-Prime yearlings ended up on the auction block in Lexington, and Bradley bought four of the colts for a total of $32,400. Although Bradley was accused in some quarters of running up the bidding for his own benefit, this seems unlikely given that his purchases included the three highest-priced colts in the sale, whose prices were probably influenced by the fact that Keene had indicated his regard for them by nominating the trio to major races in England.

None of the three proved worth shipping overseas, though Bradley did get his money back out of Boots and Saddle (purchased for $5,600) when the colt landed some nice wagers for him the following year. In the long run, however, Bradley's greatest profits came from his least expensive purchase: a wiry, nearly black colt by Domino's champion grandson Peter Pan out of Belgravia, whose sire Ben Brush had won the 1896 Kentucky Derby and whose dam Bonnie Gal was one of Keene's imported English mares. The youngster cost Bradley $1,600, a respectable price at the time but one that indicated that no one at the auction saw the colt as being particularly promising. The one person who saw him as something more may have been Bradley's longtime butler and cook, who had reportedly wheedled his employer into bestowing his name on the animal.[10] Running as Black Toney, the colt recouped his purchase price and a bit more as a juvenile when he won the Valuation Selling Stakes at Latonia and six other races from a busy schedule of nineteen starts.

Although Bradley paid $1,500 to bid Black Toney back in from the postrace auction after he won the Valuation, he had several other opportunities to sell the colt at a much better price, starting with Mose Goldblatt's offer of $15,000 for Black Toney and Boots and Saddle in July 1913. When Bradley countered by asking $25,000 for the pair, Goldblatt decided they were not worth that much and backed out. Black Toney's next opportunity to change hands came in October of the same year, when Bradley offered to sell Jefferson Livingston a three-horse package that included Black Toney for $50,000. Livingston was not interested at that price, and the colts—Black Toney included—were still on the market when Bradley entered them in the Kentucky Derby and the Latonia Derby in December 1913, though Bradley admitted at the time that he was not very eager to sell.[11]

Bradley continued to flirt with the idea of selling Black Toney through the following spring, and one can only speculate as to the changes in Thoroughbred history and Bradley's fortunes as a breeder had the colt actually changed hands. In the short term, Bradley probably regretted not making a deal, as Black Toney ran last in his intended Kentucky Derby prep at Latonia and came out of the race with a leg injury that forced him out of the Kentucky Derby. He was eventually scratched from the Latonia Derby as well and did not come back to top form until June 21, 1914, when he set a track record of 1:50⅕ for a mile and one-eighth at Latonia. A week later, he won again at Latonia and was judged ready for stakes competition.

Black Toney reached the peak of his racing career in the Independence Handicap on July 4, winning easily by three lengths over a good field of stakes horses that included 1913 Kentucky Derby winner Donerail and 1913 Kentucky Oaks winner Cream. Four days later, he was beaten into fourth just as easily in the Canadian Derby at Hamilton, for which he had been a heavy favorite, and he began to be plagued by repeated injuries.

Injury, in fact, had been the bane of the Domino male line beginning with Domino himself. Said to have raced his entire career on bowed tendons in both forelegs—the result of being worked too hard for speed as a yearling—Domino also struggled with a chronic foot problem and probably did very well to last for twenty-five starts, of which he won nineteen. At that, he was sounder than his brilliant son Commando, whose legs gave way after only nine races. Black Toney's sire Peter Pan, a son of Commando, lasted longer than his father but bowed a tendon after seventeen starts, forcing his retirement.

Had Black Toney shown a higher level of talent, he might have been retired to stud sooner. As it was, he raced on through his four-year-old season without returning to stakes-winning form. At the end of 1915, he had twelve wins from thirty-seven starts. Though speedy, honest, game, and as consistent as his physical ailments permitted, he was far below the class of his contemporaries Old Rosebud and Roamer, both members of the National Museum of Racing

Hall of Fame and both easily his superiors during meetings on the racetrack even before Black Toney's injuries started taking their toll.

The extent of Bradley's faith in Black Toney as a potential sire can be judged by the fact that the horse sired only four live foals from his first stud season in 1916 before being engaged for some of the summer handicaps on the Kentucky circuit. The horse did not make it back to the track that year, but after mating Black Toney to a few more mares in the spring of 1917, Bradley had him put back into training once again. Black Toney made three more starts, winning a one-mile club purse at Windsor on July 21, 1917, and retired with a final mark of thirteen wins from forty starts.

Nobody would normally expect a stallion to have any chance of making a name for himself off just four foals, but "Bradley luck" was operating again when it came to Black Toney. Against all odds, the young stallion came up with a champion from that tiny group. Her name was Miss Jemima, and she won four stakes races for Charles E. Rowe, who had bought her as an unraced youngster. She was widely regarded as one of the two best juvenile fillies in training in 1919, and that quickly, Black Toney went from the bottom of Bradley's stallion roster to valuable sire. As a result, the stallion's 1920 book took a marked upswing in both the quantity and quality of mares presented to him.

Despite later newspaper stories that presented the mating of Black Toney to Useeit as a misalliance, Useeit was not out of place in that book. Bradley had a marked preference for speedy mares as broodmare prospects, once commenting that any mare that could run three-eighths of a mile in thirty-four seconds or less was worth considering.[12] As a gambler, he also preferred horses that could be counted on to do their best in every race and liked to see this trait in his breeding stock.

Useeit had proven game, consistent, sound, and durable, and with thirty-four sprint wins and three track records to her credit, she was just the type of mare Bradley liked even if she lacked any European cachet in her bloodlines—probably the reason he made a point of making Al Hoots's acquaintance when their paths crossed at the Fair Grounds in 1915. Even if Bradley did not specifically offer Hoots a stallion season at that time, he was well known for his generosity to widows and orphans and would have been favorably disposed toward Rosa Hoots when she came back into contact with him, perhaps offering a free breeding to Black Toney at that time, as later newspaper reports suggested.[12]

In any event, Useeit did visit Black Toney in the spring of 1920, and on February 17 of the following year, she delivered a small, wiry black colt marked only by a fleck of white on his forehead. Alluding to both the colt's sire and the oil that was beginning to bring her not just a cash flow but wealth, Rosa Hoots named the foal Black Gold.

8

Gold and Turmoil

For all but a scant handful of people with immediate connections to him, Black Gold was just another foal out of 2,165 registered Thoroughbreds born in North America in 1921. Even the place of his birth is uncertain. Although the National Museum of Racing Hall of Fame gives his birthplace as Idle Hour Stock Farm, the *Louisville Courier-Journal* of November 15, 2008, states that he was foaled and raised at nearby Bluegrass Heights Farm. Contradicting both, an article of April 14, 1924, in the *St. Louis Globe-Democrat* specifies that he was born in Tulsa, whereas sportswriter J. L. Dempsey of the *Cincinnati Enquirer* stated that Black Gold was born at Wiggins Military Stock Farm near Lexington on March 30 rather than February 17. The best available evidence is that the colt was born on February 17 at Horace Davis's Bluegrass Heights Farm, just a short distance along Old Frankfort Pike from Idle Hour. Davis, a good friend of Colonel Bradley's, often boarded mares that had been bred to Idle Hour stallions, and Useeit is known to have been there in 1923, when she produced an Under Fire filly that died as a weanling, and in 1924, when she produced a full brother to Black Gold.[1]

Preoccupied with multiple business and charitable concerns in Tulsa, Rosa Hoots did not make the long journey east to see the new arrival, nor was there any reason to ship Black Gold or his dam to the West with Hanley Webb seeing to their care in Kentucky.[2] So—perhaps to the disappointment of later romancers—Black Gold spent his first months not running free over the Oklahoma plains but living according to the rhythms of farms whose patterns of life had been settled for generations. His babyhood was spent in quiet barns and in fenced paddocks, where he nursed, slept in the sun, and played with the other foals of his year while Useeit and the other broodmares grazed close by. Following his mother as she was taken from stall to pasture and back again, he learned to wear a halter and walk on a lead, and to let himself be handled and groomed by humans, but most of his time was spent simply learning how to be a horse among other horses.

In Tulsa, Black Gold's birth did not rate even a passing mention in the local papers. With the oil and banking industries booming, Tulsa was worlds away in culture and atmosphere from staid Kentucky, and its society was changing rapidly—too rapidly, as it turned out, for a social structure that was developing a veneer of settled gentility but underneath was seething with unresolved racial tensions from decades past. Combined with a still-present frontier mentality—at its best daring, enterprising, and energetic, but at its worst lawless, ruthless, and willing to run roughshod over the vulnerable—strained relationships between whites, Blacks, and Native Americans were enough to make Tulsa a powder keg that any spark could touch off. In the spring of 1921, the keg exploded—visibly, in a short but terrible period of open violence, and silently, in a collusion among lawmakers, law abusers, and law enforcers that would wrap some of the city's wealthiest citizens in fear for over a decade.

Tulsa's racial problems had begun during the area's frontier days, starting with the forced relocation of most of the "Five Civilized Tribes" of the American Southeast to the Indian Territory and continuing with social issues generated by the aftermath of the Civil War. White squatters on tribal land were as much a problem in Oklahoma as they had been in Kansas, and lax enforcement of treaties between the various native peoples and the federal government, accompanied by blatant disregard for Native Americans' personal and property rights, was an old story even before the Osage were forced from Kansas. Blacks fared no better, as most of them were, under the law, property (held by both whites and Native Americans) until emancipation finally reached the Oklahoma and Indian territories in 1866 following the ratification of the Thirteenth Amendment.

The twin problems of general lawlessness and open racism among the whites of the region—many of whom had moved from the South and bitterly resented both the disruption of their previous way of life and the losses they had suffered during the Civil War—were compounded by the new state government, which began passing Jim Crow laws almost as soon as it was formed in 1907. White supremacists operated with little restraint or fear of legal repercussions in the newly formed state, and their sympathizers increased in number as the oil flowing from Osage lands both made previously despised "Injuns" wealthy and attracted a class of better-educated Blacks, mostly from the North, who came to work in the growing financial and petroleum industries. These professionals and skilled workers led others of their race in building the Greenwood section of Tulsa into what was called "the Black Wall Street," a segregated enclave famous for its prosperity and its vibrant social life—and widely envied by those whites who lacked the education and skills to achieve similar success in their own community. Strict separation between the white and Black communities may have stabilized the situation temporarily as it reduced the opportunities for direct conflict, but it also made it nearly impossible for the two groups to build positive ties through personal friendships and shared activities. Further, it allowed mistaken assumptions and negative attitudes to continue feeding on themselves, uncorrected by experience.

The last bits of tinder for a potential explosion were set in place when two more events added further stress to an already tense racial milieu: a post–World War I recession that hit hardest and lingered longest in agriculture and ranching, and an influx of military veterans returning from the war in Europe. Many of the whites among the former soldiers found themselves unable to secure stable employment in a shrunken market for unskilled labor, fanning their resentments of people who belonged to what were supposedly inferior races but were more prosperous. On the other side of the racial divide, the Black veterans were having to readjust to the attitudes and disadvantages of a society that gave them less respect than they had received while fighting overseas. Compounding the anger roused by their social circumstances, many veterans of both races carried with them the lingering trauma of the things they had seen and experienced during the war, predisposing them to quick anger and hair-trigger responses to perceived threats.

Three months after Black Gold's birth, Tulsa was rocked by the so-called "Tulsa Race Riot," which began with an alleged assault by a Black youth against a white girl and a sensationalistic article regarding the "attack" (which, according to the ensuing police investigation, never occurred) in the *Tulsa Tribune* of May 31, 1921.[3] Rumors of a plan to lynch the accused youth reached the Black community, and amid the tensions of the evening, a group of armed Black men encountered a crowd of similarly armed whites in the vicinity of the jail. Words were exchanged; a shot was fired; then both sides began firing.

A few seconds later, ten whites and two Blacks lay dead, forming the epicenter of one of the most brutal racial conflicts in American history.

Responses by law enforcement and prominent white citizens were mixed, with some trying to stem the violence and others actively participating in it. Holding their ground at the jail, the sheriff and the deputies there with him did succeed in turning away the lynch mob, but city police officers not only failed to contain the violence but helped foment it by deputizing would-be lynchers. Looting, murder, and arson swept into Greenwood, where the Black defenders were outnumbered and outgunned by the white rioters; one eyewitness account even indicates Greenwood was attacked by airplanes dropping incendiaries.[4]

By noon of the following day, the Oklahoma National Guard finally quelled the rioting and restored some semblance of order, but Greenwood lay in ashes and the Black community found itself interned. Estimates of the dead have ranged from the thirty-eight individuals who could be identified by the techniques of forensic anthropology to some three hundred. The vast majority of those who perished were Black, leading modern historians to label the event as the "Greenwood Race Massacre."

Most of the residents of Greenwood were released after a few days, but the injustices done them were compounded by city planners and private developers who saw the destruction as an opportunity to rebuild the area as an industrial zone. Focused on their own potential profits, they had little incentive to rebuild the Blacks' destroyed homes, churches, and businesses; as a result, many of the newly homeless people had to spend the winter of 1921–1922 in tents. Many Tulsa residents, both Black and white, moved away at that time, and although the Greenwood district was eventually rebuilt with assistance from the American Red Cross, a pall of silence regarding the events of May 31 and June 1, 1921, settled over the remaining residents of the city. The riot was generally omitted from local and state histories and little known nationally outside the circles of academic historians, and the silence remained in place until a state commission was established in 1996 to investigate what had occurred. As of November 2022, a lawsuit seeking reparations for the few remaining survivors among Greenwood's 1921 residents and for the descendants of those known to have been living there at the time of the riot was still moving through the courts.

The year 1921 also marked a watershed in the history of the relationships between whites and the Osage community in Tulsa and its environs, and the change was not for the better. In this case, the chain of events began with the ever-increasing amounts of oil money flowing into Osage hands. Some of the recipients were prudent with that money; some were not; and some used their newfound wealth to finance trips to Europe, fancy houses and cars, and other trappings of the moneyed class. Not surprisingly, some also became victims of con artists and swindlers or made poor investments.

Overall, the Osage were probably doing neither better nor worse than most other people on newly coming into money, and there were some whites even then who voiced the opinion that the Osage were capable of managing their financial affairs without white oversight. Nonetheless, greed, envy, and paternalistic moralizing over Osages' "improvident" use of their newfound wealth found a common cause in a bill that was passed through the US Congress in 1921. Signed into law by President Woodrow Wilson, this legislation required members of the Osage Nation who had less than 50 percent white ancestry to have guardians appointed for them by local authorities. The guardians, who could legally receive up to one thousand dollars annually for their services for each person in their guardianship, were supposed to protect their wards by investing the difference between the amount of royalties received by headright (less the guardian's fee) and the headright owner's four-thousand-dollar allowance for personal use. In fact, oversight of such guardianships was so lax that guardians faced little risk of an accounting for appropriating the money that should have been invested for their wards' benefit, and many did exactly that. Some did not even scruple at seizing their wards' personal allowances, leaving people who were wealthy on paper to live in abject poverty. Forcing their wards to buy only from businesses run by the guardians' friends and relatives, usually at badly inflated prices, was another common practice to which local officials and the legal system turned a blind eye.

Because of their mixed ancestry, neither Rosa Hoots nor her two adult children were subject to the indignity of guardianship, and Mrs. Hoots's siblings and their children were also exempt from the new law. Many of their full-blooded kindred were not so fortunate, for appointments to guardianships were often determined by cronyism and bribery rather than any concern for the long-term welfare of the person being placed in wardship. Another route to guardianship was through marriage between an Osage woman and a white man, with the husband then being appointed as his wife's guardian. Although some of these marriages were founded on mutual attraction and respect, many eventually proved otherwise, adding a layer of heartbreak to an already galling situation.

Events took a still darker turn when some guardians decided that their path to riches lay through murder. Even before the passage of the guardianship law, several suspicious killings of Osages had taken place in which someone in the white community stood to benefit by the death. Following the enactment of guardianship, the frequency of Osage deaths increased as a few well-connected and powerful men realized that they could gain control of multiple headrights by murdering their wards' relatives and often their wards as well. For the full-blooded Osage, this was the beginning of the "Reign of Terror," when members of the tribe lit their houses with festoons of lights against the night and the killers who stalked them with near-impunity. The terror would not begin losing its grip until 1926, when federal investigators finally became involved at the Osages' request and began unraveling the cloak of conspiracy and corruption that had surrounded the Osage murders; it did not end for another five years after that, when the last of the related deaths is believed to have taken place.

How much Rosa Hoots was personally affected by the racial animosity and violence that pervaded Tulsa in the early 1920s is difficult to ascertain from a century later. Given her ancestry and her long history of involvement in white society, it seems unlikely that she faced any threats of physical harm. At the same time, there were doubtless those who envied her wealth and those who looked down their noses at her Osage ancestry, and she may well have had childhood friends and foster siblings who were subject to guardianship or worse. She may also have been affected in more subtle ways by the turmoil and tension of her times. She had never been one to seek the spotlight—a well-bred woman of her day seldom did, outside of genteel mention in the society columns or in connection with church or charitable activities—but perhaps it was during this time that she developed the extreme reticence that marked her later dealings with the press in the wake of Black Gold's exploits. If so, she certainly had reason.

Even if the times had been less tumultuous and her business less pressing, it seems unlikely that Mrs. Hoots would have taken more interest in the young Black Gold. The balance of the evidence is that up to the beginning of the colt's racing career, she had never been personally interested in racing except as it involved her husband; what she enjoyed about it was his enjoyment of it, as well as the chance to travel. As she told Tulsa newsman Dick Maher, "We went to Montreal, New Orleans, Lexington, and many other places in Canada and the south . . . we didn't pay but very little attention to racing at all."[5] And so, for the first two years, of his life, Black Gold never saw his owner. It was left to Hanley Webb to see to his care and, in due time, to develop him into a racehorse.

9

Three Fingers and a Chief

Webb had never been the sort of man to be sentimental about an animal; in that, he had more in common with Rosa Hoots than with her late husband. It was not that he had been unaware of Al Hoots's feelings about Useeit; on the contrary, he allowed later on that he had never seen a man so attached to a horse.[1] It was just that he saw no point in getting all wrapped up with any particular animal. His job was to take care of horses, train them, and try to make some money with them, not to make pets of them. After Al Hoots died, Husky Lad, Utelus, Gallant Boy, and a few others came and went in Webb's life, and when Rosa Hoots followed her late husband's wishes and entrusted Useeit's first two foals to his care, he set about training and racing them with perhaps a bit of rough affection but no particular attachment. Tulsa and Tuscola were just horses, and if there was anything special about them, it was mostly because of the memory of his old friend.

All that changed when Webb first set eyes on Useeit's little black colt by Black Toney. Why, he could not have said, but he returned to Davis's farm as often as he could to visit the little fellow and his mother. Black Gold soon came to recognize him, and each time Webb visited, the bond between the man and the colt grew a little stronger. When Webb left for Canada with Black Gold's half sister, Tuscola, for the summer racing season, he carried a reminder with him: a photograph of the colt, taken when Black Gold was just three days old. Increasingly creased and yellowed as time passed, the picture was mute testimony to the feelings beneath Webb's gruff exterior.[2]

The days and weeks of Black Gold's babyhood passed quietly. As he grew, he became more independent of his mother, exploring farther and farther from her side and spending more time playing or socializing with other foals. He learned to graze and to eat feed and hay, and by midsummer no longer really needed his mother's milk, though he still came back to her to nurse and for reassurance. And then the day came when men came and took them separate ways, Black Gold to a thickly bedded stall and Useeit to a new pasture, and the little black colt whinnied and hollered after his dam as she was taken out of sight and hearing. He was now a weanling, and no matter how much he flung himself about his stall and called, there was no answer from his mother. He would never see her again, and it would have been no consolation to him to know that, all over Kentucky, hundreds of foals were enduring the same separations and taking their first reluctant steps toward adulthood.

After a few days, Black Gold's distress subsided, and then another change came to his life. Ordinarily, a newly weaned foal would be left with its age-mates most of the time for the next six months or more, developing socially and strengthening bones, tendons, and muscles through normal play. Webb had other ideas. He came back to the farm, and when he left, he took Black Gold with him, leaving behind everything the colt had ever known: his barn, the familiar fields, the humans who had tended him during his first months, and his playmates among the other foals. From that time on, Webb would be trainer, groom, nurse, and surrogate parent all rolled into one.

Black Gold's new home was a stall at the old Lexington Association racetrack, where Webb was training Tuscola. Anyone around the track knew where to find Webb at any time, day or night, for he scarcely left the barn except to tend to his own needs or to take Tuscola out for a workout or race. Otherwise, he was with Black Gold, feeding him, grooming him, alert to the colt's every need and every change in behavior. At night he slept in the stall next door, a habit that would stay with him throughout Black Gold's racing career.

For all that he doted on Black Gold, Webb could hardly be accused of coddling him. In his experience, horses were rugged outdoor animals that didn't need to be swathed and blanketed just because it rained a bit on a chilly day, and he treated Black Gold accordingly. Instead of walking him up and down the shed row when it rained, Webb turned him out daily without regard to the weather so that the youngster could exercise himself. If it got cold, the trainer did not bother with putting a blanket on the colt; on the Great Plains, horses coped with winter weather far more inclement than Kentucky's without needing such things. Sure, you saw to it that your horse had shelter if a blizzard or ice storm was passing through, but ordinary cold weather didn't merit any special attention.

Webb's behavior would have passed without notice in Oklahoma, but things were done differently in Kentucky, and other horsemen muttered that he was neglecting Black Gold. Webb ignored them and continued doing things his way. After the winter passed, the muttering died down. Then the time came for Black Gold to begin training as a racehorse, and the criticism started all over again.

From the start, Black Gold hinted at talent exceeding that of his half siblings. He was intelligent, eager, and quick to learn. But the little black colt was also high-spirited and willful, and Webb, who weighed more than two hundred pounds, was too heavy to climb into the saddle and teach the fractious yearling racing manners.[3] That job fell to an old acquaintance of Webb's from the western circuit, Sam "Chief" Johnson.

Johnson was no chief, but in the cast of characters that surrounded Black Gold, he was the only "Indian" besides Rosa Hoots who actually was one, at least on his mother's side. The son of a Scots-Irish father and a Cherokee mother, he had been orphaned young and started riding not long afterward. By the tender age of eight, he had ridden his first winner at a fair near Fort Worth, Texas—or so he claimed.[4] Since there were no official records of the occasion, he might or might not have been exaggerating a bit. What is certain is that he did become a jockey, and one of the most colorful on record.

Though never a big-league rider, Johnson was daring, cat-quick, and absolutely fearless, and he more than held his own in bush races and at the half-mile "bull rings" common to the fair circuit and the minor western tracks; on one epic day, he swept all eleven races contested at a fair meeting at Saint Paul, Minnesota, a feat without parallel in racing annals.[5] A favorite with both fellow jockeys and fans, he also exercised a delightfully outrageous wit, sometimes at his own expense and sometimes at that of trainers and racing officials. He was no respecter of persons; even Marshall Cassidy, the most celebrated starter of his time and a man rather thoroughly convinced of his own importance, was not immune to the Chief's barbs. After losing an exchange with the Chief at the start of a race at Juarez, the fuming Cassidy had Johnson hauled back to the officials' stand and told him that he was "giving him the meeting" (suspending him for the balance of the race meet).

"What do you expect me to do with the meeting?" Johnson shot back. "You've had it yourself for forty-five days and ain't done so good with it." The next day, he managed to nag Cassidy into lifting the suspension and was off and riding again.[6]

Weight and injuries forced most jockeys from the saddle by their early to middle thirties, but not Johnson. A natural lightweight who could still make a 98-pound riding weight in his forties, Johnson kept riding neck-for-sale wherever he could scrounge up a mount, often taking bad actors that other jockeys wouldn't touch. Every now and then, racetrack injuries forced him into an involuntary layoff, but he always came back. Even a 1913 spill at Salt Lake City that killed his mount and put him in the hospital with a leg broken in three places couldn't quench Johnson's ardor for the track. He nearly died in the hospital and spent close to a year recovering, and he still wasn't fully healed up when he got the mount on Flying Alcroy to start his comeback at Tulsa in September 1914. Any other jockey would probably have taken it as a sign from God that he should retire straightaway when one of his stirrups broke during the first lap of the mile-and-twenty-yard event; Johnson managed to keep his seat, rode like a demon, and ended up second. He could scarcely hobble back to the paddock when he dismounted and was unable to ride again during the rest of the Tulsa meeting, but by winter he was back in the saddle and riding at Juarez.[7]

Even Johnson could not defy time forever, and he rode his last race at a track above the fair level on January 3, 1915, at the Fair Grounds in New Orleans. He went out with a flourish, all but lifting Mary H. across the finish line first in a four-horse blanket finish that Colonel Bradley later called the greatest horse race he had ever seen.[8]

Then forty-three, Johnson was ancient by jockey standards.[9] But nothing could keep him from the saddle—not age, not arthritis from old injuries, and not damaged hearing, the result of head trauma. He started earning his keep as an exercise rider and was soon much sought after in that role, getting better mounts in the morning than he had ever had in the afternoon. Perhaps the best of all the horses he ever threw a leg across was the great gelding Exterminator, whose fifty victories from one hundred starts included the 1918 Kentucky Derby.

Webb probably had a pretty good idea of Johnson's limitations, but he needed someone both lightweight and with plenty of experience for Black Gold. In addition, he needed someone he could trust personally to ride his "baby." Johnson fit those qualifications, and he was available and willing to do an old friend a favor by taking on the little black colt. Before too long, Black Gold had accepted saddle and bridle and the feel of a man's weight on his back, and Johnson was taking him out to the track daily for his first real lessons in being a racehorse.

Those lessons were not always easy on either teacher or pupil. Johnson managed to instill some basic respect for human authority into his charge, but his methods were not always gentle. By some accounts, he galloped the colt for miles, often the wrong way of the track, in a manner that other trainers figured was calculated to either kill the colt or get him fit. This may or may not have been by his intention or even by Webb's orders, for more than once, Black Gold got the bit between his teeth and took off with Johnson hanging on for dear life. Nonetheless, Johnson persevered, and Black Gold learned to harness his energy in accordance with human demands. By the time Webb moved his operations over to Dade Park in the fall, horsemen were openly admiring the handsome black youngster, admitting that the animal was "well-seasoned and thoroughly schooled" and handled his morning exercise "like an old campaigner."[10]

In spite of Black Gold's apparent health and vigor, Kentucky horsemen continued to be critical of Webb's training methods, particularly the long daily gallops that he sent the colt out for, rain or shine. Slow gallops, interspersed with jogging and breezes, were part of any yearling's normal training routine, but what Black Gold was getting was the same faster gallops that Webb had used to get Useeit into the condition he wanted after he first started training her. Useeit had blossomed under that regimen, but the horsemen eyeing Webb askance had no way of knowing that. Even if they had, they would have pointed out that Useeit was grown when Webb started training her, not a soft-boned yearling who still had a good deal of maturing to do. Those familiar with Black Toney and his lineage might also have wondered how long Black Gold's feet and legs would stand the strain, for the line of Domino did not always have the hardest of hooves or the strongest of tendons.

For Webb, his training practices were all of a piece with the kind of horsemanship he had learned in the West, and he was not inclined to change how he did things to mollify men who had never shared his experiences in a harsher world than they were used to. As writer Jack O'Donnell put it: "His experiences with horses in the oil fields and on the ranches of Oklahoma proved to his satisfaction that a good horse likes lots of work. While he didn't tell me so in so many words, he thinks the tendency of the Twentieth Century is to turn out 'sugar horses' and 'sugar men.' He is one of that school of trainers who believe that the way to make a good baseball pitcher is to work him often, and the way to make a good horse is to race him often."[11]

Regardless of the controversy, Black Gold apparently continued to thrive on the unconventional treatment even after he went on to the Fair Grounds in December 1922. The colt quickly gained note as one of the most promising youngsters in New Orleans. Rumor had it that he had already attracted the attention of Colonel Bradley, who had supposedly offered $10,000 for the son of Black Toney but had been turned down.[12]

Webb paid no more mind to rumors than he needed to. His job was to get Black Gold ready to race, and the last step was schooling the colt at the barrier and in the saddling area so that his manners would pass muster with the track stewards. And with that test passed, the trainer began looking for a spot for Black Gold's first race.

10

Baby Steps

Horses generally had much heavier racing schedules in the 1920s than they do now, but even in Black Gold's day, most leading trainers would have argued against racing a promising two-year-old in January instead of waiting until May or so. Then as now, opinions were divided as to the humanity and utility of racing two-year-olds, especially during the first half of their juvenile seasons. Some felt that it did no harm and might even strengthen bones and tendons provided a young horse was basically sound and sufficiently mature, and others believed that early racing often resulted in early injury and burnout. There was (and is) probably truth on both sides, depending on the horse and the trainer.

Any arguments on the subject would have been lost on Webb, whose knowledge of horses' responses to training and racing was limited to his own experience and observations. His view was simple: If a horse seemed fit to race, you raced it, and there was no reason to wait a minute longer than you had to. He may also have felt pressured by the presence of Rosa Hoots's son, Alfred Augustus Hoots, who had come to New Orleans from Skiatook and was presumably there in anticipation of seeing Black Gold begin his racing career.[1] On December 31, 1922, Webb dropped Black Gold's name into the entry box for the Rightway Purse, a January 1 race for two-year-olds, and the only reason that Black Gold didn't race on his official second birthday was that the race failed to fill.[2]

The irony of the situation was exquisite. Just a few days earlier, horsemen at the Fair Grounds had petitioned the meeting's organizers, the Business Men's Racing Association, to card up to four two-year-old races daily to accommodate

57

all the youngsters they had brought to the meeting.[3] But as *Louisville Courier-Journal* racing writer C. J. Savage observed, "The presence of Black Gold . . . scared all of the others out as the trainers with two-year-olds under their care did not care to chase their charges after him right now."[4] That was no overstatement. Only one other colt had been entered in the Rightway Purse out of close to two hundred rising juveniles quartered at the Fair Grounds, at Jefferson Park, and at private stables in the surrounding area. It was the first time since the Fair Grounds had resumed racing in 1915 that an opening-day juvenile race had been forced to cancel for lack of entrants.

Webb kept trying to find a race for Black Gold, but to his frustration, the same thing kept happening over the next several days. Part of the problem was that Black Gold's reputation continued to frighten off possible rivals, but another part was persistent rain. Webb probably didn't see why that should have been an issue, since he worked Black Gold rain or shine. Nonetheless, the other youngsters weren't getting schooling that they needed, and Fair Grounds officials decided that it was better to delay any juvenile races than to have green two-year-olds "running half-wild" on a muddy, slippery track.[5]

At long last, the sun came out on January 7 and started drying out the track, aided by a stiff breeze. Everyone knew that Black Gold would enter the first juvenile race for males that came open, but after a week's forced inaction, other owners and trainers were getting impatient enough to take a chance on facing him. Nine youngsters' names were dropped into the entry box for the first race on the January 8 Fair Grounds card, a three-furlong dash for maiden colts and geldings. Black Gold's was among them, and he went to the post as a heavily bet 1.20–1 favorite. His rider was Henry Burke, a solid journeyman who had been among the leading riders in New Orleans the previous year.

For a skittish young Thoroughbred used to the relative quiet of morning workouts, the noise and scent of more people than he had ever seen in his entire life put together was enough to ramp nerves to fever pitch. The colt had no way of knowing that the city was on holiday for the anniversary of Andrew Jackson's victory in the Battle of New Orleans, meaning that the crowd was much larger than normal for a Monday racing card, nor would he have cared. All he knew or sensed was the activity and excitement of many, many humans, and the presence of a strange man on his back at a time of day when he was usually resting quietly in his stall.

In company with six other nervous, keyed-up youngsters (two others had scratched from the race), Black Gold lined up behind the same sort of web barrier that his mother had faced so often; there were no starting gates at the Fair Grounds until 1928. Any start was still an opportunity for chaos, and never more so than when a group of juveniles faced the barrier for the first time in their lives.

Thanks to Webb's schooling, Black Gold had some idea of what to expect. Even so, when the webbing flew up, he hesitated a fraction of a second. In the same fraction, one of his rivals bolted for the outside rail and dumped his jockey; another leaped straight forward but not fast enough to avoid a traffic tangle that knocked him back and out of contention. Responding to the tug of the reins and a shift in his rider's weight, Black Gold steered clear of the trouble and lengthened stride. In seconds, he was in front and drawing off. He had no rival but his own shadow as he flashed by the winning post, six lengths in front of his nearest pursuer.

Black Gold felt the reins tighten, telling him to slow down; then they guided him into a long, looping turn, back toward a place where a group of humans waited for him. A photograph taken by H. C. Ashby in 1923 captures how he may have looked as he pranced back to the judges' stand, full of his first victory: a light, lithe animal with head up, ears pricked, straining eagerly against a tight rein. He had run his first three furlongs in competition in 0:35⅖, good time considering the track condition (officially "good," meaning that it still retained some moisture but was not muddy) and his inexperience.

Newspapers as far away as New York took notice of the auspicious debut, though with reasonable caution. Winter racing was often short on quality, and even when good horses were involved, extreme precocity was not always the herald of greater things to come. Just two years earlier a much-touted youngster named Lord Allen had been a flashy maiden winner at the Fair Grounds, set a new track record of 0:34⅘ for three furlongs in his next outing . . . and then fizzled. Besides that, Black Gold just wasn't physically impressive. He was small and lightly made, and some horsemen felt Webb was training him down too fine on top of it.[6]

Still, there were those who felt that Black Gold had the potential to be something special. "He's the most level-headed baby I ever laid my eyes on," said Jimmy Brown, who had been covering races since the 1880s and was held to be "one of the ablest judges of thoroughbreds in the country" according to the *Buffalo (NY) Courier.* "[He] is built along the most approved lines and runs close to the ground, just like a deer. He'll be heard from on the northern tracks next season if no accident befalls him."[7]

Aside from such positive opinions, Webb could also take encouragement from the fact that Will Land, third in Black Gold's maiden race, broke his maiden in his next outing on January 12. That race was restricted to maidens, however, and there were no more races carded for which Black Gold was eligible until January 26. That day's lineup included the Nursery Purse, a three-furlong allowance race for juveniles, and Webb got Black Gold in with Henry Burke again engaged to ride the colt.

Unlike handicaps, in which weights are assigned by the racing secretary, allowance races modify the base weight to be carried by all entrants with set increases or decreases (called penalties and allowances, respectively) based on the contestants' previous performances. As a previous winner, Black Gold picked up the maximum weight in the race and carried 118 pounds; nonetheless, he was a 1.10–1 favorite at post time. The second choice at 2–1 was C. T. Worthington's colt Worthmore, a son of Useeit's old rival Lady Moon'et. After scratching out of an earlier maiden race on January 22—in which he would have been a short-priced favorite—he was one of several first-time starters in the eleven-horse field. Like Black Gold, he had gotten the reputation of being a "flyer" before he ever raced, and he had just 108 pounds in the saddle including jockey Bill Kelsay. Perhaps significantly, he was being bet heavily by his owner and his owner's friends.

Worthmore lived up to his reputation in a way that would have made his dam proud. After two minutes of jockeying at the post, he got off sharply and was never headed, winning by four lengths. His time was just one-fifth of a second off the track record, and most observers agreed that, had he been pushed, he could have established a new mark.

Black Gold's race was much stranger. He broke well but was then taken back sharply—an odd tactic for a three-furlong baby race, especially with a veteran like Burke in the saddle and no apparent reason for checking the colt given by either the charts or newspaper accounts. Further, he was taken over to where the going was deepest and most tiring. When finally given his head, he closed well to finish third, a half length behind the filly Edna V., but drew a comment of "given bad handling generally" from the official chart caller.[8] His race also drew comment from C. J. Savage, who stated, "Black Gold . . . did not look the same youngster that won his previous start in such easy fashion."[9] Later, a report came out that a nail had been found in the frog of one of Black Gold's feet following the race.[10]

Later, novelist and racing official Horace Wade would paint Black Gold as having been born on a night when a comet streaked across the sky, an evil omen that led "H. M. Hoots" to prophecy a life of ill fortune for the colt and all who handled him.[11] Given that the real Hoots had been in his grave more than three years before Black Gold was ever born, Wade's account was clearly more than a little fanciful, a fact that seems to have escaped later writers who drew on him as a source for Black Gold's story.[12] Nonetheless, the tale held a germ of truth, for Black Gold and bad luck—or what seemed to be bad luck— were never far apart from the running of the Nursery Purse onward. There would be no official investigation of Burke's ride or of Black Gold's reversal of form. Early-season juveniles were unpredictable, and Worthmore had won so easily that there seemed no point in looking for excuses for his beaten rivals. Nonetheless, Black Gold's second race was the beginning of a pattern of his losing races that, on paper, he had an excellent chance to win . . . and most of them were races where Worthmore was involved.

11

Hot Property

Whatever the cause of the misfortunes Black Gold had encountered in connection with his second race, the nail in his foot may have been the one with the most serious implications for his future. Puncture injuries to the frog of a horse's foot—a triangular mass of elastic tissue that forms part of the foot's shock absorption system—can range from minor to serious, depending on the depth of penetration and whether infection sets in. Both mechanical injury from a deep wound and nagging infection can compromise structures deeper in the foot, and this may well have happened to Black Gold; more than a year later, Webb admitted that the foot had never fully recovered from the nail incident.[1]

How much of the lingering effects of the injury can be laid at Webb's doorstep is anyone's guess. Most trainers of his time were accustomed to treating their horses' minor injuries themselves rather than seeking out one of the few veterinarians available, and Webb was no exception to that rule.[2] Although it is likely that the trainer made use of the time-honored methods of poulticing and tubbing to clean the foot and bring any infection to a head that could be lanced and drained, whether he continued any treatment after the colt was relieved of any obvious lameness is unknown. Decades later, veteran horseman Olin Gentry, then Colonel Bradley's farm manager, would recall that Bradley had been concerned enough to send his own veterinarian around to administer a shot of tetanus antitoxin and offer advice, but Webb refused the assistance and, as always, did things his own way.[3] Within a few days, Black Gold was galloping again, seemingly none the worse for his experience.

Webb was a man who chewed on grudges the way other men chewed on plugs of tobacco, and jockeys who turned in a bad ride on one of his horses—especially a suspiciously bad ride—soon found that he neither forgave nor forgot. When Black Gold came out for the Dixie Junior Purse in February 12, Burke was replaced in the saddle by rising Fair Grounds apprentice B. "Red" Harvey. Worthmore was not entered, and Will Land, said to have been working exceptionally well, scratched. That left Black Gold to face seven rivals over a muddy, heavy track as a 1.20–1 favorite.

Mud is a great leveler of Thoroughbreds, and both Useeit and Black Toney had lost races on wet going to horses they could handle easily under drier conditions. Given that heritage, some experienced bettors probably thought Black Gold was an underlay—a horse going off at odds shorter than its performances and competition warrant. Black Gold proved otherwise. Breaking smartly, he showed speed from the outset as Harvey steered him over to the rail—the shortest way home but also the deepest going on a muddy track. It didn't bother the colt at all; in fact, he seemed to relish the soggy footing. Skimming effortlessly over the surface, Black Gold drew off to win "well in hand" by four lengths over Edna V.[4] His time of 0:35⅗ for the three furlongs was just a tick off what he had posted in his maiden win over a much faster surface.

The Fair Grounds meeting closed on Mardi Gras Day, February 13, and Black Gold and the other horses there moved over to nearby Jefferson Park for the remainder of the New Orleans racing season. With Black Gold back in winning form, Webb wanted to get another start in him quickly. A February 19 allowance over three and one-half furlongs looked ideal, but there was one problem: Harvey could not ride the colt, probably due to contract obligations with owner-trainer John Ward. Thus, Webb found himself hunting for a rider for the third time in four races. He settled on Lawrence McDermott, a capable jockey who was coming off a good year in 1922.

Six juveniles, Black Gold included, turned out for the race, the opener on the day's card. Thanks to his last-out victory, the colt picked up a five-pound penalty and carried 123 pounds against 118 on Will Land, 115 on Edna V. (who got a three-pound sex allowance), and 107 to 110 pounds on the other three starters.

Perhaps feeling the weight, Black Gold was uncharacteristically slow in breaking into stride and trailed his field early. In the meantime, Will Land had broken sharply and was flying on the lead, setting a hot pace of 0:11⅘ for the opening furlong and 0:23⅖ for the first quarter mile. Then Black Gold started picking it up, coming relentlessly around the outside. As he drew up on Will Land's flank, the gelding responded to the challenge with a fresh spurt, hitting the three-furlong mark in 0:34⅘. It should have been a winning move, but Black Gold came right back at him. Under hard urging from McDermott, the black colt surged past the tiring leader. Seventy yards from home, he swerved left, crowding Will Land's path slightly, but his momentum was too great to be denied. At the finish he was two lengths in front, with Will Land second and Edna V. another six lengths back in third.

Hearty cheers greeted the result, and then the applause turned into a roar as the time was hung out. In spite of the slow start and his weaving steps in the stretch, Black Gold had run the distance in a sensational 0:40⅘, shattering the previous track record by 1⅗ seconds. The following day, Black Gold's race made it into newspapers from Canada and New York to California, along with the news that the Hoots colt had been nominated to several stakes at Aqueduct and Jamaica off his record-breaking performance.[5]

Not everyone agreed that his race had been quite as impressive as it looked. Several private timers had recorded times of 0:41⅕ or 0:41⅖ for the race, and it was also noted that Black Gold had benefited from a strong tailwind.[6] In addition, second-place Will Land, whom Black Gold had impeded slightly during the stretch run, finished close enough to have also beaten the former mark. Nonetheless, even the slowest of the private clockings had Black Gold breaking the track record by at least a full second, and that track record had been set by a future stakes winner who had carried nine pounds less than Black Gold had shouldered. C. J. Savage summed up the general consensus when he opined, "He [Black Gold] is about the best juvenile seen on a New Orleans race course in many years."[7]

In the excitement following the record-breaking performance, no one seemed to pay any attention to Black Gold's tardy start or his duck toward the rail late in the race. True, he had not shown similar behaviors before, but two-year-olds were often erratic and unpredictable. If there were any whispers on the backstretch speculating as to whether the colt might be sore, they never made it past the backstretch to the newspapers, and Webb kept his own counsel. The next day, Black Gold was out for exercise as usual, seemingly none the worse for wear, and innocently unaware that he had just become a hot property.

Breeding a good racehorse is a matter of catching lightning in a bottle; the same mating that produces a champion one year may the following year yield a full sibling that can't run fast enough to work up a decent sweat. Because of these vagaries, many owners never trouble themselves with the breeding end of the sport, leaving it to others to take the risks of trying to come up with something that can actually run. But let a breeder start racing a youngster that flashes real talent, and there is usually a line at the door hoping to buy a ready-made racehorse.

In Black Gold's case, the line started forming the day after his eye-popping win at Jefferson Park, beginning with Kansas City's rising political boss, Thomas J. Pendergast. Like many of the other big-city bosses of his time, Pendergast was a heavy gambler and had developed a taste for horse racing. By 1919 he was actively involved as an owner, and by 1922 he had his first good horse, a two-year-old named Bo McMillan, who became a stakes winner at Saratoga. Pendergast was targeting the 1923 Kentucky Derby with Bo McMillan, but he had not built up his political career or his contracting business by stopping with initial successes. He wanted more, and so he contacted Rosa Hoots, offering $20,000 for Black Gold.[8] He was not a man who was often refused, but this time he was, and apparently flatly enough that he did not bother to try raising the offer. Other would-be owners put out tentative feelers without making specific offers, but they received no encouragement; according to one story circulating through the newspapers, Mrs. Hoots had said, "I know if my husband lived he would not give up a son of his love-pony for all the money in the world."[9]

Not long afterward, the *Tulsa Tribune*'s Dick Maher arranged a rare interview with Rosa Hoots on April 7, 1923, to talk about her horse.[10] Knowing something of the Hootses' previous involvement with racing, and perhaps having read the already-widespread romantic version of the colt's origins— including the part that claimed that Mrs. Hoots believed that her dead husband's spirit was riding the colt to victory—Maher went in expecting sentiment to predominate during the interview.[11] He was in for a surprise. After the topic turned from preliminaries about Al Hoots and Useeit to Black Gold himself, what he got was disinterest, even disdain. "What do I care about Black Gold?" Mrs. Hoots asked bluntly. "I don't know much about the racing game and I don't care to loaf about the stables or the track. . . . I haven't seen him nor any of the horses for several years."

Maher was equally unprepared for her continuing with a cool-headed evaluation of her colt as an asset. Black Gold was still "on trial," she said, and needed to prove himself against the better competition awaiting him in Kentucky before she made any long-term decisions regarding his future.

Based on personal experience, Mrs. Hoots had reason for her skepticism about Black Gold's merits; nine years earlier, she had watched Useeit struggle in Kentucky after proving herself the best sprinter at the Fair Grounds. She also knew that Tulsa and Tuscola had not come to much after decent maiden wins; in fact, Tulsa had been claimed and was racing for another owner, an event that was apparently of little concern to Rosa once it became obvious that Tulsa lacked the ability to fulfill Al Hoots's dream. Nonetheless, Maher wanted to see something more than apparent indifference. "Aren't you going back east to see your colt run?" he asked.

"I haven't thought about it. I'm too busy here," came the bland response.

Maher found himself fishing for another question with which to conclude the interview. At the time, Harry Sinclair was president of the Exchange National Bank of Tulsa and deeply involved in regional oil production through his Sinclair Consolidated Oil Corporation. He also owned Rancocas Stable, and his star colt Zev was considered a top candidate for that spring's Kentucky Derby. Perhaps with that in mind, the question Maher came up with was, "How would you like to see him enter the Kentucky Derby in another year?"

Rosa Hoots only smiled.

12

One Man's Dream

Mrs. Hoots may have found Maher's closing question amusingly premature, given her own cautious nature and the fact that Black Gold was only a two-year-old who had yet to prove himself in stakes company. Yet the fact that Maher had asked it at all signaled a far-reaching change in the status of the Kentucky Derby, a race that had been on the verge of extinction two decades earlier. That it survived to become the national obsession of Thoroughbred racing in the United States is a remarkable story in itself—one that, like Black Gold's, began with one man's dream. That man was Colonel Meriwether Lewis Clark Jr., the creator of the Kentucky Derby—and very nearly its destroyer.

Born in Louisville in 1846, Clark came of a lineage as aristocratic as any in America. His father, the senior Meriwether Lewis Clark, was a successful architect and the son of William Clark, second-in-command of the famous Lewis and Clark expedition and later the first governor of the Missouri Territory. His mother, Abigail Churchill, was the daughter of Kentucky state legislator Samuel Churchill and a granddaughter of Kentucky pioneer Armistead Churchill, whose plantation was one of the earliest in the Louisville area.

The Churchill family was involved in Kentucky horse racing from the state's beginnings, and Samuel Churchill was one of the founders of Louisville's old Oakland Race Course in the 1830s. Clark developed his own interest in this part of his family's heritage after the untimely death of his mother, whose family raised Clark after his father found himself too affected by his bereavement to raise his children alone. The young Clark spent a great deal of time with his bachelor uncles, John and Henry Churchill, and learned the love of fine horses and racing from them, a love that deepened during the first of two trips to Europe.

Having both inherited money and married it (though his first wife died young, as did his second), Clark could afford to indulge in patrician tastes for fine dining, sumptuous parties, and good horseflesh. He also had a certain sense of noblesse oblige, making him inclined to listen when he was approached by several prominent Kentucky breeders in 1872 on the subject of attempting to revive horse racing in Kentucky.

Horses and horse breeding had been a part of Kentucky's traditions since the state's earliest days, but the state's breeding industry was in serious trouble. Many of the state's best horses had been casualties in the Civil War, forcing some horsemen out of the business entirely. The rest were facing uncertain times. Oakland Race Course had shut down even before the war, and other tracks were either operating only sporadically or had shifted to trotters. Kentucky's last remaining major race track for Thoroughbreds, Woodlawn, had closed in 1870; New York, New Jersey, and several of the midwestern states that had been essentially undamaged by the Civil War were moving ahead of Kentucky in the horse-breeding market; and the need was urgent for a track where locally bred racehorses could be showcased and the market for them revived.

Clark was not a breeder, but he had something else the group needed—a charismatic presence, accompanied by name recognition and blood ties to Louisville society. He also had money, connections in the banking industry, and the energy of youth. In the breeders' view, there was no better man to spearhead an organization to bring Thoroughbred racing back to the state. Their question was simple: would he be interested?

Clark was, but though he could be impetuous and high-handed, he sensed that this was a matter that would take some thought. Thus, instead of plunging straight into the challenge, he traveled back to Europe with the specific purpose of studying not just the world's great horse races and courses but the rules and customs under which European racing was conducted. This tour took him over a year, but it proved time well spent, for he knew exactly what he wanted to create when he returned in 1873. What he envisioned was a race meeting that would re-create his experiences at venues such as Epsom Downs, Longchamp, and Chantilly, combining the highest class of racing with the elegance and luxury of a great social occasion.

His plan won the support of his Churchill uncles, who agreed to provide the land on which the new racing plant would be built, and in 1874, the

Louisville Jockey Club was organized with Clark as president. Membership in the club was by subscription, with 320 individuals agreeing to pay one hundred dollars each for a share in the new enterprise. The first race meeting was slated to begin on May 17, 1875, and to run for six days. Its opening-day showpiece would be the Kentucky Derby, a race for three-year-olds modeled after England's classic Derby Stakes. A counterpart for three-year-old fillies, the Kentucky Oaks (named after England's Oaks Stakes), would run later in the meeting, along with the Clark Stakes, a race later open to older horses but initially modeled after the oldest of England's classic races, the St. Leger Stakes.

Fifteen horses contested that first Kentucky Derby, representing major owners all over the Midwest and South. Under the eyes of a crowd estimated at up to twelve thousand, a small chestnut colt named Aristides took the lead after stalking the pace for the first mile. Repelling a challenge by Volcano, he stayed in front the rest of the way to win by a length. The time of 2:37¾ was believed to be a new world's record for a three-year-old over a mile and a half.

For his colt's efforts, Price McGrath received a purse of $2,850 and a massive sterling silver punch bowl valued at $1,000. The following day, the newspapers gave glowing reports of the racing, the new track's facilities, and the color and gaiety of the occasion, much to the pleasure of Clark and his associates.

Although McGrath's two-horse entry was favored in the betting, Aristides's victory was considered an upset as he had been entered to prompt the pace for his more heralded stablemate Chesapeake—the first of a long string of Derby favorites that "couldn't lose." Still, it was popular, and as the 1875 racing season progressed, it became apparent that Aristides was a much better horse than anyone had thought. By the end of the year, he was widely reckoned to be the best three-year-old in the country. Over the next six years, three more colts acclaimed as national champions claimed the Kentucky Derby as one of their prizes—Vigil, Baden-Baden, and Hindoo—and the prestige and reputation of the race rose accordingly. Clark's dream had become a reality.

For Clark and the Louisville Jockey Club, these were excellent years. Each spring, the Kentucky Derby drew in fine horses and their owners from across the country, along with the cream of local society. Clark's opulent pre- and post-Derby parties became legendary, and his tall, massive figure strode through the festivities with the air of a lord surveying his domain. Occasionally his auto-cratic temper flashed, sometimes to the point that he drew a gun to threaten the object of his ire, and once he paid for his lack of emotional restraint with a bullet in the chest, the souvenir of an altercation that developed after Clark angrily accused prominent breeder Thomas G. Moore of failing to pay his entry fees at the track. Still, the racing itself was conducted with strict integrity, the race meetings were a great social success, and for some time, the people who counted in Louisville were inclined to overlook Clark's more outrageous actions. He was, after all, one of their own.

Nonetheless, Clark's prestige and connections did not compare to those of the northeastern elites who dominated American racing in the late nineteenth century, and as early as 1882, there were hints of a growing rift between the Clark regime and the eastern establishment. That year, the powerful Dwyer Brothers stable had the top colt in the country in Runnymede, but the heavy-betting Dwyers were unsatisfied with the auction pools that were the primary means of betting at the Louisville Jockey Club's track. A popular form of betting in early Kentucky racing, auction pools were run by pool sellers, who "sold" each horse in the race in a kind of fantasy auction. Following the race, the bidder who had "bought" the winner received all the money in the auction pool, less the pool seller's commission of 5 percent. Multiple pools could be sold on each race, as many as the demand occasioned, but each pool was separate from all others.

Auction pools were satisfactory to the locals, but the Dwyers were unused to them. They wanted bookmakers, and they threatened to withdraw Runnymede unless they could bring bookies from their native New York. They got their way but not the win as Runnymede was beaten by a half length by the unheralded gelding Apollo, a horse that had run second in a selling race only a month earlier. Though they made no complaint regarding the outcome of the race, there were no more Derby runners for the Dwyers until 1896, when Mike Dwyer (who by then had parted ways with his brother Phil) won with Ben Brush.

That was bad enough, but four years after the Runnymede affair, a track official—possibly Clark himself, according to one account—made an enormous gaffe regarding James Ben Ali Haggin, the largest owner-breeder of his time and a force to be reckoned with in both eastern and Californian racing circles. After Haggin's Ben Ali won the Kentucky Derby in 1886, Haggin was heard complaining about the lack of on-track bookmakers (who were on strike due to a dispute regarding licensing fees). His complaint reached the ears of a Louisville Jockey Club official, but instead of being conciliatory, the man injudiciously belittled Haggin and finished his comments with "to hell with him anyway."[1] Word of the official's response got back to Haggin, and shortly afterward, every horse Haggin had brought to Kentucky was on its way back to New York. The withdrawal of Haggin's stable left gaping holes in the entries for the remainder of the meeting, with an inevitable negative effect on betting handle. Worse, Haggin's complaints regarding his treatment were soon common knowledge among his peers in the East, who joined Haggin in giving Clark's track the cold shoulder for the next quarter century.

Without eastern support, the Kentucky Derby inevitably declined in prestige, essentially becoming a regional prize. The Louisville Jockey Club, too, declined in prestige and condition. The track had never been a money maker; in debt from the day it opened, it paid a dividend to its shareholders only once during the years Colonel Clark was in charge. With the lack of eastern horses leading to smaller fields and lesser handle, there was no money to spare to repair or upgrade the facilities, which by 1883 had acquired the nickname "Churchill's Downs" in reference to its family connections.[2] The poor physical condition of the racing plant increased dissatisfaction among racegoers and local horsemen and made the track even less attractive to both. In an effort to keep the track going, Clark repeatedly bypassed collecting his salary as track president and dipped into his own pockets to cover losses at the track's meetings.[3]

In hindsight, the downward slide of the Kentucky Derby was driven by the same man responsible for its initial success. At the race's beginning, Clark was just what was needed: a visionary with the energy, drive, money, and connections to carry out the grand idea he had conceived. The problem was that he was not a man suited to the task of transitioning the glittering start into an ongoing success. Aside from the embarrassing difficulties created by his quick temper—which were eroding his family's support—he was too often rude and arrogant with those he considered beneath his station, creating rifts between himself and horsemen from outside the local area, small breeders, potential subscribers to the race meetings, and some members of the press. He made few new friends for himself or the track, and his insistence on maintaining personal control over what he had created inevitably brought him into conflict with anyone who might have been able to give him needed if unpalatable advice. Compounding the problem, he lacked both the business skills necessary to ground his creative vision in fiscal reality and the marketing skills needed to attract more favorable publicity and more investment.

Not all of Clark's decisions were bad ones. Unlike some other racetrack operators, he encouraged the attendance of women of all classes, reasoning that if the ladies enjoyed a day at the races, their male escorts would also do so and would make betting (then restricted to men) part of their enjoyment. He also made plans to update betting options and reduce corruption by bringing pari-mutuel machines from France, though this idea had to be shelved when local bookmakers protested this threat to their businesses. Years after Clark's death, his pari-mutuel machines—and a legislative loophole that he and friends in the Kentucky government had engineered to permit their use—allowed betting to continue when bookmaking was shut down by a hostile city government just before the spring race meeting of 1908, saving the Kentucky Derby and Churchill Downs from threatened bankruptcy.

Nonetheless, Clark was unable to stop the track's financial hemorrhaging, and his failure to govern either his temper or his elitist attitude became too much of an embarrassment to his Churchill uncles to be ignored. As they still owned the land on which the track existed, they had the leverage to force a change and eventually did. In 1894, the New Louisville Jockey Club, a group headed by former newspaperman Charles F. Price, took over the management of Churchill Downs and named William F. Schulte as the track president; Price became the track secretary. Clark was retained as presiding judge, but a few years later, in worsening health and increasingly isolated, he committed suicide at the age of fifty-three. He died less than two weeks before the twenty-fifth Kentucky Derby, won by Manuel.

On taking over from Clark, the New Louisville Jockey Club poured money into an attempt to save the Downs. Spending some one hundred thousand dollars on the renovations, they built a new grandstand on the west side of the track. Capable of seating 1,500 and providing standing room under cover to another 500, the grandstand was topped with what became the symbol of Churchill Downs: its iconic twin towers, designed by architect Joseph Dominic Baldez. The management also freshly whitewashed the stables and fencing.

Even after that, only four horses contested the 1895 Derby, won by Halma. The small field led to one more change being made. After twenty-one renewals contested at the mile and a half of the original Derby Stakes, the distance for the 1896 renewal was dropped to the modern distance of a mile and a quarter. Horsemen greeted the change enthusiastically, making 171 entries; eight started, the largest field in seven years.

It was encouraging, but it was not enough to reverse the slide; over the next decade, the average Derby field was just five horses. Churchill Downs continued to lose money year in and year out, and the investors were losing what little patience they had remaining. By 1902, they had had enough and were ready to shutter the track.

No one in that group would have given the Kentucky Derby a wild long shot's chance of surviving. But Derby dreams die hard, and somehow Colonel Clark's vision had found a new home in the heart of a Louisville tailor. Matt Winn not only became the race's unlikely savior but took the Derby to a new level, transforming it into the grand pursuit of American horse racing.

13

Mr. Derby

While famed sportswriter Joe Palmer jocularly credited Matt Winn with inventing the Kentucky Derby—along with bourbon, hickory-cured ham, and Stephen Foster—Winn was still a month away from his fourteenth birthday when the first Kentucky Derby ran in 1875. His father, Patrick, was one of hundreds of Louisville residents who took advantage of free parking for their wagons and carriages in a section of the track infield, and the boy watched the race from the seat of his father's grocery wagon.

Like most of the other attendees, young Winn expected the big, handsome Chesapeake to win. Instead, as he watched Aristides hurtle down the stretch to victory, something caught fire in his soul. He found himself in love, not with a horse but with the Derby itself. It was a passion that lasted throughout his life, earning him the nickname of "Mr. Derby."

Winn's passion did not translate into a career in the horse business, at least not at first. He was too big to make a jockey and lacked the skills and connections needed to make a go of it as a trainer or breeder. His interests lay in business, and at fourteen, he left St. Xavier High School to enroll in Bryant & Stratton Business College. After graduating a year later, he worked briefly as a bookkeeper and as a clerk before becoming a traveling salesman for the wholesale grocery firm of Stege & Reiling. He held that position for close to a decade, traveling by horse and buggy through the mountain counties of Kentucky to make his rounds.

Winn did well in sales, and anyone observing him at this time in his life would probably have said that he had found his calling. But every year, no matter what his circumstances, he made his pilgrimage back to Churchill Downs for the Kentucky Derby. To him, there was something irresistibly romantic about the race and its setting: spring sunshine and flowers, beautifully dressed women turned out for a gay social occasion, men engaging in friendly chaffing as they argued the merits of their favorites, bettors generating excitement and tension around the betting ring. Above all, there were the horses and their thrilling displays of speed and courage, culminating in the day's showcase: the Derby.

In 1887, Winn gave up the life of a traveling salesman for a more stable one as partner with Ed Langan in the latter's Louisville tailor shop. As Winn later admitted, he knew nothing about tailoring; that was Langan's end of the business. What Winn brought in was less tangible than skill with a needle but just as important. He knew the money side of business, and he knew how to market the goods he sold. He also knew how to connect with the customers, applying a bit of Irish charm here, entertaining with a well-told anecdote there. Soon, the shop was prosperous and a favorite with Louisville's businessmen, sportsmen, and politicians.

The closing years of the nineteenth century were good ones for Winn. He had married his sweetheart, Mollie Doyle, in 1888 and was raising a family. He had a business he understood and enjoyed as well as an increasing number of useful connections with Louisville's upper class. He had money enough to enjoy the diversions and luxuries available to a respectable businessman, and he could afford to gamble on a bit of sporting action if he chose to spend a pleasant afternoon amusing himself with a trip to the races. He even had racehorses of his own from time to time, and every year he continued making his annual trip to the Derby to take in the spectacle that had captivated him since boyhood.

Perhaps at times during those years, there was talk that the New Louisville Jockey Club was not doing so well. Thanks to the clientele that patronized the Winn & Langan Tailoring Company, Winn would almost certainly have known of any rumors to that effect. Nonetheless, so long as the Derby kept running, he was unconcerned about the track's problems. Then an old friend paid him an unexpected visit in 1902, and without warning, Winn found himself with the Kentucky Derby's fate in his hands.

Winn was in the tailor shop when Charles Price came by, and one look at his friend's face told Winn that Price had not stopped in to exchange pleasantries.

Without preamble, Price dropped a bombshell: Churchill Downs, he said, was about to shut down for good. Then he dropped an even bigger one. He wanted Winn to buy the track.

The request made no sense. Winn had no experience in track management, and Price knew it. It was insane to ask a complete novice to take on a challenge that had broken the hearts and wallets of experienced racing men—but Price also knew about his friend's private obsession and framed his proposal in terms of the one thing that might sell it. Buy the track, he said, and the Kentucky Derby would survive. Let Churchill Downs go down, and the Derby would die with it.

Winn hesitated, but only for a moment. As he later admitted, if it had been only a matter of saving Churchill Downs, he would have refused—but he could not let the Kentucky Derby go. He asked for a few days to think it over, but he already knew what he was going to do. If Price couldn't come up with another buyer at the last minute, Winn would act as best he could to save the Derby by saving Churchill Downs.[1]

As he expected, Price was unable to find anyone else willing to buy the track, and Winn stepped in as Price had hoped he would. Even so, Winn was too cautious to take on the expense of trying to save the track by himself. Instead, he used the marketing skills he had developed during his years as a salesman and businessman to persuade other prominent citizens to join forces with him, organizing them into a syndicate. Between them, they ponied up the forty thousand dollars needed to buy the racing plant. Charles Grainger, the mayor of Louisville, became the new track president, but he was mostly a figurehead. Officially Winn was vice president, but in all but name, Churchill Downs was his to run.[2]

And run it he did. Although he held on to his tailoring business for the first year, Winn put most of his prodigious energy into long-overdue renovations to the track's facilities. By the time the 1903 meet rolled around, Churchill Downs had a new clubhouse, an improved café, and a refurbished grandstand, making it an attractive place for Louisville society and out-of-town guests to see and be seen. The changes proved popular, and when the receipts were totted up after the close of the fall meeting, Churchill Downs had turned its first profit in many a long year.

After 1903, Winn could no longer keep up with both the tailoring shop and the management of the track. With some reluctance, he let the former go, committing himself to the racing world. He was now officially Churchill

Downs's general manager as well as its vice president, and having gotten a feel for what people wanted and expected of a racing facility, he began branching out. Over the next several decades, he would become involved with managing other tracks, including Douglas Park (two miles across Louisville from Churchill Downs), City Park in New Orleans, Empire City in New York, Laurel Park in Maryland, and Terrazas Park in Mexico. He would also become the president of the American Turf Association, which gained control of racing dates and rules for practically all the major tracks from Chicago and Kentucky to New Orleans after a struggle with the older Western Turf Association.

In the middle of all Winn's other duties and ventures, the Kentucky Derby remained the love of his heart, and he worked tirelessly to improve and promote it. Nonetheless, he went through nearly a decade when he could do little more than keep the race alive. The 1903 edition (won by Agile) drew just three starters, and the Derby remained a regional prize for years after. It was not even the biggest race in Kentucky, as the Latonia Derby offered larger winners' purses than the $4,850 earned by the Kentucky Derby winners of 1896 through 1912.

Unlike Colonel Clark, Winn knew the value of following a sound business plan and building goodwill, and he kept to a long-term strategy pursuing both ends rather than rushing out to boost the purse or provide other short-term incentives. He continued making improvements at Churchill Downs and sought out new investors to bolster the track's financial health. He built good relationships with the local press and their colleagues in Cincinnati, Chicago, St. Louis, and New Orleans, and he also spent time courting the best newspaper reporters and sports columnists of the day whenever he was in New York, plying them with free meals, drinks, and promises of expenses-paid trips to the Downs if they cared to come and visit.[3] When some took him up on the offer, he considered himself well repaid by their increased interest in covering racing at his plant.

Then Winn got an unexpected break from an unexpected source: the same antigambling movement in politics that had nearly closed Churchill Downs in 1908. In the fall of 1910, New York joined a wave of states that had effectively shut down horse racing thanks to new laws outlawing most forms of gambling. With the richest and most prestigious racing circuit in the country closed, the major owners who had been racing there had three choices: they could disband their stables, they could ship their horses abroad (mostly to England and France), or they could send their racers to Kentucky, Maryland, or Canada to participate in what North American racing was still available at a level above the fair circuit and the bush. Knowing opportunity when he saw it, Winn drew on the friendships he had struck up with owners all over the East, letting them know that their horses would be heartily welcome in Kentucky.

Richard Carmen was among the New Yorkers who decided to send horses to Churchill Downs, and in 1911, his Meridian became the first Kentucky Derby winner since Joe Cotton in 1885 to be reckoned the year's outstanding three-year-old colt. The next year, Worth (owned by H. C. Hallenbeck of New York) became the first nationally acknowledged juvenile champion to compete in and win the Derby since Ben Brush. Then Donerail came along in 1913. A local runner, he was no champion, but he became the longest-priced horse ever to win the Kentucky Derby, and news of his record pari-mutuel payoff of $184.90 on a two-dollar win ticket gave the race valuable publicity.

Racing reopened in New York within a few weeks of Donerail's victory, but Winn's luck held in 1914 as the best two-year-old of the previous season, Old Rosebud, just happened to be owned by Churchill Downs track secretary Hamilton Applegate. The morning before the Derby, track superintendent James Ross and his staff literally sponged away the remnants of a torrential downpour to put the track into fast condition for the big race, and Old Rosebud rewarded their efforts with a new track record that stood until 1931.

The turning point that elevated the Derby to an event of national standing came in 1915. That year, Winn scored his biggest coup yet by persuading the popular and influential Harry Payne Whitney to enter his champion juvenile filly, Regret, in the Kentucky Derby. Whitney's fellow New Yorker James Butler—personally connected to Winn as the owner of both Empire City and Laurel—sportingly followed suit by sending his champion juvenile colt, Pebbles, and the two champions ran one-two around the racetrack in front of the largest Derby field ever, with the filly triumphant by two lengths.[4] Following Regret's victory, Whitney exulted, "I don't care if she ever wins another race, or even runs again, for she has done enough this afternoon by winning America's greatest race."[5]

That declaration was the moment Winn credited with making the Derby "an American institution."[6] Whitney's enthusiastic endorsement of the Derby was all that eastern owners needed to be convinced that this was a prize worth pursuing. For more than twenty years, until the threat of World War II curbed field sizes somewhat, fields of fifteen or more runners were the rule rather than the exception. Names such as John Sanford, Fred Johnson, Willis Sharpe

Kilmer, and Commander J. K. L. Ross, all familiar to New York racing, joined the ranks of those whose horses had become Kentucky Derby winners. They were lured not only by the Derby's ever-increasing prestige but by its purse, which swelled from $10,000-added in 1915 to $50,000-added by 1921.[7]

The one top owner Winn could not charm into sending a runner was Samuel Riddle, who in 1920 declined to send the legendary Man o' War in quest of the roses; he felt that the race fell too early in the year to ask a three-year-old to carry 126 pounds over a mile and a quarter.[8] Nonetheless, the great colt's absence may have benefited the Derby more than his presence, as a likely field of no more than five or six runners swelled to seventeen. Some forty-five thousand patrons showed up to watch Ral Parr's gelding Paul Jones defeat Upset (the only horse ever to defeat Man o' War) by a head after a gritty front-running performance. The following year, Colonel Bradley scored a popular one-two finish with Behave Yourself and Black Servant, and in 1922, Benjamin Block brought in his undefeated juvenile champion Morvich to gallop off with the prize—a double coup for Winn as Block bypassed the Preakness Stakes, which was run on the same day that year.

As the spring racing season approached in Kentucky in 1923, Winn could look back on what he had accomplished in just twenty years with pride, but he was not sitting on his laurels. He seemed to be everywhere, inspecting the latest set of renovations and improvements to the Downs, checking in with Ross's successor, Tom Young, as to the condition of the racing strip, maintaining contact with city officials, courting owners of high-profile three-year-olds to ensure that as many as possible sent their colts to the Derby. And when he was not otherwise occupied, he was keeping a close eye on the rising two-year-olds and their owners around the country, already thinking ahead to what he planned to make the grandest Derby yet: the Golden Jubilee, celebrating the race's fiftieth anniversary. Many of the youngsters deemed most promising had yet to make their racing debuts, but after the New Orleans racing season closed, he already had one "early bird" on his radar—Black Gold, now on his way to Kentucky.

14

Kentucky Trial

Black Gold settled in well after making the trip from New Orleans to Lexington in late March, and his barn was soon drawing regular visitors—some attracted by a chance to get a look at the colt, and others looking for a chance to partake of some of Webb's cooking, which had a more than ordinary reputation among Bluegrass horsemen.[1] Webb enjoyed showing off both his colt and his culinary skill to his backstretch cronies and basked in the praise for both his food and his colt's appearance and condition.

Nonetheless, by the time the Lexington meeting opened on April 28, much of the hoopla surrounding Black Gold's track-record performance in New Orleans had died down. Racing is a "what have you done for me lately" game, and the colt had not raced since that effort, though there was no reason to suspect anything was amiss; he had turned in a sharp breeze shortly before leaving Jefferson Park, going three furlongs in better than track-record time.[2] The reason that he had not been in competition was that from February 20 through the closing day of the Jefferson Park meeting on March 17, the only juvenile races carded had been for maidens, claimers, or fillies. That was a left-handed compliment to Black Gold, who was the likely reason that the track could not get a field together for another juvenile allowance, but it meant that, by the time he was entered in the Spring Station Purse on Lexington's opening-day card, he had not raced in more than two months.

Still unconvinced of Black Gold's ability to handle Kentucky competition, Rosa Hoots remained in Tulsa; though she was getting regular updates on the colt's training and condition from Webb, she would await news of the outcome of an actual race before making any further decisions. The Kentucky crowd apparently did not share her doubts, especially since Black Gold had already proved himself under the rainy conditions prevailing on opening day and had been working well at the Lexington oval. They made the colt a heavy favorite even though he had 118 pounds aboard against 113 on Will Land, the only other previous winner in the four-furlong sprint. The other contestants, still maidens, were assigned 110 pounds, though several ended up carrying more than their required imposts because their jockeys were unable to make the weight. Unfortunately for Webb, he could not get Lawrence McDermott to ride as the jockey was under contract to the stable of Howard Oots, and he ended up settling for Jack Howard as Black Gold's pilot in the colt's first Kentucky start.

Black Gold won respect that day but not the race. Whether because of poor handling by Howard or a lack of focus on his part, he was "caught unprepared" at the break in what was officially termed a "bad" start for the field.[3] With the inside lanes blocked by the horses that had outbroken him, the colt was forced to race wide throughout. In the meantime, Digit, breaking from the second post position, had a perfect trip on the front end. That proved to be the difference. Black Gold came flying in the stretch, but the ground ran out a head too soon. His chart notation read, "Much the best," rare praise indeed for a losing effort.[4]

Far away in Oklahoma, Rosa Hoots was nursing a freshly broken arm from a riding accident.[5] Nonetheless, she received Webb's report of Black Gold's performance with an interest that she had not revealed to Dick Maher. Black Gold had proved that he could run with Kentucky horses, and he had an engagement coming up in the Tobacco Stakes, the first juvenile stakes race of the Kentucky season. Perhaps it was a good time to see for herself what she had and to decide whether Useeit's little black colt was the one who could transform her late husband's dream to reality.

A few days later, Mrs. Hoots was on a train headed east, accompanied by her son Alfred.[6] Her business in Tulsa could wait; she had more pressing business in Lexington, where Black Gold would meet stakes company for the first time.

May 7 came in with clear weather but colder than expected for the time of year; two days later, there would be a trace of snow on the ground.[7] Webb shrugged off the unseasonable nip in the air as he saddled his colt for the

Tobacco Stakes and gave the jockey a leg up: a new rider, Black Gold's fifth in six starts. With Howard having joined Webb's grudge list for his poor break in the colt's last outing and with McDermott still unavailable, Webb had gone for experience and engaged Danny Connelly, a respected veteran who had taken several important races on champion Old Rosebud in 1917 and had won the Kentucky Oaks in 1920 and 1922.[8]

Rosa Hoots had made an uneventful trip from Tulsa, touched by bitter-sweet memories; she had scarcely left Oklahoma since her husband had died, and Lexington was both familiar and changed since Useeit had last raced there in 1915. Now it was Alfred rather than Al by her side as she sat among the crowd enjoying the day's races. She had gotten her first look at Black Gold earlier in his stable, with Webb hovering like any proud and slightly anxious parent as he showed off his "baby." The colt had looked good then, but any horse could look good when it was merely posing. So, as the field filed out onto the track for the day's feature, Rosa watched the slim black colt with a keen, assessing eye as he paraded by the stands with six others. He was smaller than most of the others, but he gleamed like oil in the sun, his coat a handsome contrast to her silks of old rose jacket, crossed white sashes, white bars on sleeves, black cap. He was alert and eager, ready to go; Connelly handled him calmly, wasting no energy. In a few minutes, they were at the post.

Connelly timed the barrier's rise perfectly, getting Black Gold away in stride—and in the next split second hauled back on the reins as Mack Garner came slamming over on Black Satin to shut off the inside route. Checked hard, Black Gold dropped back into safe space, but now he was near the rear of the pack. His misfortune was Edna V.'s fortune; with George Yeargin gunning her to the front and clear of the trouble, the speedy filly was skimming along on an uncontested lead along the rail. Forced to come wide, Black Gold was running fastest of all at the end but ran out of ground. With a neck to spare, Edna V. reached the finish line in 0:47, just a fifth of a second off the four-furlong track record. Once again, the Hoots colt's chart entry read "much the best," but without the win to show for it.[9]

Neither the Hootses nor Webb blamed Connelly for the loss, and Black Gold appeared to have suffered no harm from the rough opening to the Tobacco Stakes. The one ominous note was that the colt was wearing front bandages in a workout photo taken a few days after the race, but though such bandages were used to support sore legs, they could also have been protecting minor cuts or scrapes, and there is no mention in the newspapers of any obvious lameness.[10] A week later, Connelly was back in the saddle as the colt went out for the West Point Purse, an allowance race at Churchill Downs. This time Black Gold got away from the barrier without any trouble, and Connelly was able to track the early pace of Brilliant Cast before taking command in the stretch. After that, collecting the purse was a formality. Over a track rated "heavy," Black Gold had still not been asked for his best when he crossed the finish line eight lengths in front, a big margin for a race of only four and one-half furlongs.

It was Black Gold's first win in three starts since coming to Kentucky, but virtually every horseman around conceded that with better racing luck, the colt could just as easily have been three-for-three since his arrival in the Bluegrass. As it was, Black Gold boasted an overall record of four wins, two seconds, and one third from seven races, and Webb proudly let it be known that the colt would race next in the Bashford Manor Stakes at Churchill Downs on May 19—Derby Day.

Rosa Hoots approved his plan, which fit in with her own decision to attend the big race for the first time. Maher had asked her about the Derby; now she would see for herself what the race was about, and whether she had a horse worthy of it—and worthy of Al Hoots's dream.

The forty-ninth Kentucky Derby drew another huge crowd to Churchill Downs, along with twenty-one of the best three-year-olds in the country. Among the racegoers, most of the talk centered around the Preakness winner, Vigil, who had run a powerful race in the Baltimore classic on May 12. He was not the favorite; that honor went to the four-horse Greentree Stable/H. P. Whitney entry.[11] Walter Salmon's colt was the second choice, though, with third choice riding on the seven colts in the mutuel field.

All but forgotten in the betting was Harry Sinclair's Zev, who had flopped badly in the Preakness—his first start at more than six furlongs. The champion two-year-old of 1922 had come back to win a sprint over good older horses three days later, but with only four days' rest from that effort, most racegoers who thought of Zev at all dismissed him as a sprinter who was in the Derby only to let Sinclair collect a bet from Colonel Bradley. Bradley routinely offered odds of 4–1 against a given two-year-old from the previous season even making it to the Derby starting gate, and Sinclair had bet five thousand dollars that Zev would beat those odds.[12]

Whispers around the track said that Sinclair's trainer, Sam Hildreth, had even more riding on the race; if Zev won, he and his friends stood to make as much as five hundred thousand dollars from winter book bets.[13] Nonetheless, when the big day rolled around, neither Sinclair nor Hildreth was present, an indication that neither thought much of Zev's chances. Sinclair, it was said, was "detained" in New York, and Hildreth deputized assistant Dave Leary to saddle Zev.[14]

Sinclair was one of several big-name owners who had not come to the Derby, but there were plenty of other glittering or notorious personages present in a crowd estimated at seventy thousand or more. European royalty lent its cachet to the great event in the persons of the Prince and Princess of Hesse, who were the guests of Xalapa Farm owner Edward Simms. Politicians included US Representative Harry Hawes and Black Gold's would-be owner Thomas Pendergast, who was running Bo McMillan in the big race. The major Kentucky breeders and owners were there in force, rubbing elbows with financial barons and captains of industry, while society writers circulated amid their elegantly dressed wives. Adding to the spectacle, the US Army dirigible *TC-1* circled the grounds.

No one in the crowd paid any attention to a tall, quiet woman in her middle fifties who looked more staid than fashionable, other than perhaps to cast a sympathetic glance in passing at the cast that still immobilized one arm. The reporters and society columnists buzzing around the Downs had other stories to pursue, and that was as Rosa Hoots preferred. Escorted by Alfred as before, she took in the sights and sounds of Derby Day as she patiently waited for Black Gold's race.

In contrast to the unseasonable cold of just ten days earlier, the day was sunny and hot. Around most of the racing plant, the crowd was packed so tightly that the breeze could barely waft through the throng to cool sweating bodies. Nonetheless, the racegoers were in a festive mood. The racing action was as hot as the day, and the spectators cheered lustily for each race and each winner. They had been treated to three good contests before the Bashford Manor came up, and an excited buzz greeted the nine colts and geldings that stepped out onto the track for the day's secondary feature.

From her comfortable anonymity, Rosa Hoots watched her colt intently. What she was looking for, only she could have said. Perhaps she was merely hoping for better luck than when she had seen him last; perhaps she was watching for an omen.

After two minutes of milling and jostling at the barrier, the field was in line and still. Eight young Thoroughbreds erupted out of that stillness as the barrier flew up. The ninth was Black Gold. For a crucial split second, he stood flat-footed as groans burst from his supporters. Then he, too, was charging down the track.

His pursuit seemed hopeless. The race's distance was only four and one-half furlongs, and Black Gold was dead last behind a wall of horses. There was nothing Connelly could do except wait, keep his mount balanced and ready, and hope for an opening. Through the first quarter and into the turn, Black Gold continued to trail while Digit and T. S. Jordan fought it out on the front end. Then Connelly saw a gap as the field began to string out in the stretch. He gave Black Gold his head, signaling "Go!" with voice and hands and heels—and hung on as Black Gold took off.

Rosa Hoots watched as her colt became black lightning. He burst through the opening, leaving the other two trailers behind. In seconds five more rivals dropped back beaten, one after another. With a hundred yards to go, Black Gold was third and flying, but so was the leader. Two and a half lengths ahead, Digit was stretched to the utmost with T. S. Jordan driving at him. Seventy yards to go, and Digit was done; Black Gold caught him, passed him. Ahead, Jack Howard was riding like a demon, driving T. S. Jordan for the wire. His mount was tiring, but surely Black Gold was too. No mere two-year-old could sustain that kind of charge.

All around Mrs. Hoots, the spectators' roar reached the level of frenzy as the impossible happened. With fifty yards to go, Black Gold surged to the lead. He was a half length in front, a length, and now daylight showed between him and T. S. Jordan. He was still drawing off when he flashed beneath the wire, two lengths to the good. As *St. Louis Post-Dispatch* sports editor John Wray described it, he had won "with consummate ease" and was "10 or 15 lengths the best."[15]

A mighty cheer rose from both the stands and the infield as Connelly brought Black Gold back to the judges' stand with the colt still dancing and eager. A second cheer erupted as the time was hung out: 53 seconds flat, just two-fifths of a second off the track record. The next day, the official chart would read, "Won easily; second and third driving."[16] It also reflected that Zev had won the Kentucky Derby at odds of 19.20–1, taking his field gate to wire.

Rosa Hoots was an intensely private woman. There was no newspaper interview following the Bashford Manor, and she left Kentucky as quietly as she had come, without revealing her thoughts to anyone except her son and her trainer. But the day after Black Gold's spectacular victory, Webb declined an offer of $50,000 from an unnamed eastern turfman on her behalf.[17] Not too long afterward, Alfred Hoots told a writer for the *Oklahoma Farmer* that he hoped to see Black Gold in the 1924 Kentucky Derby.[18]

15

Summer of Futility

After his tremendous effort in the Bashford Manor, Black Gold rested for the remainder of the Churchill Downs meeting before moving over to nearby Latonia, where he was engaged to run in two stakes races: the Harold Stakes on June 23 and the Cincinnati Trophy on June 30. He was greeted as the king of the Kentucky juveniles when he arrived, but with reservations as to how long he might hold his throne. Already, one challenger had emerged: Ruddy Light, who on June 2 had scored a spectacular win in a five-furlong maiden race. Sailing in by eight lengths while eased up, the filly equaled the Churchill Downs five-furlong track record of 0:59 flat, leading C. J. Savage to opine that she "probably could tie Black Gold . . . in a knot."[1] Ruddy Light followed up by winning the Clipsetta Stakes on June 9 with Black Gold's old rival Edna V in the beaten field, setting a new stakes record.

While the *Lexington Leader* claimed that Rosa Hoots "most feared" Ruddy Light as a rival for her colt, Webb did not seem overly concerned about the filly, sending Black Gold about his work as usual.[2] Given that Ruddy Light had been "straight as a string" to beat other fillies by a diminishing length in the Clipsetta, he may well have suspected that she was likely to regress in her next outing.[3] In any event, she was not eligible for either of the stakes races Black Gold was targeting.[4] A more immediate concern was Worthmore, working toward his first start since his defeat of Black Gold at the Fair Grounds. The speedy colt was catching the eye of the railbirds with his quick works, and there was another colt at Latonia who was beginning to draw marked attention even though he had not yet started his first race. His name was Wise Counsellor, and it was a name that would haunt Hanley Webb for many months to come.

Wise Counsellor came onto the racing scene with a backstory nearly as improbable and romantic as Black Gold's. It began in Missouri, where a Kentucky-bred stallion named Mentor had been banished. Mentor had good bloodlines, as he was a grandson of the great nineteenth-century runner Hanover through that horse's son Blackstock, a talented but unsound horse who had been a stakes winner in New York; his dam, Meta, was a daughter of the good stakes winner and sire Onondaga and had produced a nice stayer named Sunny Slope. But as Hall of Fame trainer John E. Madden observed, "Once you've tried a horse and found out that he is no good, his relatives don't help much."[5] Mentor fit that saying, which was why he was standing for a pittance at the St. Louis–area farm of Dr. William C. Gadsby in 1920 rather than at a reputable farm in the Bluegrass.

Rustle was among the handful of mares presented to Mentor in the spring of 1920, and she had credentials not much better than his. An undersized daughter of the fast runner but moderate sire Russell, she numbered two little selling stakes among her eleven wins as a juvenile, but that was the peak of her form. By the time 1920 rolled around, she had produced seven named foals, all by Mentor, and none had proven worth the feed it took to raise them as racehorses.

Mentor was sold off to the US Army Remount Service that fall, and by then, Rustle's owner, Fred Meier, had had enough of her too. Convinced the mare had not conceived from her most recent mating to Mentor, he sold or gave her and two of her daughters by Mentor to Dr. Gadsby, who shipped them off to Lexington's December sale of horses of all ages. When her turn came up in the auction ring, the aging mare could not draw a single taker at her opening price of one hundred dollars.

Among those watching Rustle being led around the ring were Lexington mayor Thomas C. Bradley and his friend Charles H. Berryman, the manager of Elmendorf Farm. Seeing that Bradley was mildly interested, Berryman decided to throw his two cents in and offered to give Bradley a free season to Ballot if he would go ahead and buy Rustle.[6] Ballot, then standing at Elmendorf, was quite a good racer and sire, and that was sweetener enough for Bradley. He bid one hundred dollars. No one followed up. After another minute or two of silence, the auctioneer concluded no further bids were coming and slammed his gavel down, making Bradley Rustle's new owner.

A few months later, it became obvious Rustle was not barren after all, and not long afterward she produced a chestnut colt. She was then taken off to her promised assignation with Ballot, which apparently came up empty. Three years and another mating later, she finally produced a Ballot foal, a filly that received the name Faithful Friend and ended up winning just one of twenty-seven races. By then the property of Milton Snyder (who had become a partner in the mare after Wise Counsellor's birth), Rustle lived on and bred a few more foals, finally dying in January 1932.

In the meantime, Rustle's surprise colt lived and thrived. Perhaps not entirely trusting his luck with this gift horse, Bradley sold a half interest in the youngster to his brother, Dr. Ernest Bradley. In due time, the Bradley brothers turned their colt over to Auval "Jack" Baker for training, and soon the whispers began around Lexington that the strapping chestnut with the white right hind foot was a real runner.

Baker was patient in getting Wise Counsellor ready to race, and the colt did not make his first start until June 20 at Latonia. Such was his reputation off works alone that he was a solid favorite in the five-furlong maiden event. He ran second by three-quarters of a length, but virtually every horseman watching the race conceded that had the inexperienced colt not gotten himself shuffled back early, he would have beaten Energy, who had the benefit of a previous start and turned in a more focused race. Following the race, Thomas Bradley received several "huge" offers for the colt but turned them away, stating, "Wise Counsellor is not for sale at any price."[7]

Three days later, Wise Counsellor was in the field for the Harold Stakes, and this time he was not favored; that honor went to Worthmore, who was coupled in the betting with stablemate Will Land. Racing as the C. T. Worthington entry, the pair went off at 2.20–1. Weighted down with 127 pounds after his spectacular score in the Bashford Manor and forced to concede from eight to seventeen pounds to his ten rivals by the conditions of the race, Black Gold was the second choice at 2.85–1, while Wise Counsellor (who ran coupled with a colt named Keegan) was held at 6.40–1. Still entitled to the maximum allowance for being a maiden, Wise Counsellor carried just 110 pounds, while Worthmore carried 117.

Eleven colts and geldings answered the call to the post. It took four minutes of milling and jockeying at the barrier before the field was sent away, and the instant the webbing snapped up, Worthmore and his jockey Bill Kelsay charged over from the number 6 position, tangling up everything to the colt's inside as he grabbed both the rail and the lead. Whether that was Worthmore's idea or Kelsay's was a moot point, but the net result was that three colts caromed over onto Black Gold in a chain reaction as he tried to get in stride from post position 2, nearly knocking him to his knees.[8] The only colt who fared worse was Valley Land on the rail; he was bounced all the way back to eleventh, with Black Gold just ahead of him and trapped at the back of the pack.

Wise Counsellor had not entirely escaped Worthmore's interference as he broke from post position 5, but jockey Earle Pool was able to steady him quickly and secure racing room at midpack. That was all Wise Counsellor needed. Sweeping by Worthmore in the upper stretch, the big chestnut drew off effortlessly to win by two lengths while "pulled to a walk."[9] His time of 0:59 equaled Latonia's track record for five furlongs. As for Black Gold, there was no miracle finish for him that day; trapped in a pocket until the final furlong, he was "running over horses at the finish" but could only get up to fourth before the ground ran out.[10]

Black Gold lost little respect by this effort, as evidenced by his being sent off at 1–2 in his next start, a June 26 allowance race called the Dayton Purse. This time Danny Connelly was able to get him away from the break without incident, and the colt ran on top all the way to win the race "well in hand."[11] Shouldering topweight of 122 pounds, he had conceded fifteen to eighteen pounds to all five of his rivals, among them the future major stakes winners Befuddle and Altawood.

Anticipation was running rampant among horsemen, fans, and journalists as Black Gold and Wise Counsellor met again on June 30 in the Cincinnati Trophy, the top juvenile prize of the summer Latonia meeting. Under the race conditions, they met as equals, each carrying 127 pounds. In spite of his earlier defeat by Wise Counsellor, Black Gold still had enough adherents that he was favored at 2.10–1; Wise Counsellor was second choice at 3.30–1. Worthmore, getting a nine-pound weight concession from the top pair, went off at 5.65–1.

Worthmore started inside both Black Gold and Wise Counsellor, and he caused no problems as he shot out to take his usual front-running position on the rail. Wise Counsellor stalked him almost casually, settling in to cruise just off his rival's withers. In the meantime, Black Gold, away a step slowly, was forced to bide his time at midpack while in close quarters. Nonetheless, he had less than four lengths to make up on the leaders—if he could.

He could not. As Worthmore began to tire in the stretch, Wise Counsellor disposed of him with ease and continued to the finish with Pool doing only enough to keep him from loafing. Once in the clear, Black Gold answered Connelly's call willingly in the final furlong to pass Worthmore but could make up only another half-length on Wise Counsellor before the chestnut sailed under the line with three lengths to spare.

No one made any excuses for the results, which were generally regarded as fair and decisive. As Bob Saxton of the *Cincinnati Enquirer* put it, "The Hoots colt is a good one, but Wise Counsellor took his measure yesterday, and it is likely that he can do it any day of the year."[12] There was reason for that confidence. According to the venerable handicapping reference *Ainslie's Complete Guide to Thoroughbred Racing,* a commonly used rule of thumb is that at sprint distances, a four-pound difference in weight equates to slowing a horse by a fifth of a second, enough time to traverse a full length.[13] Using that formula, Wise Counsellor's three-length margin suggested that he was Black Gold's superior by at least twelve pounds over the six furlongs of the Cincinnati Trophy—and with that, Black Gold's brief reign as the top juvenile in Kentucky ended.[14] In the eyes of Kentucky turfmen, the king, though not dead, was clearly deposed; long live the new king.

After his two big wins, Wise Counsellor disappeared from the racing wars until the fall. Worthmore, however, was still around to be a thorn in Black Gold's side. The two met again on July 5 at Latonia in the Cleves Purse, an allowance that drew most of the better juveniles remaining at the track. Under the allowance conditions, Worthmore had to carry just 107 pounds to Black Gold's 122. Nonetheless, the bettors made Black Gold the favorite at 1.35–1.

The betting public was probably correct that Black Gold was the better animal even at the weights, but this time the colt was his own worst enemy. For the third time in his last four races, he lagged at the start, resulting in his getting shuffled back early. In the meantime, Worthmore set the pace up front. With no Wise Counsellor to pressure him, he cruised easily on the lead, brushing off a brief bid from Chilhowee. He hit the five-furlong mark in time that tied the existing track record for the distance while still running strongly along the rail. Black Gold was in hot pursuit, but he was forced to circle the entire field as he made his run and still lacked a length and a half of catching Worthmore when the ground ran out. The final time of 1:05⅗ was just a fifth of a second off the track record for five and one-half furlongs.

After that, Worthmore and Black Gold parted ways for a time, with Worthmore closing out the Latonia meeting with a defeat by Chilhowee in an allowance on July 7 before being given a break. Black Gold, who had made seven starts within the preceding ten weeks—more than Wise Counsellor and Worthmore put together—probably needed one himself, and initially it seemed he would get it; according to the *Lexington Herald* of July 6, Webb had announced that Black Gold would be taken to Lexington and turned out for the remainder of the summer.[15] But on July 8, Webb shipped the colt up to Chicago's Hawthorne track and entered him in an allowance race slated for July 11.

For once, luck was on Black Gold's side, though with a Delphic twist. On the morning of the race, Webb woke up and went into Black Gold's stall to start his normal routine, only to find that the colt had hurt a foreleg sometime during the night. The cause of the injury was never determined, though there was no evidence of foul play. Although it was intimated by at least one observer that the colt could possibly have run anyway, he was withdrawn by Webb, who was unwilling to risk aggravating the problem.[16]

Black Gold's injury looked like one more piece of the bad luck that seemed to dog his steps, but it was probably a blessing in disguise. Webb fussed over his pet and kept him in his stall, and if the trainer fretted that the injury was not healing as fast as he could wish, at least the colt was getting a much-needed rest after a series of hard races. Further, the timing could hardly have been better. Black Gold had no more important engagements until the fall season for the Kentucky circuit, so he was losing little by not racing in Chicago, and he still had plenty of time to be brought back to top condition for the Lexington fall meeting.

With Black Gold on the sidelines, few people spent much time thinking about his history of misfortunes on the track, especially at the starts of his races and in the first few crucial strides. To racing fans and bettors, Black Gold was simply "unlucky," and Webb and most of his fellow horsemen saw nothing untoward other than Black Gold's having developed a bad habit of being hesitant at the break, which naturally cost him position early in a race. If racing officials noticed that Black Gold's luck was especially bad when larger prizes were on the line, they wrote it off as coincidence. Nonetheless, one man had become certain that Black Gold's bad racing luck was not luck at all. The problem was that J. D. Mooney might have been the one man that Webb was least inclined to listen to, because the jockey had been on Hanley Webb's bad side for nearly three years—and there were no indications that Webb would change his opinion any time soon.

16

J. D. Mooney

Racing was in John James Mooney's blood. Born in New Orleans on November 24, 1901, he was the son of Irish immigrant Alexander Mooney, a riverboat man who was later the sexton of the Fireman's Cemetery. The sexton's job included the care of the coach horses used for the firemen's funerals, and Mooney first learned to ride on these stolid animals. He also learned to drive, and his earliest memories of the track were of taking his Grandma Mooney to the Fair Grounds in the family buggy. There they would watch the races together, with the boy drinking in the excitement and enviously admiring the cocky, daring jockeys in their bright silks.[1]

Alexander Mooney died in 1910, leaving his wife, Emelia, to raise six children as best she could. To a wiry boy from a struggling family, the lure of potential fame and money at the track was too much to be resisted, especially after his older brother Joe became an apprentice jockey. Responding to that siren call, Mooney soon found work with a Fair Grounds trainer as a stable boy.

Being a stable boy meant doing all the hard and dirty work of caring for horses, from mucking stalls to hauling buckets of water, as well as any other chores that the trainer saw fit to assign. There was no oversight from child labor laws (then nonexistent) or track officials, and many of the "boys" were runaways, orphans, or youngsters who were pushed out of too-large families trying to live on too little. Working for meager pay at best and bare-bones room and board at worst, they were at the mercy of whatever trainer was willing to provide them employment. If fortunate, they got a decent place to sleep, enough to eat, and an education in horsemanship that gave them some hope of earning a living. If not, they might be beaten, starved, or otherwise misused with little chance of the abuser's sins ever catching up to him.

There was no fixed timetable for moving from "stable boy" to "exercise rider" to "apprentice jockey." Some boys never got as far as becoming exercise riders, either because they were already showing signs of growing too large or because they failed to master the rudiments of handling a horse. Others could ride well enough to exercise an animal but lacked the quick reflexes, fearlessness, and instantaneous judgment necessary to a race rider.

Even after a boy officially became an apprentice, his life was still controlled by the trainer who held his contract, and apprentice jockeys often continued to do a stable boy's chores in addition to riding. An apprentice's contract could also be sold without his knowledge or consent, and more than one apprentice found out about such a transaction only after his new master came over and told him to move whatever possessions he had to the new stable. It was not until a rider became a journeyman—after a year as an apprentice or his fortieth victory as a jockey, whichever came first—that he could focus mostly on riding, and even then he was answerable to whatever trainer he had contracted with for first call on his services before he could accept mounts from another stable. It would be several more decades before the contract system gave way to freelancing as the norm for most jockeys.

Compared to other jockeys of the time, Mooney got off to a late start. Many started riding when they reached the legal minimum age of sixteen—assuming one believed what was written on their licenses, which often as not padded a boy's age by a year or two. Mooney was eighteen when he rode in his first official race at Churchill Downs on May 10, 1920. Riding for Freddie Stanton (who had also employed Joe Mooney), Mooney finished fifth on Marasmus in a six-furlong claiming race. He had his first winner within a week, piloting Speedster to victory on May 17, and by the fall had a decent reputation on the Kentucky circuit. From there he went to New Orleans, where he became a leading rider of the 1920–1921 winter season. It was sometime during this period that he became known as "J. D. Mooney," a designation used in the racing charts to avoid confusion with Joe Mooney.

Mooney was never one of the stars engaged by the big eastern stables; for most of his career, he was just another journeyman, freelancing in between contracts with one modest stable or another. Nonetheless, he was respected at the tracks in Kentucky, Louisiana, and Canada where he did most of his riding—at least, as respected as most jockeys ever got in an era when veteran riders in their thirties were still commonly referred to as "boy." Nicknamed "Sit Still Mooney," he had a cool head and the ability to bide his time during the running of a race.[2] He was known as a "money rider," a jockey who seldom took a horse that didn't have a decent chance of finishing in the top three, and that made his presence in the saddle worth noting when it came to placing bets. He also had the reputation of being a strong rider at the finish, perhaps in part due to the extra muscle granted by his size; tall and lanky for a jockey, with large hands that betrayed the size of his frame, he stood five feet, eight inches, a height that made keeping to a riding weight of 105 pounds or so an agonizing struggle fought with laxatives and endless miles run in rubberized suits.[3]

Mooney was far from the only rider who battled constantly with the scale. Constant reducing to make riding weight was the lot of most jockeys, and it may well have killed more riders than racing accidents did. Mooney's methods were commonplace among his peers, and others tried even more unhealthy tactics. Limitation of fluids was routine, resulting in severe dehydration and its accompaniments: irritability, dizziness, loss of muscular coordination. Any number of methods of increasing sweating and urination were used. Diets that the most rigorous of monks would have considered ascetic were often employed; some jockeys tried to live on a few leaves of lettuce or a glass of wine or champagne daily for days or even weeks at a time. For those who could not abide by such strict regimens, self-induced vomiting—"flipping"—was often the method of choice to rid the body of excess food, corroding tooth enamel and sometimes creating stomach ulcers or permanently scarring the esophagus.

The results were devastating. Although jockeys sometimes managed to drop seven to ten pounds within a single day, they paid the price in physical weakness, headaches, cramps, and sometimes complete collapse—even sudden death, as happened to Frank Hayes. After going through severe reducing to make weight for a steeplechase race at Belmont on June 4, 1923, Hayes won his first victory aboard Sweet Kiss only to slump over in the saddle as he was pulling up his mount. He was probably already dead when his body hit the track; the verdict of the racetrack physician was "heart failure."[4]

Other jockeys did not die so suddenly, but they died all the same, their weakened bodies falling prey to pneumonia and tuberculosis. Another grim shadow that followed riders was suicide, a natural corollary to depression created by both the physiological effects of severe reducing and the harsh realities of scraping out a marginal existence. Some turned to alcohol as a means of managing physical or emotional pain, in some cases merely a slower form of self-destruction. And every race meeting was attended by accidents, leaving the injured, the crippled, and the dead behind them. Those who survived the initial physical trauma of a spill or other mishap were often at the mercy of their employers when it came to whether they got treatment or not; insurance for jockeys was nonexistent, and few had the savings to pay for hospital care, let alone any prolonged period of recuperation. Some jockeys, fearful of being replaced by a trainer or owner, rode with concussions or broken bones. Protective gear was next to nonexistent; even the skullcaps jockeys wore were no more than cardboard or pressed fiber beneath the exterior silk, and that was assuming that the jockey hadn't cut out the protective lining to save on weight.

Some got out before the inevitable damage became too great, recognizing that weight or moderate talent would never allow them to reach the heights. But for some, the chance of both danger and glory astride a powerful Thoroughbred outweighed the hardships. The racetrack held out the same hope for small, light boys that the boxing ring did for brawnier youths from the steel towns—a chance that your athletic ability, skill, and determination could pay off and lift you out of mere existence to wealth and fame. The brass ring was there, just waiting to be grabbed.

Mooney managed to survive both his apprenticeship and the transitional period that followed it, when trainers who had been riding an apprentice for the sake of the weight allowance granted a "bug boy" (a nickname gained from the asterisk, or "bug," that marked an apprentice rider on the racing program) suddenly became less willing to ride a new journeyman. He was generally liked by both his peers and the fans, and in 1923 he was at as close to a happy medium as he would ever achieve, still young enough to have less trouble making weight than he would later, yet old and seasoned enough to know both the skills and the tricks of his trade.

Those tricks were employed often. Mooney did his share of rough riding, though some of it could be chalked up to self-preservation; as he wryly observed in 1961, not one race out of a typical six-race card in his day would have gotten past a modern film patrol.[5] That may have been an understatement. From big names like Earl Sande and Laverne Fator to the lowliest bug boys, jockeys of the 1920s routinely employed tactics that would put a modern rider's license at serious risk. Mooney himself once recounted giving another horse a well-timed shove with a booted toe during a hotly contested stretch run, sending the animal staggering toward the opposite fence while Mooney steered his own mount straight on toward the finish.[6] Other illicit but frequently used maneuvers included grabbing hold of a rival horse's saddlecloth or tail to retard the animal's progress and gain a brief tow for one's own mount; locking legs with another jockey to keep a rival from passing; and use of the whip to discourage other horses as well as encouraging one's own. The whip was not always confined to use against equines, either; more than one rider returned to the jockeys' room after a race with welts adorning arms, thighs, or buttocks. Even worse, if a rider had seriously angered his peers, he might find himself the victim of gang tactics with his mount being repeatedly bumped, boxed in, or even forced into or over the inside rail, putting horse and rider at serious risk of injury or death.

Mooney served a few suspensions when his tactics caught the attention of track officials, and a few more when his temper got the better of him in conflicts with officials or fights with other riders. Still, he was respected as a hard worker and a sharp observer, getting up before most of the other riders were out of their bunks so that he could watch morning workouts and perhaps hustle up a ride or two—or avoid being put on a horse that was unsound or dangerous. He was also an amusing storyteller and perfectly willing to share a tale at his own expense, such as the one about the race at New Orleans in which his mount bolted from the post parade, shot through the gap leading back to Shed Row, and went tearing into the stable area with Mooney still aboard. The commotion brought the resident bootlegger out of his den in one of the sheds, and as the runaway careered by in a circuit around the barns, Mooney yelled at the man to get him a drink ready. On the next lap, Mooney snatched the drink from the bootlegger's hand, gulped it down, and went back to the business of getting his mount under control—much to the amusement of the other race riders and starter Harry "Old Man" Morrissey, who were watching the entire escapade from their vantage point at the starting line as they waited for the errant racer and his jockey to rejoin the field. Apparently, Morrissey could match Mooney for both wit and savoir-faire, for when Mooney finally cantered up and brought his horse into line, the starter blandly quipped, "I hope you didn't forget to tip the bartender!" before sending the field away.[7]

Mooney's sense of humor was not uncommon among jockeys, who often used a joke to gloss over the dangers of a profession in which inches sometimes separated glory from death. What he had that was less common was a virtue not always found among jockeys below the top tier: Mooney was essentially honest, a man who could be counted on to ride to the best of his ability regardless of the betting or any attempted bribery.[8] Others were not always so scrupulous, among them Joe Mooney, who was ruled off for life in 1925 for his part in a race-fixing scandal at Latonia.[9]

Exactly when J. D. Mooney and Hanley Webb first met is not known, though it could have been as early as June 1920, when both were plying their trades at the Latonia summer meeting. They had certainly met by November 1920, when Webb put Mooney up on Black Gold's older half brother, Tulsa, at the Churchill Downs meeting. Mooney won with the gelding on November 10, but two days later he finished fifth of six after Tulsa broke poorly and then got cut off when Mooney tried to send him through a hole on the rail. Mooney felt he had done his best to try to win and wrote it off to bad racing luck, but Webb apparently saw it otherwise. He was angry, and he refused to give the young jockey any more mounts.[10]

Mooney didn't think about it any further at the time; Webb didn't have enough horses to be a regular source of mounts, and the Kentucky racing season was nearly over anyway. But two years later, when Webb brought Black Gold down to New Orleans to start his racing career, that second ride on Tulsa came back to haunt the jockey. One look at Black Gold convinced him this was an animal with more potential than anything he had ever thrown a leg across, but when he put out a feeler about getting the mount on the colt, Webb angrily slapped it down. Still convinced that Mooney had cost Tulsa any chance that day in 1920—and perhaps suspicious that he had tried to throw the race—Webb was not about to let Mooney anywhere near his pet, no matter what the jockey tried to get back into the old man's good graces.

With Webb giving him the cold shoulder, the closest Mooney got to Black Gold that winter was when he was schooling another youngster alongside him at the barrier. For Mooney, it was like watching one of Barney Oldfield's race cars from the seat of a Model T.[11] He wanted the mount so badly he could practically feel Black Gold prancing under him, but even after Webb had sacked Henry Burke for his ride in Black Gold's second race, he still wouldn't talk to Mooney. Even Mooney's first big stakes win, this aboard Amole in the 1923 Louisiana Derby, failed to get Webb to give him the time of day, much less a chance to ride Black Gold.

Mooney had to be content with observing Black Gold from a distance, sometimes when the colt was at exercise, sometimes watching his races from the rail or from the backs of rivals. After that odd ride from Burke in the colt's second start, he also kept his ears open, and by the end of the Lexington meeting, he didn't like what he was hearing around the track and in the jockeys' room. The talk was that there was money to be had by getting Black Gold beaten—as much as a thousand dollars a race—and it was as simple as arranging for another rider to bump his mount into Black Gold right after the start, providing an excuse to check the colt and get him into a bad position early.[12]

Going to the stewards wasn't an option. Mooney had no proof, and he knew that making the accusation would probably be the end of his riding career once the other jockeys heard about it. Going to Webb wasn't going to work either; he'd figure it was just another of Mooney's ploys to get on Black Gold. Then the racing moved to Churchill Downs, Webb hired Danny Connelly, and Black Gold's fortunes seemed to improve. Mooney ended up riding well-beaten rivals in the West Point Purse and the Bashford Manor Stakes at Churchill Downs before finishing up the track on Valley Land in both of Black Gold's losses to Wise Counsellor at Latonia. Nobody was blaming Connelly for the mess Worthmore had caused in the Harold Stakes, and nearly everyone except a few die-hard fans agreed that Black Gold had been outrun on his merits in the Cincinnati Trophy.

By that time, Mooney's dream of getting the mount on Black Gold was more a daydream than a serious hope. Webb's grudge against him was as strong as ever, and Mooney knew he wasn't going to get a chance with the colt anyway as long as Connelly kept doing well with him. Even so, he was happy with his life. He had been acquainted with Canadian horseman Jim Heffering for a couple of years, and in the spring of 1923, he married Heffering's daughter Marjorie. He was also riding some good horses, including Carl Weidemann's promising In Memoriam, who was being pointed to the Kentucky Derby by trainer George Land. Mooney and In Memoriam could do no better than eleventh in the Derby, but after his agreement with Land ended at the close of the Churchill Downs meeting, Mooney next became the regular rider for Whiskaway, a horse from the powerful stable of Harry Payne Whitney and one of the best three-year-olds of the previous year.

As a four-year-old, Whiskaway had become a sulker who didn't always feel like running, but Mooney got on with him well enough to ride him to a couple of stakes wins at Latonia before heading up to Canada for a visit. He ended up staying through September, winning a number of races including the Dominion Handicap on Spot Cash. Then it was back to Latonia, and another meeting with the little black colt that had never left the back of his mind.

Mooney resumed his watch on Black Gold the moment he arrived at Latonia. Within days, he knew that Hanley Webb was looking for a jockey—again. That was good news for him, but there was other news that was not so good. Black Gold's bad "luck" was back, and worse than ever. Worse still, it had changed him, and not for the better. The black colt was getting the reputation of a "coward," a horse that wouldn't assert himself if everything didn't go his way.

Mooney knew it wasn't the colt's fault; he was becoming what humans were making him. He also knew he could do something about it if given a chance. Nonetheless, all he could do was watch and wait, hoping to catch a break that would bring him and Black Gold together.

17

Converging Paths

Even if Mooney had not gone to Canada, there would have been no chance of his picking up the mount on Black Gold that summer—not because of Webb's intransigence, but because the colt was not running. Although the injury he suffered on July 11 had been initially considered slight and there was even some talk of his going to Saratoga for a crack at the big-name eastern colts, July slipped into August and Black Gold still had not returned to the track.[1] By the time he began working again in the second week of August, it was too late to consider taking him east. Perhaps his lameness was slow to work out to Webb's satisfaction, for although the trainer went ahead and shipped Black Gold down from Chicago in advance of the Lexington fall meeting, the colt was not pushed to show speed for another few weeks. It was not until just a few days before the Lexington meeting was to open on September 15 that Black Gold turned in a smart workout of five furlongs in 1:03⅔, causing the correspondent for the Chicago sporting periodical *Collyer's Eye* to comment, "Never looked better."[2]

Other paths were also converging on Lexington and its tempting fall prize, the Breeders' Futurity. Wise Counsellor was not eligible for the race, but Worthmore and Chilhowee were on the grounds and said to be training well. Adding spice to the mix, prominent eastern owner Gifford Cochran had nominated two stakes colts to the Breeders' Futurity, Sun Flag and Sunspero, and Mrs. Walter Jeffords had Diogenes as a Futurity prospect after winning the rich Hopeful Stakes with him at Saratoga. All three potential eastern invaders were reportedly under strong consideration for the race.

Anticipation was running high on opening day, with several of the best juveniles at the track slated to collide in the Danville Purse, the sixth race on the card. Only five ended up passing the entry box, but among them were Black Gold, Worthmore, and a fast filly named Alchemy who was unbeaten in four races and had such a reputation that she ruled as favorite over the colts.

Danny Connelly was riding at the Lexington meeting and did not have a mount in the Danville, but he and Webb had apparently had a falling-out, for it was Lawrence McDermott who guided Black Gold to the post for the five and one-half furlong race, his first time aboard the colt since Black Gold's track record performance at Jefferson Park. He got his mount a decent break, but it was Alchemy who shot to the front with Worthmore right behind her. Electing not to join the speed duel, McDermott eased back, letting Black Gold fall four lengths behind the leaders as they blazed through the first quarter in 0:22⅗, heads apart.

Alchemy began inching away from Worthmore, stretching her lead to a length at the half-mile point, but the first quarter had told on her; she ran the second quarter in 0:24⅖, and Worthmore was clearly going the better of the two. The slowing pace let Black Gold pick up ground on the leaders without being pushed, and he was just half a length behind Worthmore as the horses swept through the turn for home, with a split-second opportunity to cut the corner and shoot through on the inside. In the next split-second, Bill Kelsay veered Worthmore into Black Gold's path, forcing McDermott to check his mount sharply.[3] The instant Black Gold dropped back, Kelsay gunned Worthmore to the lead. Once in the clear, Black Gold launched a furious rally that took him past the weary Alchemy, but he was still a nose short of Worthmore at the wire.

There was an unspoken code among jockeys that you didn't claim foul against another rider, no matter how egregious the offense.[4] For once, McDermott didn't care. He was livid, and as soon as he unsaddled, he marched back to the officials' stand to make his case. He got no satisfaction from the stewards, who let the results stand.[5] The next day, the chart for the race bluntly stated that Black Gold "was best but was blocked by winner in the stretch and had to go around losing enough ground to cost him the race."[6] Journalists were equally scathing; C. J. Savage fumed in his racing coverage that "Black Gold was pounds the best and should have won."[7] Likewise, the writer for the *Cincinnati Enquirer* characterized Worthmore's win as "fluky."[8]

It might have been fluky, but when it came to Worthmore and Black Gold, flukes were the norm. From the questionable ride Black Gold got from Henry Burke in the colts' first meeting to Worthmore's left turn at the start of the Harold Stakes and Black Gold's poor break in the Cleves Purse, Worthmore had gotten more than his fair share of assistance from Black Gold's misfortunes and had yet to outfinish the black colt on pure merit. The Cincinnati Trophy was their only meeting in which Black Gold had gotten a reasonably clear run, and that time he had led Worthmore home, though Wise Counsellor had gotten the better of them both.

The thread of odd events tracing through the colts' mutual histories took another peculiar turn in their next meeting. On September 21, both came out for the Orchard Hall Handicap, a race over the same track and distance as the Danville Purse. The track was heavy and muddy, and only two other youngsters came out to contest the issue. They were never a factor. With McDermott back up, Black Gold got a clean trip as the 0.60–1 favorite and, after tracking his rival through the first half, came on in the stretch and defeated Worthmore by four easy lengths "under restraint."[9] Adding to the apparent decisiveness of the victory, Black Gold carried 122 pounds to Worthmore's 118. Under the conditions of the race, the weight assignments indicated that the Lexington track secretary thought Black Gold would win by about a length if all other conditions were equal; the colts' actual performances suggested that the secretary would have needed to give Worthmore a sixteen-pound weight advantage to put him on even terms with Black Gold at the finish.

Although most observers took the race as clearly showing Black Gold's superiority, not everyone agreed that the case was as one-sided as it looked. Even Black Gold's more ardent supporters had to concede that the off footing had probably been in his favor, though since Worthmore had never been tested over heavy going, there was no previous line on his form under such conditions. Worthmore had also run wide on the turn for home and quit abruptly in the stretch.[10] Both were behaviors he had not shown before, though in fairness he had set an exhausting pace in the early going—one that would have been considered lively on a fast track, much less a deep and muddy one—and may simply have gotten leg-weary.

A bigger question than whether the race was a true line on the colts' relative merits was whether C. T. Worthington's colt had ever been intended to show his true form at all, a question raised after Bill Kelsay was called to the stewards' stand immediately after the race to give an account of his ride on the 2–1 second choice. The reasons were not specified in the day's racing coverage, but the September 27 edition of the *Cincinnati Enquirer* stated that the stewards had suspected that Worthmore had not been ridden to win.[11] Two days later, *Collyer's Eye* came just short of explicitly declaring that something crooked had been afoot, alleging that the "wise Boys" around the track had scented that something was up when four thousand dollars in last-minute bets came in on Black Gold and that Kelsay had turned in an "amateurish" attempt to cover what the paper implied to be a deliberately subpar ride.[12] That the chart caller had made no note of anything unusual about Worthmore's behavior or his handling by his rider made no difference to the unnamed accuser.[13]

Later events suggested that the stewards were not entirely satisfied by Kelsay's explanation that his colt had been unable to handle the track conditions, but after quizzing the jockey as to the riding instructions he had received, they let Kelsay go with a warning that another suspicious ride would get him a suspension.[14] That left speculation to run loose as to whether or not Worthington had simply sent out a "short" horse (one not fully fit) for needed sharpening. That was a legitimate tactic, so long as a reasonable attempt to win was made, and under those circumstances, it would have been permissible for him to tell Kelsay not to push the colt if he was obviously beaten. The darker alternative was that Worthington had meant for his colt to lose in the hope of getting longer odds in the big race to come and had instructed Kelsay accordingly.

What Webb thought of the situation was not recorded, but he had other things to consider as he put his colt through final preparations for the Breeders' Futurity. Most of the track buzz centered on Chilhowee, who had become Lexington's "now" horse after equaling the track record for five and one-half furlongs in a front-running victory on September 19. That was not necessarily bad news as far as Black Gold's supporters were concerned; as Worthmore also liked to run in front, there was a fair likelihood that he and Chilhowee would burn each other out in a speed duel. The eastern invaders were also getting attention and were perhaps more worrisome; though Mrs. Jeffords had decided against sending Diogenes, Cochran's two colts were in, and so was Infinite, another New York stakes horse.

Webb was keeping an eye on the competition, but his most immediate problem was one he had faced repeatedly throughout the season: securing a new jockey for Black Gold. He was not dissatisfied with McDermott, but McDermott wasn't available; as the contract jockey for the Howard Oots stable, he was obligated to ride Oots's colt Just David in the Futurity. That left Webb hunting through the available freelancers and those contracted jockeys whose employers were agreeable to allowing them to pick up an outside mount. With less than twenty-four hours to go before the race, the trainer finally secured Ivan Parke, who had been the hottest apprentice in New Orleans earlier that year and had continued riding well after moving up to Kentucky.

The track came up muddy on Futurity Day, September 26, and the bettors took note. Chilhowee, said to be a good mud runner, was the favorite off his track-record performance at 2.20–1, with Black Gold, a proven commodity over wet footing, second in the betting at just over 3–1. The Cochran entry of Sun Flag and Sunspero was at 4.85–1, Just David was fourth choice at 8.40–1, and everything else sported double-digit odds—among them Worthmore, who was held at 21–1 after his lackluster effort five days earlier under similar track conditions.

Six of the seven fields on the Breeders' Futurity card got away cleanly. The exception was the Futurity. It took four increasingly tense minutes to get the twelve-horse field lined up, and chaos broke loose again in the same split-second that starter William Hamilton sent the barrier skyward. Worthmore, timing the break perfectly, shot away with a clear advantage and grabbed the early lead; Black Gold was away badly and caught in the rear of the pack; and Chilhowee was practically left at the post. Rushed up to get into contention, he went wide on the turn, finishing his chances.

Parke started working Black Gold up the inside, saving ground, but up front, Worthmore had winged through an opening quarter in 0:22⅘ before Kelsay eased him back and let the long shot filly Say No take a short lead. The brief breather was all Worthmore needed. At the top of the stretch, Kelsay called for his best, and Worthmore responded. Showing no signs of tiring in the stretch as he had in his earlier races, the Worthington colt ran on strongly and won by a length and a half from Say No. Black Gold, third at the stretch call, made a valiant effort to better his position but tired near the finish and ended up another length back. Struck by another horse at some point during the chaotic start or the early running, he came out of the race bleeding "profusely" from cuts to his hind legs.[15]

The following day, the sportswriter for the *Cincinnati Enquirer* called the race "unsatisfactory."[16] He was not the only one who saw it that way. Immediately following the race, both Kelsay and Worthington were called before the stewards, who demanded an explanation of Worthmore's sharp reversal of form. Neither jockey nor trainer could explain to the stewards' satisfaction why the colt had turned in such different showings five days apart over the same track and under much the same conditions, and both were slapped with indefinite suspensions pending further investigation.[17] Henry Burke, who had ridden Energy in the Futurity, also came in for the stewards' ire, drawing a ten-day suspension for rough riding.[18] Yet at the same time, no investigation was made into the rough start that had cost both Black Gold and Chilhowee so dearly while giving Worthmore an early advantage. Perhaps it was merely because no particular horse could be singled out as the chief offender, but the whole affair left a sour taste in observers' mouths.

It had also left a mark on Black Gold, though not physically; to Webb's relief, the colt's injuries proved to be minor. His mental state was another question. He had already been showing signs that he was increasingly afraid at the start of a race, especially when in a field of more than a few horses. The same colt who had been a quick, eager starter in New Orleans had become more and more hesitant at the break throughout his time in Kentucky; worse, he was developing a habit of refusing to extend himself if bumped about or forced to race inside horses.[19] His small size made the problem worse, as a larger, stronger rival could easily knock him off stride or simply crowd and intimidate him. He needed to be able to get off to a clean start and find racing room early, and that had not been happening. Now he had actually been hurt while racing, and his fear of being roughed up or trapped by his rivals was worse than ever.

Webb needed help, but he had no idea where to turn. To get Black Gold turned around, he needed a jockey both he and the colt could trust—someone who was a good enough horseman to analyze the colt's behavior and correct it, someone who was wholly honest as a rider, and someone who was available and willing to commit himself to Black Gold as more than a pickup mount. The problem was that, between the jockeys Webb had already tried and sacked and the ones that had contract commitments elsewhere, the trainer was running out of options.

For Mooney, the situation represented a golden opportunity, but there was just one hitch. Webb still wouldn't talk to him, and without some outside intervention, it didn't look as if he ever would.

18

Slim Chance

Mooney had one thread of hope that he might get Webb to listen to him if he could only get a hearing: Webb was getting desperate, and the pressure on the old man was ratcheting up with each day that passed before Black Gold's planned start in the Queen City Handicap on October 27. It was the showpiece of the Latonia fall meeting, and it was Black Gold's last chance to grab both prestige and a big purse before the fall racing season closed in Kentucky. Webb needed Black Gold's behavior problems fixed before then, and Mooney had an idea as to how he could do just that. All he needed was a chance to try his plan.

The jockey was still mulling over the problem of how he could approach Webb when luck and an old acquaintance stepped in to take a hand. Slim Stewart was hanging around Latonia, and he knew Mooney from when he had been the young jockey's agent. Now Stewart had a wife, a child, and no money or job. Since he wasn't currently acting as agent for anyone, he didn't have a track badge that would give him access to the backstretch and old friends there who might help him hustle up some work, and he couldn't afford to pony up admission to the grounds. So, when he saw Mooney coming out of the track one evening, he struck up a conversation, hoping the jockey might be his ticket to a badge and perhaps a little money.

It took only a moment's talk for Mooney to realize that Stewart wanted something. That was fine; everyone around the track made use of these "I'll scratch your back if you'll scratch mine" relationships from time to time. In fact, it was more than fine, because Mooney was about to make use of this one.

Stewart was an old acquaintance of Webb's, and to Mooney that connection was worth a lot more than anything Stewart was likely to ask for. After hearing Stewart out, Mooney agreed to arrange for Stewart to get a badge, then pulled out fifty dollars and handed it over—with one condition. He wanted Stewart to go to Webb and ask the trainer to give Mooney a chance as Black Gold's rider.[1]

Stewart agreed to act as a go-between, and Mooney went on back to his lodging and got something to eat before the phone rang. The landlord answered, then called Mooney over. It was Stewart. He had been as good as his word, and he had good news: Webb was at least willing to talk if Mooney would come on over to the stable.

Another man might have hurried straight over, but Mooney hadn't waited most of a year for this opportunity without thinking ahead as to what he might do if it came. He knew about Webb's liking for drink, and even though Prohibition was in full swing, it was a rare racetracker who didn't know where he could get liquor. Mooney liked an occasional nip himself, so he went by his favorite watering hole before making his way to Black Gold's stable with a pint flask of whiskey tucked away under his coat.

Webb was waiting for him, and the two men sat down in the stall that served Webb as office, tack room, and bunkroom. Soft rustling noises came from the stall next door as Black Gold moved about, shifting the straw bedding. Mooney brought out the whiskey and passed it over; Webb found a couple of cups and poured. His face wasn't showing much, but at least he was listening as he settled back, drink in hand.

Mooney knew better than to start off with openly asking for the mount. Instead, he began with what was nearest to Webb's heart: Black Gold himself. While he didn't come out and accuse the other jockeys who had been riding the colt of being crooked, he pointed out what Webb had already been seeing for himself, that the other riders were letting Black Gold get bumped about. As Mooney explained it, that was why the colt had gotten hesitant at the break and shy about being near other horses, especially if he had to run inside of them; he didn't want to be hurt again.

That had Webb's interest, and then Mooney revealed his plan. Let him ride Black Gold, he said, and he could use his spurs to straighten the colt out and get him running from the start.[2]

Spurs in the 1920s were not the blunt-tipped articles that jockeys used later; when used vigorously, they could leave bleeding gouges in a horse's sides. At the mention, Webb stiffened, but Mooney had anticipated this response and had prepared for it. He showed the trainer his spurs, pointing out where he'd filed them down. As he told Webb, he couldn't cut the colt's hide if he wanted to; all he wanted the spurs to do was to help keep Black Gold's attention on his rider's cues. With the colt's mind on what his jockey was asking instead of on his own fears, Mooney was sure that Black Gold would do the rest.

The talk and the whiskey both ran out around midnight. Finally, Webb gave in. A few days later, on October 25, 1923, Mooney rode Black Gold for the first time. The race was the Catlettsburg Purse at Latonia, a six-furlong allowance intended as a prep for the Queen City Handicap.

For Mooney, it was like making his riding debut all over again—excitement, nerves, thinking about what he wanted to do, trying not to overthink. He had the mount he had been angling for all year, but he knew that if he made one bad move on Black Gold, Webb would dump him faster than a moldy sack of feed. Everything he had been working for came down to the start of this one race—his one chance to win Webb's confidence and, even more important, to start winning Black Gold's.

There were seven races on the Latonia card that day, and the Catlettsburg was the sixth on the schedule. The first four were claiming races, and Mooney had mounts in the second and fourth. They weren't much; he finished third on both; but they had served a purpose, for he now knew to an inch how the muddy track was playing. He sat out the fifth race, and then it was time to walk to the paddock and get Webb's instructions. He listened quietly. The expression on the trainer's weathered face was carefully neutral, but Mooney didn't miss the glint in Webb's eyes, the one that said, *You do right by my colt, or else.* Then Webb was cupping his hands, and Mooney cocked his knee to accept the boost onto Black Gold.

Black Gold fidgeted as he felt Mooney's weight settle into the saddle, but he responded obediently and with increasing eagerness as Mooney guided him out of the paddock and down the path that led onto the track. Only four others followed, and Mooney was only concerned with one of them: Energy, who had broken his maiden at Wise Counsellor's expense and had the reputation of being a very quick horse at the break.

Aside from the chart, there is no surviving observer's account of the Catlettsburg Purse. It is left to imagination to see Black Gold lined up at the start, restive but obedient to this strange new human on his back—Mooney tightening the reins just the fraction needed to signal the colt to stand—the jockey's arms and thighs and back tensing, matching the coiled tension of his mount—the starter's shoulders bunching as he grasped the trigger for the barrier. . . .

Mooney's timing was perfect. As the barrier flipped skyward, he simultaneously gave his mount both his head and a prod with his blunted spurs. Startled, Black Gold leaped forward, leaving Energy and everything else in the small field flat-footed. From his perch atop the colt's withers, Mooney felt the rush of his mount's speed and power and knew right then that he had never been on a horse like this one. Never.

Now that he was clear and in stride, Black Gold wanted to keep going full-out, piling speed on speed. Mooney felt the same, but there was another lesson he needed to teach. Before Black Gold had gone a dozen strides, the jockey applied a bit of restraint, letting Energy rush up from the outside to prompt the pace with his nose at Black Gold's throatlatch. Black Gold's ears flattened, and he pulled against Mooney's hold; he didn't like being between the rail and another horse, and he wanted to put distance between himself and his rival. *Wait*, Mooney's hands insisted. *Wait*.

Henry Burke on Energy must have wondered what was going on, seeing the hold Mooney had on Black Gold. Mooney was keeping an eye on Burke, of course; he wasn't about to let Black Gold become the victim of dirty tactics. But most of his attention was focused on his colt, sensing the moment when Black Gold started to relax just a little. That was what Mooney wanted—the hint that the little black colt was becoming more confident, no longer intimidated by having another horse running next to him. He kept Black Gold under wraps a little longer, until the half-mile mark, and then he let the reins out a single notch. With that, Black Gold simply galloped away from his pursuers while Energy, spent and discouraged, dropped back. The black colt was still under some restraint when he crossed the line five lengths in front of Battle Creek, who had overhauled Energy for the place.

It had been a visually impressive performance, though the time was a slow 1:15⅘ and the field was mediocre. Still, Black Gold had once again handled an off track with smooth ease; he had broken well under Mooney's handling; and he could hardly be blamed for running no faster than the competition warranted, especially over muddy going. Following Webb's prerace orders, Mooney sent the colt on through what was essentially a paid workout with another furlong in 14⅓, finishing seven-eighths of a mile in 1:30. Black Gold came back clean and full of himself—and, as Mooney had promised, there wasn't a mark on the colt's gleaming black hide when Webb checked over his "baby" back at the stable.

There was no doubt that Webb was pleased with Mooney's ride and the way Black Gold had responded; it showed in his brief, toothless smile and his thawing attitude toward the jockey. There was only one problem; Mooney could not ride Black Gold in the Queen City Handicap, as he had already given J. T. Weaver his word that he would ride Colonel Gilmore back after winning with him on October 23. Mooney knew that Webb wasn't likely to hold a grudge for that; the trainer's own code of honor didn't have room for broken promises. Nonetheless, it left Webb scrambling yet again for a jockey for Black Gold, and that left Mooney with mixed emotions. He wanted the colt to do well in the Queen City, but he didn't want someone else to do so well with him that the newcomer ended up walking off with the prize mount. Still, he had done what he could to convince Webb that he should become Black Gold's regular jockey. All he could do now was to wait things out while he plied his trade elsewhere, hoping that he would have another opportunity with his dream horse after the big race was over.

19

Season's End

As was so often the case with Black Gold, fate once again had a slap to deliver just as it seemed the colt's fortunes might be looking up. Good jockeys who were still free to take a mount were in short supply at Latonia with a big field and a $10,000-added purse on the line, and in the end, Webb had to settle for giving Jack Howard the mount on Black Gold in the Queen City. Given that Howard had ridden Black Gold poorly back in April and had probably cost him a win then, Webb had to be hard up indeed to give him a second chance when he had written off other jockeys permanently for no more cause.

Even if Mooney had been available to ride, Webb's confidence in Black Gold would have been tempered by his awareness that Wise Counsellor would be in the race. He knew that Black Gold had never looked like beating the Mentor colt in the Cincinnati Trophy at level weights, and even though Wise Counsellor had not raced since then, his reputation and his most recent works were such that the Bradley brothers had demanded—and gotten—$66,000 for him in mid-October.

The price tag was high for the times, but it reflected the status of the colt's new owners as well as his own merits. The buyers were John S. Ward and his silent partner, wealthy Chicagoan Fred Burton, and it was no secret that Ward intended to point Wise Counsellor for the 1924 Kentucky Derby after the colt completed his fall engagements. Adding to the difficulty of Black Gold's task, Ward also intended to run Worthmore, acquired for $22,000 when C. T. Worthington dispersed his racing stable at Latonia in the wake of his suspension. Both colts were under the care of the well-regarded trainer

Roscoe Goose, who as a jockey had won the 1913 Kentucky Derby aboard Donerail.

As if the Ward entry would not have been plenty to contend with, virtually every Kentucky two-year-old with any pretense of class was targeting the Queen City. The best of the local contingent other than Wise Counsellor and Black Gold was probably Chilhowee, who had bounced back from his own tough run in the Breeders' Futurity to win the Ft. Thomas Handicap over future Hall of Fame member Princess Doreen on October 13. He was being ridden by Clarence Kummer, famous as Man o' War's regular rider in 1920, and another top eastern jockey was also present; this was Laverne Fator, who would ride the Rancocas Stable's speedy New York stakes winner Bracadale.

Wise Counsellor was rumored to be having trouble with one of his feet, and he had missed his intended prep race in the Ft. Thomas for reasons that his connections did not disclose.[1] Nonetheless, when the entries for the Queen City were taken on October 26, his was one of sixteen names making up the list, though his stablemate Worthmore had gone lame and was not entered after all. As expected, Ward's colt had the top weight assignment with 125 pounds against 122 on Black Gold and Bracadale, 119 on Chilhowee, and 113 or less on everything else. Adding to the challenge facing Wise Counsellor, he drew the far outside post, giving him the longest distance to travel, with Black Gold two places to his inside. Bracadale got post position 3, a good spot for a speedster, with Chilhowee just to his outside.

The weather was cloudy but dry on race day, October 27. Mud would have encouraged Black Gold's backers, but without it, he drifted out to third choice in the betting at odds of 5.60–1. Wise Counsellor was favored at slightly over 3–1, Chilhowee was at 5.20–1, and Bracadale was the only other entrant at less than double-digit odds.

As it turned out, Wise Counsellor should have been at much lower odds. It took only one minute to get the big field lined up and away, and when the favorite broke cleanly, the race was as good as over. Only one colt, Bracadale, had outbroken him, and Ward's colt flashed by his impertinent rival in a matter of strides. From there, he sailed along in regal isolation. If anyone had thought the mile distance might bring him back to the others, they were soon disillusioned. Never fewer than three lengths in front at any call of the race, the big chestnut widened his lead to as many as eight lengths before Earle Pool took him in hand. Battle Creek, in closest pursuit throughout, settled for second, beaten five lengths as Wise Counsellor simply galloped in. Bob Tail and King

Gorin II closed from farther back to be third and fourth, respectively. The time was a moderate 1:39⅗, but it was generally conceded that Wise Counsellor could have gone substantially faster had he been asked to do so.

Wise Counsellor's victory made perfect sense. Already acknowledged as the best colt in Kentucky going into the race, he had if anything matured and improved during his time away from the track. What did not make sense was Black Gold's dreadful showing. All three of Wise Counsellor's closest pursuers were colts that Black Gold had beaten easily earlier in the year, and on previous form, the Hoots colt probably should have been a clear second. Instead, he straggled home ninth, beaten some fourteen lengths, and the only good thing that could be said of his performance was that he had led Chilhowee home by two lengths. Colonel Gilmore, with Mooney aboard, was another twelve lengths farther back, next to last.

The common opinion of Black Gold's race was summed up by the correspondent for the *Brooklyn Standard-Union,* who sniffed that Black Gold "quit at the quarter pole."[2] Offering a more nuanced view, C. J. Savage stated: "Black Gold was poorly ridden and he had no chance to run at any stage of it. Every time that he made a move he was shut off."[3] Nonetheless, even he had to acknowledge that once again, when put into close quarters and bumped about, Black Gold had shut down and refused to fully extend himself. It was a dismal omen for anyone looking for a possible Kentucky Derby hopeful, and the bookies took note as they started thinking about early betting for the Golden Jubilee.

Fortunately, Black Gold emerged from the Queen City unhurt, and on November 9, Webb took him back to Churchill Downs for the final meeting of the Kentucky season. The colt seemed to appreciate the change, working with more enthusiasm and sparkle than he had shown over the Latonia strip.

Wise Counsellor had made the short journey to Churchill Downs as well, though the wise guys around the track were now certain that he was sore in his right hind foot.[4] Sore or not, he was headed to the $5,000-added Golden Rod Handicap on November 10 and then the Kentucky Jockey Club Stakes on November 17, the last rich race of the Kentucky racing season for two-year-olds, where he was slated to meet the Rancocas Stable entry of Mad Play and Bracadale along with Battle Creek, Chilhowee, and his stablemate Worthmore.

Black Gold had not been nominated to either race, which left him on the outside looking in. Perhaps that was as well. Wise Counsellor was a no-show for the Golden Rod, for which he had been assigned 132 pounds, but twelve other juveniles showed up, and the race was won by the filly Glide with Chilhowee, Worthmore, and King Gorin II in the beaten field—certainly a group that Black Gold could have defeated, but by no means a sure win.

The Kentucky Jockey Club was another story. Wise Counsellor was there, and he turned in a sensational performance, even though he raced on a cracked right hind hoof held together by a leather strap and a bit of cotton batting.[5] Summoning all his courage to turn aside the challenge of the improving Mad Play, the Mentor colt won by a neck for his fourth victory in five outings. His time of 1:37⅕ was said to have been a new record for a two-year-old at any of the Kentucky tracks, and even though he had not raced outside Kentucky, he was generally acknowledged as sharing the national championship among the year's juveniles with New York's darling, St. James, who had won Belmont Park's historic Futurity Stakes with 130 pounds aboard. The only other youngster mentioned in the same breath with the leading pair was Mrs. William K. Vanderbilt's Sarazen, a brilliant speedster who went through the season unbeaten in ten starts but in lesser races. Although there had been talk of a possible match race between Sarazen and Wise Counsellor to be run after the Kentucky Jockey Club Stakes, nothing came of it, leaving the question open as to how Sarazen stacked up against the very best of his peers.

Wise Counsellor's heroics ended up overshadowing Black Gold's final race of the season, which took place against much less heralded company on November 13. Sent out for the one-mile New Albany Purse, Black Gold had to face only five rivals, the best of which was King Gorin II. He also had Mooney back in the saddle, and when Mooney got him a clean break, that was all Black Gold needed. Kept under restraint all the way, he romped in by two lengths. The time over a fast track was 1:38⅗, considered quite good for a juvenile but about seven lengths short of Wise Counsellor's time four days later.

In the wake of the adulation surrounding Wise Counsellor, Black Gold's absence from the Kentucky Jockey Club Stakes was little remarked, as was Rosa Hoots's declaration that her colt would be pointed to the 1924 Kentucky Derby.[6] A few days later, the little black colt was on a train back to New Orleans, ending his year in the place where it had begun with such promise.

20

The Road Less Traveled

For horses owned by the upper class of the Northeast, winter was the season of rest. This was partly making a virtue of necessity, given the weather of the region, but it was also a luxury that testified to the wealth of people who could afford to race horses purely for sport. If their horses did not race for several months, that was no hardship to those whose livelihoods did not depend on their animals' earnings. They could find other amusements while the two-year-olds of the previous season grew into more adult frames and the older stars healed from nagging injuries, and the prizes available in the winter months had neither the prestige nor the purses to be worth rushing a promising colt or filly. Thus, winter racing had little attraction to the elites of the sport. They might watch other people's horses run as they wintered in New Orleans or Miami, but March was generally thought soon enough for their own stables to start serious preparations for major events that would not take place until May.

Horsemen from less exalted social strata had a different view. Many depended on their horses as their meal tickets and could not afford to suspend their operations for months at a time. Others, though not technically reliant on their stables, were not inclined or able to support them through prolonged periods of idleness when they could be earning money. Winter racing in Mexico, California, Louisiana, and Florida might not be lucrative or prestigious, but it paid the bills and furnished a medium for betting—often the primary rather than the secondary source of income for a cagey trainer or owner. Consistent or amusingly quirky horses that entertained the crowds during the months when the top runners were in their winter quarters became popular heroes in their own right, and if the stars of winter racing generally faded when the warmer months came around and the competition stiffened, that was only to be expected.

Given the nature of winter racing in the 1920s, the appearance of a newly turned three-year-old at one of the winter venues was generally taken as a tacit admission that not much was expected of the animal later in the year. Of the Kentucky Derby winners through 1923, only 1904 victor Elwood had raced during the winter season, and that was at a time when the Derby carried much less prestige. So, when the word got around that Black Gold would be pointed to the Louisiana Derby on March 17, those bookies who had already started taking bets on him at odds of up to 100–1 in their winter books for the Kentucky Derby smiled comfortably.

Their complacency reflected their assessment of Black Gold's chances. It wasn't that anyone thought he was a bad colt. His record of nine wins from eighteen starts was commendable, his win in the Bashford Manor Stakes had been exceptional, and most horsemen thought he was unlucky not to have several more wins on his record. Looking at all he had accomplished, no less a judge than veteran sportswriter Joe Palmer ranked him fifth among the two-year-olds of 1923, not just in Kentucky but with the whole nation in view.[1] Nonetheless, the colt had a history of being unable to handle bumping and crowding, sure occurrences in a big Derby field. Add to that the handicaps of his small size, a pedigree that most experts thought leaned more toward sprinting speed than stamina, a history of injury and intermittent soreness, and, worst of all, a trainer with a reputation of having no idea of how to handle a good horse, and the consensus was that he had no more than an outside shot, assuming he made it to the Derby at all. Since winter book bets were nonrefundable, the bookies' odds were based on the perceived likelihood of a horse's actually making it into the race as well as its perceived merits, and many felt that with Black Gold starting to race so early in the season, he had little chance of staying sound until the big race.

In spite of the naysayers, a surprising number of people were willing to put money down on Black Gold's nose, but most of the bets were relatively small— twenty dollars here, fifty or a hundred there—and were placed by everyday people: shoeshine boys, elevator girls, cab drivers, oil workers, and cowboys. Only a few of the oddsmakers noted that those little bets on Black Gold were adding up to substantial sums, and none of them seemed alarmed; they were secure in their own judgment. Yet a few keen-eyed observers had noticed two things. One was that Black Gold had never been beaten at Churchill Downs and had run far better there than he had at Lexington or Latonia. The other was that he was an easy two-for-two with Mooney in the saddle—and Mooney was known for riding at Churchill Downs better than he did anywhere else.[2]

Based on the betting patterns, Black Gold was far more popular than most of the "experts" realized, but at the end of 1923, there were only two people in the public eye who seemed to believe in the little black colt without reservation. One was Rosa Hoots, whose now-unwavering faith in Black Gold was patronizingly dismissed as "superstitious credulity."[3] The other was J. D. Mooney, now also in New Orleans and eagerly anticipating the call to return to Black Gold's saddle.

Black Gold did not return to racing immediately after arriving in New Orleans, but there was no rest awaiting him. Despite more or less constant rain over the area, the black colt was soon out daily at Jefferson Park, with or without his lone stable companion, Tuscola. Other horsemen shook their heads, watching as the increasingly muscle-sore animal galloped day after day—not an easy lick, but a hard, punishing gallop over the churned-up, muddy track.

The treatment was intentional, though the intent was not cruel. "Webb . . . insists that the only way to build up an iron constitution in an animal is to build within him, by hard work, muscles that are superlative in power," observed a correspondent for the *Winnipeg Evening Tribune.*[4] Whether by intent or not, Webb's insistence reflected the ethos of the "physical culture" movement of the late nineteenth and early twentieth centuries, which advocated strenuous exercise methods as a means of developing the human body to peak fitness and which was then receiving fresh attention thanks to the burgeoning popularity of bodybuilder Charles Atlas.

Regardless of what influenced Webb's determination to develop Black Gold's muscles to the fullest extent possible and his methods for doing so, the desire for those muscles was not mere whimsy. Webb knew he had a good colt, but unlike Rosa Hoots, he had already concluded that unless the track was muddy, Black Gold was no match for Wise Counsellor on raw talent, and he had his doubts regarding his colt's ability to handle the best of his other possible rivals.[5] As he saw it, his one chance to fulfill Rosa Hoots's dream of making a Kentucky Derby winner of her colt lay in making Black Gold fitter than his rivals. Knowing that longer races were coming up ahead, Webb may also have been seeking to lay a foundation for stamina that would overcome any distance limitations inherited from Useeit.

Webb continued the hard work through most of December before finally giving Black Gold a rest that many observers felt was long overdue. A few weeks' break resulted in "a decided change"; though no taller, Black Gold was visibly thicker and more muscular.[6] But now the pendulum swung to the other end as Webb seemed in no hurry to put the colt back into hard training, even though other candidates for the Louisiana Derby were already ready to race. Some observers were unconcerned, among them the clocker for *Collyer's Eye*, who in mid-January mentioned that Black Gold was "going along slowly" but was getting enough work to indicate that he was "the best 3-year-old at the track."[7] The *Louisville Courier-Journal's* correspondent also gave a sanguine report on the colt, stating that "the rail birds there [at Jefferson Park] report that he moves along like a flying express."[8] Others—ironically, in view of earlier criticisms—accused Webb of "babying" his charge.[9]

Webb, in fact, was playing out a delicate balancing act between Black Gold's fitness and his soundness, aided and abetted by Albert "Pinky" Brown, who had replaced Chief Johnson as the colt's exercise rider after the Chief, perennially restless, headed back out to ride races on the fair circuit. Still in the early stages of a career as an exercise rider that would span more than fifty years and see him gallop eight Kentucky Derby winners, Brown got his nickname from his unusual appearance; an albino, he sported a bushy mass of white hair, pale pink skin, and startlingly blue eyes. He didn't have the best of eyesight even as a young man, a consequence of his albinism, but he had strong hands and an uncanny ability to use hearing as well as the feel of the animal underneath him to analyze a horse's gait and pace. He was already doing most of his galloping for Ben Jones, who would take him along when he went to train later on for Woolford Farm and then Calumet, but he had enough time to spare to ride Black Gold for Webb for a few weeks while the colt was in New Orleans. Brown apparently formed a high opinion of the colt during his short time with him, for in a 1964 interview, he named Black Gold as his third favorite among all the top horses he had galloped, following only Triple Crown winners Whirlaway and Citation. He also stated that he thought Black Gold could have won a million dollars under the racing conditions of the early 1960s—quite a compliment, considering that only a handful of horses had won that much money at that time.[10]

Webb needed all the help he could get in managing Black Gold, for even with Brown's aid, things were not going well. While the trainer was publicly putting a good face on his colt's condition, the urge to unburden himself was apparently overwhelming when Fair Grounds assistant manager Joseph Murphy stopped by one morning and asked how Black Gold was doing. Pulling Murphy aside for a private conversation, Webb confessed the truth. "Black Gold is not doing well," he said. "He pulls up sore, and I am trying to find the trouble."[11] It was not until several days later that Webb, looking relieved, buttonholed Murphy with glad news: "I have found the trouble in his feet. I have had the heels too high."[12]

With the colt's feet trimmed and reshod, Webb believed he had corrected the cause of his soreness. He continued sending Black Gold to the track daily, sure that any remaining trouble would work itself out. Others continued to see evidence that something was still not right. By February 6, Black Gold was far enough along for his first real speed drill of the year. Sent out for three-eighths of a mile around the "dogs" (markers placed on the track to prevent horses from working on the inside paths near the rail), Black Gold "fairly flew," getting a quarter mile in 24 seconds flat and completing his work in 37 seconds.[13] That was considered good time for Jefferson Park, especially under the conditions, but the correspondent for *Collyer's Eye* noted that it had taken the spurs to get the colt to extend himself.[14]

That was ominous enough, but worse, it was common knowledge by mid-February that Black Gold was training in bar shoes.[15] Named for the stabilizing bar connecting the heels of the horseshoe, bar shoes were used to support a cracked or weakened hoof and, thus, were a sure sign that all was not well with the colt's feet. Not too long afterward, veteran trackman Jimmy Brown wrote to Lally Collyer, telling him that "he [Black Gold] comes out 'dickey' on his legs every morning and it does not seem likely that he can be gotten ready in so short a time."[16] The noted St. Louis bookmaker Tom Kearney likewise had his reservations, offering Louisiana Derby odds of 4–1 on Black Gold against 2–1 on Thorndale, a recent winner over older horses.[17] Even so, Black Gold's trouble was apparently intermittent, for not everyone saw his works the same way. Writing in the same issue of *Collyer's Eye* that cited Jimmy Brown's observations and Kearney's odds, Walter Pearce opined, "Black Gold is sure to be seen in action before the season comes to a close and it is highly probable that he will be crowned the champion of the three-year-old division."[18]

Lameness in a racehorse can be frustratingly difficult to diagnose and treat even in modern times, when X-rays, ultrasounds, and other diagnostic tools have been added to the resources of trainers and veterinarians. It was harder in the 1920s, when all a trainer had to go by were his observations of his horse's gait and behavior and his skill at analyzing what he saw. Horses can't describe their pains to humans, and adding to the complexity of the task of diagnosis, some animals would lose their lameness as they warmed up; others were sore on one day and apparently sound on another. Still others, poor movers at their slow gaits, seemed fine when they galloped, or might run straight and true during a race only to start limping after the adrenaline of competition wore off. Sometimes, a trainer might successfully relieve one cause of pain or lameness only to find that the horse had developed another trouble spot in its attempts to ease stress on the original injury.

There were a few trainers who seemed to have a sixth sense regarding their animals' physical problems and gained the reputation of being "wizards" who could keep horses of questionable soundness racing, even ones that other good trainers had given up as hopeless. Webb was not remotely close to being in that class, nor was he an expert farrier as some of his peers were. Whether he was singularly incompetent compared to the average trainer of his time can be debated, but he was certainly no better than average when it came to managing a horse's routine physical problems and was probably out of his depth at handling anything more serious. Nonetheless, he was never intentionally cruel or brutal. As far as he knew, any aches and pains Black Gold still had were no more than the ones he himself felt in the morning before he got limbered up, and he was confident he would have Black Gold racing-ready or close to it well before time for a final decision about a Louisiana Derby start.[19]

Black Gold went out for a three-furlong spin on February 29, working in the same 0:37 of his earlier drill at the distance but in "handy style," certainly an improvement over needing spurs to get him to stride out.[20] That was encouraging, but the next day did even more to vindicate Webb's judgment. That morning, with J. D. Mooney in the saddle, Black Gold turned in a "sensational" seven-furlong workout at Jefferson Park, getting the distance in 1:28 while easing up during the final sixteenth of a mile.[21] Equally important, he pulled up "perfectly sound," as the correspondent for *Collyer's Eye* saw it.[22] After Black Gold cooled out, Webb was all smiles. "The Derby won't even be close," he predicted. "Black Gold has too much class for the others, and he is going to run away and hide from them."[23]

Three days later, Black Gold was still sharper. With Mooney again riding, the colt repeated his seven-furlong work and clipped a full second from his time, then galloped out an additional furlong under restraint to complete a mile in 1:45⅘. The quality of his effort reportedly left local horsemen "agog" and caused the *Cincinnati Enquirer's* J. L. Dempsey to term it "the most phenomenal work of the season."[24] The following day, Webb did two things: he dropped Black Gold's name into the entries for the six-furlong Sarazen Purse at the Fair Grounds, signaling the colt's readiness to complete his Louisiana Derby preparations in action on the racetrack, and he told Mooney to get ready to ride.

21

Laissez Les Bon Temps Rouler

Mooney was ready when Webb's call came. Though later romance might claim that he did not ride at all that winter, fearing that an injury or suspension might keep him from being able to ride Black Gold, reality insisted otherwise. Mooney and his wife still needed to eat, and so he rode a few races here and there during the Fair Grounds meeting, enough to keep the bills paid and Mooney in riding trim until Black Gold was ready to run. If there were any doubts about the jockey's readiness to ride for the big money, they were laid to rest on Fat Tuesday, March 4. Not only did he pilot Black Gold during his impressive second workout, but he rode Flint Stone to victory in the Mardi Gras Handicap over at the Fair Grounds that afternoon.

After that, no one was surprised when Webb made it official on Wednesday morning: Mooney would ride Black Gold for the rest of the New Orleans racing season, which would take place at Jefferson Park. That afternoon, Mooney steered Tuscola to a second-place finish in a $700 allowance race, an event far less significant for the small purse Tuscola earned than for Mooney's assessing how the Jefferson Park track was playing under racing conditions.

Five colts turned out on March 6 to oppose Black Gold in the Sarazen, a race honoring champion golfer Gene Sarazen rather than his equine namesake. With the human Sarazen in Miami for an international tournament, Black Gold was the attraction of the day and drew a sizable audience to the saddling area. His appearance was something of a disappointment to the experts, who noted that he was still small and unimpressive-looking.[1] Nonetheless, Rosa Hoots, who had been following Black Gold's training closely, was completely confident and had already told her friends in Tulsa that she expected to hear that Mooney and Black Gold had won "hands down."[2] The crowd, likewise expecting the race to be a paid workout, bet him down to 0.70–1.

According to the *Louisville Courier-Journal*, Black Gold "should have been 1 to 100."[3] Biding his time in third place early, the colt took the lead on the turn for home and was taken in hand once clear of his rivals in the stretch. From there on in, Mooney was occupied with two things: looking around for challenges that never came, and trying to keep Black Gold from pulling his arms out of their sockets. The official chart shows Black Gold won by three lengths in 1:12⅖, just a fifth of a second off the Jefferson Park track record, and no one doubted he could have gone faster had his rider desired; as it was, he finished "as fresh as a daisy" and jogged back to hearty applause from the stands.[4] Following the race, Webb announced he had arranged to ship Black Gold to Churchill Downs on April 1.

The only people unhappy with Black Gold's win were those members of the Louisiana bookmaking fraternity who had heard about the colt's foot problems and assumed that he would not be ready to win so early. They paid for their lack of confidence in Webb and his horse, especially "Big Store" operator Nick F. (known as "The Greek"), who took a bath reported at anywhere from $40,000 to $56,000. He and his colleagues would not be caught out so easily a second time. While they were still on the hook for the odds they had given in the early Louisiana Derby betting against Black Gold, the smarter ones were hedging their Louisiana Derby bets as best they could. Unlike their colleagues to the north and east, they were also getting some Kentucky Derby money down on Black Gold while the odds were still long enough to help offset the bets they had already taken.

Those of the midwestern and eastern bookies who figured that one sharp race against indifferent opposition was no real cause for concern felt justified after Black Gold came out again four days later for another allowance race on March 10. Facing six rivals over a mile and seventy yards, Black Gold only took command after trailing Fredericktown's pace for a mile and stopped the clock in the moderate time of 1:46⅘.

Given that the track was only rated "good" and that Black Gold's field posted the sharpest internal fractions of any of the three races over more than a mile on that day's card, the colt's showing may not have been as mediocre as many experts proclaimed. Nonetheless, they had clearly expected more from him after the Sarazen, and the same people who had been declaring Black Gold a sure winner of the Louisiana Derby after that race were now looking around for another choice. Among those suddenly writing Black Gold off was J. L. Dempsey, who, while criticizing Mooney for "blundering handling," felt the little black colt might not be up to the 126 pounds he would be required to carry in the Louisiana Derby.[5] He was more impressed by the larger and more powerful Thorndale, who worked a mile in 1:42 under "a heavy boy" just prior to the first race on the March 10 card and pulled up "in splendid shape."[6]

Benjamin Block, Thorndale's owner, was not nearly as sanguine about his colt's chances and made what was termed "a flattering offer" for the Black Toney colt.[7] (He was politely refused.) He was influenced in his opinion by his own trainer, Fred Burlew, who "practically conceded victory [in the Louisiana Derby] to Black Gold" despite the colt's having been less than spectacular.[8] Other experienced eyes may have judged that not all of Mooney's "blundering" was his own fault. The correspondent for the *Louisville Courier-Journal* noted that Black Gold seemed to race "in spots," and either unhappiness at an inside position or resentment of being asked to rate off the pace may have been factors in his performance.[9] A recurrence of his soreness cannot be ruled out either, although there were no postrace reports of lameness.

Rosa Hoots apparently had no misgivings. She arrived at Jefferson Park from Tulsa on March 10, ready for a week's enjoyment of the sights and sounds of New Orleans before the Louisiana Derby.[10] After being burned earlier, the local oddsmakers were not inclined to dismiss Black Gold either. Although early betting had made Black Gold and Thorndale virtual cofavorites at 1.40–1 by March 16, the professional handicappers opened the Louisiana Derby betting with Black Gold favored at odds of 1.20–1 despite the fact that the allowance conditions of the race required the colt to concede nine to fourteen pounds to each of his ten rivals. The question now was which Black Gold would show up—the one who had looked sore in February, the one who had looked unbeatable in early March, or the one who had looked a little vulnerable on March 10. The answer would determine whether Black Gold would go on to Kentucky or would drop by the wayside, just another would-be contender whose pretensions had been exposed.

The motto of the city of New Orleans is "*Laissez les bon temps rouler*"—in English, "Let the good times roll"—and the people who came to Jefferson Park on the closing day, March 17, were not about to let a small thing like a little drizzle dampen their spirits. A St. Patrick's Day crowd estimated at seven thousand showed up, ready to cheer for a real horse race in the day's feature, the Louisiana Derby.

Whatever had caused Mooney to ride at less than optimum form in Black Gold's second prep race, it apparently had not damaged Webb's trust in the jockey, as Mooney was back aboard Black Gold for the big race. Although Tuscola was entered in the third race on the card, neither Webb nor Mooney wanted to take a chance on an accident that might keep Mooney from riding Black Gold for the big money, and Webb engaged another jockey for the mare.[11] In the meantime, Mooney idled away his time in the jockeys' room as he waited for the Derby, the fourth race of the day. After each race, the other jockeys were coming in looking more and more bedraggled, and Mooney smiled to himself, knowing what that meant. It was even better when he went out to join Webb and Black Gold in the paddock. The morning drizzle had become an all-day rain, and a track that had been officially "fast" for the first race was now "soft and sloppy."[12] To Mooney and Webb, it was the luck of the Irish, for that was just the sort of going that Black Gold liked better than any other.

Bettors seemed to view the weather otherwise, perhaps thinking that the Hoots colt might have trouble coping with his weight assignment under the tiring conditions. By post time, his odds had drifted upward to 1.60–1, with Thorndale closing as the second choice at 2–1. Nonetheless, the crowd cheered vigorously when the favorite made his appearance at the tail end of the post parade, last in the field of ten colts and one filly.

Every minute that a horse must carry more weight than its rivals is to the advantage of those rivals, and the other jockeys in the race had no intention of making things easy on Mooney and Black Gold. With one eye on the favorite, they jostled for advantage for five minutes before getting off to a clean, even start. After that, they had no trouble keeping an eye on Black Gold—or at least, on his hindquarters. Breaking eagerly from his outside post, the colt was in front in a matter of strides, skimming over the muck with joyous ease. Behind him, his rivals faced another rain, made of the globs of mud that Black Gold's hoofs scooped up and threw over horses' coats and jockeys' silks. Strain as they might, none of them could get anywhere near to being close enough to return the favor. All along the backstretch, Black Gold led by two or three lengths, and Mooney had yet to let him loose.

An approving roar burst from the crowd as the black colt turned into the stretch alone, still racing along under a snug hold. He was pulling, asking to run faster, but was reluctantly obedient as Mooney began gathering him in instead. His mouth open as he hauled against the bit, Black Gold was already pulling up as he finished the nine furlongs in 1:57⅕, six lengths in front of Brilliant Cast in second. Thorndale, never closer than five lengths to the flying leader, gave up the chase early and finished eighth. As Mooney looped his colt back and cantered back past his defeated rivals toward the winner's circle, his white breeches and the colt's black hide gleamed through the gloom of the late afternoon, insolently clean. Black Gold had won the Louisiana Derby, and with it his right to go on to Kentucky.

22

Kentucky Bound

Among the sportswriters, Dempsey, at least, was gracious in defeat. In his next-day account of the Louisiana Derby, he acknowledged the little black colt had performed "as if much the best" and had handled the weight that was supposed to be too much for him "with utmost ease."[1] The correspondent for the *Buffalo Courier* was similarly impressed, reporting Black Gold "ran a field of ten others ragged."[2]

Most of the other newspapers also offered praise but in more perfunctory fashion; for many, the account of the race was a bare-bones recital that could be compressed into a couple of inches of column space. The lack of weight they attached to Black Gold's victory and their low regard for his connections may perhaps be measured by their referring to his owner as "Mrs. A. Hoyt," "Mrs. H. M. Hoots," and "Mrs. R. A. Hoot," sometimes not even getting the spelling consistent within the same article. Likewise, the colt's trainer became "C. Webbs" and "Harry Webb."

If most journalists were not overly impressed, they probably felt they had reason. As decisive as Black Gold's victory had been, Tom Kearney expressed the opinion of many observers when he said, "Black Gold didn't beat a thing in New Orleans."[3] His statement was exaggerated but not far wrong. Thorndale and third-place Rinkey (the lone filly in the field) were both stakes winners later in the season, but none of the others managed to win a stakes event that year. On a more general note, sportswriters also cast a dubious eye on the quality of the racing in Louisiana, noting that, over the past several season, several colts that had come out of races in New Orleans with high reputations had flopped badly when facing tougher company later in the season. While the journalists conceded that 1917 Kentucky Derby winner Omar Khayyam had wintered in New Orleans, where he began his training for the spring racing season, they pointed out that he did not race there, opening his three-year-old season in more orthodox style at the Lexington spring meeting. No horse had ever gone on from the Louisiana Derby to finish in the money at Louisville, much less win the roses; in fact, Damask, fourth in the 1920 Kentucky Derby, was the first Louisiana Derby winner to even start in the great race.

Nonetheless, New Orleans bookies wasted no time in slashing Black Gold's Kentucky Derby odds in their future books from the prevailing 40–1 to as low as 15–1. Bookies in Louisville, Chicago, Cincinnati, and St. Louis were a little slower to follow suit (most went to 20–1 or 25–1 over the next few days), but even they admitted that if track conditions turned up sloppy or muddy on Derby Day, Black Gold would be a hard colt to beat. That was more than jubilant Louisiana racing fans thought Black Gold would need. They had adopted Rosa Hoots's colt for their own, calling him the "Little Big Train."[4] Rain or shine, they figured that he had the Kentucky Derby as good as won, and within hours after the Louisiana Derby, money from New Orleans and the Osage country in Oklahoma began pouring in on the little black colt as bettors sought to get their money down while the odds were still attractive.[5]

Most bookies weren't alarmed, even when it became obvious that Black Gold was drawing unusually heavy play, substantially more than the other horses offered at close to his odds. There were still two months to go before the Kentucky Derby, and a lot could happen in that time. The colt had been gotten into racing form much too early to keep his edge all the way until mid-May; he might go stale, or his off-and-on soreness might return even though he appeared to have come out of the Louisiana Derby sound. Even if he stayed fit and healthy, there were far better horses than the ones he had beaten only just starting to get worked into shape; the top Derby hopefuls—Wise Counsellor, Sarazen, and St. James—had not even started serious galloping.

Four days after the Louisiana Derby, Webb made another decision out of line with conventional wisdom. Virtually any other trainer of a major Kentucky Derby hopeful would have seen to it that his horse was placed in a special horse car and transported by express train to its destination, minimizing bumps and jolts that might damage delicate legs or throw a sensitive animal off its feed; transporting a good horse by ordinary freight simply was not done.[6] Webb reasoned differently. Abandoning his previous plans to ship his colt to Kentucky in April, Webb loaded Black Gold, Tuscola, and his stable pony into a boxcar that was part of an Illinois Central freight train on the morning of March 21.[7] They were bound to Louisville on a slow journey that Webb felt would let Black Gold acclimate gradually to the colder weather farther north without delivering a shock to his system.[8]

As the train ran north, rumor ran even faster. Before Webb and his charges arrived in Louisville on March 23, a story was already spreading like wildfire out of New Orleans about an early-morning trial that Black Gold had run at Jefferson Park just before getting on the train. By the time the Universal Service's Sam Whitmire hit print with the story on March 24, the word was out from the Crescent City to Chicago that with the full Kentucky Derby weight of 126 pounds up, Black Gold had run the Derby distance of a mile and a quarter in 2:05.[9]

To put that time in perspective, of the thirty-eight horses that had won the Kentucky Derby since its distance had been cut from a mile and a half in 1896, only seven had equaled or bettered 2:05 for the ten furlongs—and Jefferson Park was widely considered to be a slow racetrack, not conducive to speed. Given the surface and the time standards of the 1920s, it would have been a phenomenal trial. There were only two problems with the story. One was that the bookies in Kentucky and the Midwest uniformly continued to post odds in the same range of 20–1 to 25–1 that most had offered since March 18 or 19, suggesting that they were unaware of such a work despite their networks of sharp-eyed clockers and tipsters. Given that the bookies' livelihoods depended on their information chains, it would be a rare thing indeed for a serious workout by a Kentucky Derby contender to escape their notice. The other was that when he arrived at Churchill Downs, Webb himself denied the trial had ever taken place, telling the *Daily Racing Form*'s reporter that Black Gold had not even had a saddle on since the Louisiana Derby.[10]

To this day, Black Gold's supposed trial remains an enigma that may or may not be tied in with Webb's sudden decision to take Black Gold on to Louisville well before he had originally planned to do so. If the work did not happen, then how the rumor came about becomes a question. Black Gold was a well-known horse, unlikely to be mistaken for another—even assuming there was another horse in New Orleans capable of showing that kind of speed— and there seems to be no reason or motive for anyone's having fabricated the story from thin air. If it did happen, then the reasons behind Webb's setting up a clandestine trial for his colt and then attempting to keep it from public knowledge are secrets he took with him to the grave.

Regardless of what had happened, Black Gold took the trip to Kentucky in stride, eating and sleeping without any apparent distress under Webb's watchful eye. On March 23, he arrived safely in Louisville, ready to begin preparing in earnest for the fiftieth Kentucky Derby.

Although Black Gold's arrival in Louisville drew due notice, he was only a forerunner for an anticipated flood of horses and horsemen into Kentucky. In 1924, 152 three-year-olds had been nominated to the "Golden Jubilee" Derby, the largest pool of nominees since the "Silver Anniversary" renewal in 1899. They represented the cream of the eastern stables as well as the best that the West had to offer.

Leading the pack with nine nominations each were Harry Payne Whitney, who had made it a quest to try to repeat Regret's 1915 victory, and Harry Sinclair's Rancocas Stable. They were followed by Whitney's sister-in-law, Helen Hay Whitney, whose Greentree Stable had nominated eight, and William Woodward's Belair Stud with six. Colonel Bradley, the largest of the western owners, had four nominees. Other major owners who had named multiple horses to the Derby included John E. Madden, Gifford A. Cochran, Joshua S. Cosden, and Oak Ridge Stable.

Of course, not all of these horses were expected to start. Some were unraced and had yet to show that they belonged in a selling race, much less the Derby. Some were already being dropped from consideration by March for any of a number of reasons—injury, sickness, and, most commonly, lack of talent. Others would be used up helping to hone the speed and stamina of more favored stablemates, often by running in relays against the stable stars so that talented but reluctant workers would be deceived into thinking they were in actual competition and would exert themselves accordingly. Such use of numbers was just one of the advantages a wealthy and powerful stable had over smaller outfits like the Hoots Stable in preparing its top Derby contenders. With deep pockets to draw on, big stables also had ready access to the best in trainers, farriers, and exercise riders, as well as contracts with the best jockeys.

After being humbled for two straight years by colts representing eastern interests, horsemen and racing buffs from west of the Appalachians felt they had a real shot at turning the tables in the regional rivalry that had become part of the Derby since Regret's triumph. Nonetheless, many observers felt that the strength of the potential Derby field lay in the East, where Sarazen—who had reportedly wintered extremely well—was at the top of most bookies' offerings at about 5–1. St. James was also well-regarded at about 12–1, and Mad Play, considered the strongest candidate from the Rancocas Stable, was held at 15–1 as the Derby horses began their spring preparations in earnest. Black Gold was one of the western runners conceded to have a legitimate chance but was overshadowed by Wise Counsellor (who opened in the March books at 6–1) and no better than equally regarded with Colonel Bradley's Pimlico Futurity winner, Beau Butler, commonly offered at 20–1.

Bookmakers offered odds on horses, not owners, but if any had been offering bets as to which owner would hoist the Kentucky Derby trophy, Rosa Hoots probably would have been at longer odds than her colt. Only one woman before her had owned a Kentucky Derby winner, and that was back in 1904, when Elwood carried Lasca Durnell's colors home at a time when the race carried much less prestige.

In 1924, female owners were no longer a complete novelty, and five had nominees to the fiftieth Derby. Nonetheless, there was a marked disconnect between sportswriters' treatment of those women who belonged to the eastern aristocracy and that accorded to those who did not. Those women who were members of the elite might be intruding on what was considered a man's game, but they were often accomplished equestriennes in other horse-related activities, and their wealth and social connections ensured that they could buy and hire the best for their stables. They might not be taken quite as seriously as the men of their level, but they could not easily be discounted or ignored.

Rosa Hoots was a different case. She was wealthy, acknowledged as a good horsewoman, and well accepted in Tulsa society. Nonetheless, by the standards of the eastern establishment and big-city elites, she was a provincial from the frontier and was further set apart from their class by her racial and cultural heritage. Her history of involvement in business dealings together with her husband and independently as a widow was likewise mostly outside their experience; although her adult life overlapped that of the noted female financier Hetty Green—a woman who several times kept New York City's finances afloat by extending the city short-term loans—Green was the exception to the rule of well-off women generally confining themselves to social rather than business pursuits.

Thus, because of her sex and origins, the "Indian woman" was often seen more as a curious figure in the romantic story of her colt's origins than a person to be taken seriously in her own right. Black Gold was certainly good enough to give her hopes for him some credence, but that she might have assessed the available facts and used them to draw reasonable rather than sentimental conclusions as to her colt's chances appeared to occur to no one. She was too emotionally attached to her undersized colt and her no-name trainer to be thinking rationally, at least according to the "experts." And so, when Mrs. Hoots let it be known that she had already made her arrangements for the Kentucky Derby—in fact, had made them back in January—most of the "experts" chalked it up to superstitious faith in her late husband's vision.[11] If they needed more copy regarding Black Gold, it was as easy as tossing out an article rehashing the popular tale about Black Gold's history; after that, they moved on to chasing news about the horses they believed were the real contenders and the glittering men and women who owned them.

23

Preparations

From the moment Black Gold arrived at Churchill Downs, Hanley Webb made it plain he was taking no chances regarding his colt's welfare. As soon as he had Black Gold and Tuscola bedded down in their stalls, he sent someone looking for Tom Young with a specific request: he wanted an axe. Young obliged, and within the hour, Webb had chopped an opening between Black Gold's stall and the empty one adjoining it, where Webb intended to live and sleep.[1] It was no longer enough for him to simply be close by; he wanted to be alert to his charge's every move, and he couldn't do that with a wall between them. And if anyone thought he might get access to Black Gold during those times when the trainer was sleeping or had to be elsewhere, he soon found there was another guardian on duty: an Irish terrier named Teddy Roosevelt, who combined a toothy grin worthy of his namesake with a suspected willingness to use those teeth on anyone who didn't belong near Black Gold.[2]

With the living quarters for man and beast arranged to his satisfaction, Webb took Black Gold and Tuscola out for a little light exercise, letting them limber up muscles that might have stiffened aboard the train; he asked no more of his colt than that. For the next several weeks, he would have no reason to push Black Gold. Unlike his rivals, the colt already had a solid foundation under him; he was as well-muscled as Webb could desire; and he had no excess weight from winter idleness to work off.[3] Nor was he going to be pushed to make any of the traditional Derby prep races at Lexington or anywhere else; Rosa Hoots and Webb were in accord that the best plan for Black Gold was to keep him in light training until shortly before the Kentucky Derby, when

134

the work would be thrown to him to put him on edge.[4] In the meantime, the colt could afford to take time to rest, heal up any nagging little issues, and acclimate to what was turning out to be one of the coldest, wettest springs Kentucky had seen in decades.[5]

The one thing that was disturbing was that Black Gold once again seemed footsore. Other trainers at the track did not regard the problem as serious, and some even thought that the lameness might stem from soreness in the colt's shoulders rather than his feet. Nonetheless, Webb had Black Gold's shoes pulled, believing that they might be pinching the colt's feet.[6] It would do Black Gold no harm to go barefoot while he was only in light training, especially since the loamy Churchill Downs track was held to be easy on a horse's feet. If it was sloppy or muddy out, well, Black Gold liked that even better, and there was no need to ask him for speed. Not yet.

With his feet feeling more comfortable, Black Gold was quite lively within a day or two of his arrival in Louisville—more so than Webb, who had gotten sick almost as soon as he got off the train.[7] Fortunately, he had brought help with him in the form of veteran exercise rider Charley Akers, who had taken over Black Gold's exercise after Pinky Brown left New Orleans with Ben Jones.[8] Then in his early fifties, Akers—known as "Pop" in the racing community—had been riding on the Ohio fair circuit when he was ten years old. A year later, he rode his first sanctioned race at Lexington, and during the following years he had ridden all over the Midwest and Upper South, in Canada and Mexico, and even in England. During his heyday, he had ridden against champion jockeys such as Isaac Murphy and Snapper Garrison, and his mounts had included the great Salvator, the best American racehorse of 1889 and 1890. Akers knew a good horse when he saw one, and as soon as he got off the train from New Orleans, he confidently predicted that Black Gold would win the Derby.[9]

Webb could not have asked for a better right-hand man in managing Black Gold during the long weeks between the Louisiana Derby and the Kentucky Derby. Akers handled Black Gold's morning work on his own while Webb recovered from his illness, and the ex-jockey had his hands full with his eager mount. After watching Black Gold canter under Akers's restraint on March 30, C. J. Savage wrote: "If there is anything wrong with Black Gold it would be a difficult task to discover it. He eats well, is as frisky as a kitten at all times, and he is desirous of 'turning on' at full speed every time he comes on the racetrack."[10] Even so, the pundits and the bookies remained mostly unconvinced that Black Gold had more than an outside shot, and with nearly seven weeks still to go before the Derby, most of them continued to look elsewhere for a winner.

Webb read as many newspapers as the next man, and when he was not busy with Black Gold, he was keeping up with what the colt's potential rivals were doing. If he felt a bit smug over what he was learning, he could be forgiven, considering the scorn he had gotten for Black Gold's handling during the winter. All through March, the unseasonably cold, wet weather plaguing much of the United States had kept most of the other Derby prospects off the tracks, getting their exercise by being walked and jogged along the shed rows or ridden over tanbark paths in their stable areas. Even Sarazen, taken down to Miami for the winter by trainer Max Hirsch, had not gotten beyond conditioning gallops by the time Black Gold won the Louisiana Derby. As the month drew to a close, sportswriter G. F. T. Ryall estimated that most of the New York–based Kentucky Derby candidates were a week to ten days behind in their training schedules.[11]

The Kentucky contingent was not faring much better, but as March slipped into April, other colts besides Black Gold were beginning to show up on the morning work tabs. Naturally, the one drawing the most attention was Wise Counsellor, the Derby favorite of virtually every horseman and journalist west of the Appalachians.

Wise Counsellor had actually made the news back in January when he and his stablemate Worthmore were among thirty-five horses that escaped a stable fire that destroyed two barns at Churchill Downs.[12] He appeared to have taken no injury from the incident, and when John Ward got Wise Counsellor onto the track in March (having taken over his horses' training from Roscoe Goose), the colt appeared to have developed well over the winter. Those expressing concerns over the bad right foot that had plagued the Mentor colt in the fall could take assurance from Ward's assistant, W. E. Welsh, who stated that the colt had entirely grown out the quarter crack that had troubled him and was "as sound as a bell of brass."[13] Others, however, were not so sanguine. Among them was Goose, who heartily praised his former employer's training skills and Wise Counsellor's talent but nonetheless pointed out that the colt had weak feet, saying, "I would not want to bet that the son of Mentor gets to the [Derby] post."[14] There were also observers who commented that the big chestnut had gotten a bit fat since closing his juvenile campaign. According to the correspondent for *Collyer's Eye*, the wagering among backstretch observers was that it was even money as to whether Wise Counsellor would make the big race.[15] To sportswriter O'Neil Sevier, those were short odds, his estimate was that it was 6–1 against Wise Counsellor's starting in the Derby, much less winning it.[16]

Ward ignored the naysayers, and Wise Counsellor took to his Derby preparation with apparent zest and good energy. He was said to have been galloping on the tanbark oval surrounding the Churchill Downs barns even before he started working on the main track, and the reports reaching New York were sufficiently glowing that Max Hirsch made a special trip to Kentucky to look the colt over.[17] Wise Counsellor's stablemate Worthmore was also making a favorable impression, his lameness of the previous year having been chalked up to "excessive training."[18] When Ward wasn't actively training his two stars, he was showing visitors to their stalls and basking in the compliments he was receiving on their health and appearance.

Hirsch returned to New York impressed with Wise Counsellor but still convinced that he had the better horse. Nonetheless, he was now fighting against time to get Sarazen fit and ready for the Derby, especially after his charge had to miss several days of training due to a slight ankle injury. Building up Sarazen's stamina was also a concern, for the gelding was an undersized specimen that had even less in his bloodlines and appearance to suggest suitability for the Kentucky Derby distance than Black Gold did. In fact, his background was as suited for a "rags to riches" story as either Black Gold's or Wise Counsellor's. Sired by the very fast but unsound High Time, a Domino grandson who scored his only stakes win over five furlongs, Sarazen had been produced from Rush Box, whose sire Box had done his best running in the seven-furlong Carter Handicap. How far Rush Box could run was not known, for she had never raced and had reportedly been broken for farmwork before being bought cheaply as a mate for High Time, then just starting his stud career.

From there, Sarazen's story took an upward turn. Bought at a modest price by Phil Chinn, whose eye for a horse and wheeling-dealing ways were both legendary, Sarazen showed brilliant speed in his first few races and was then sold for $35,000 to Mrs. Vanderbilt's Fair Stable. After the youngster defeated good older horses in a one-mile stakes race at Pimlico to cap off his unbeaten juvenile season, no one was surprised when Mrs. Vanderbilt and Hirsch declared their intent to win the Derby with him. There was good reason behind that plan. As a gelding, Sarazen was not eligible to the Preakness or the Belmont Stakes, so the Derby was by far the biggest spring prize that was open to him—if he could get the mile and a quarter.

With no time to spare in his schedule for being finicky about the weather or the track conditions, Sarazen went out for one-mile gallops over off going on April 5 and 7, showing substantial improvement between the two works, and by mid-April had been sent for a gallop over the full Derby distance. His time of 2:18 was still far off the standard needed to be a Derby contender, but Hirsch let it be known that he was pleased with the gelding's progress—or at least, that was what he told the newspapers. The one sign that all might not be well in Sarazen's camp was a May 2 report in the *Brooklyn Daily Eagle* that Mrs. Vanderbilt had tried to buy the promising colt Ladkin from August Belmont, offering $75,000.

New York's other top hope was the aristocratic St. James, though the connections of the handsome bay colt were giving enigmatic signals as to his status with regard to the Derby. Those who sniffed at the plebeian breeding of Wise Counsellor and Sarazen and the supposed "range pony" background of Useeit pointed to St. James's impeccable English bloodlines as certain to enable him to get the Derby trip, even though he had never raced farther than six furlongs and, although touted as "well advanced" in his training, had only begun what was termed "light exercise" by mid-March.[19] The miserable weather was partly responsible, for it was already well known that St. James could not handle off going, but the real question was whether owner George Widener and trainer Andrew Joyner would even send the colt to Kentucky. They had nominated their colt to the Derby and to the Preakness as well, but both were more interested in winning New York's Belmont Stakes, the original counterpart to the Derby Stakes, than some upstart race in Kentucky. By March, it was common knowledge that though St. James might contend for the Derby or the Preakness if he was sufficiently fit and the weather was dry, Widener and Joyner were perfectly ready to bypass either or both of May's big races if necessary to attain their desired goal. There were also questions as to just how sound St. James might be, given that he had bypassed a strong chance at the rich Pimlico Futurity in late 1923 after coming out of his big Futurity Stakes win with what O'Neil Sevier termed "disquieting leg symptoms."[20]

As uncertain as St. James's Derby status appeared, getting a line on him was easy compared to trying to get a clear idea of where Mad Play stood, for he had essentially vanished after his closing second to Wise Counsellor in the Kentucky Jockey Club Stakes. Along with the other Rancocas Stable horses, he did his winter training on Rancocas's private track, where he could be brought along as fast or slowly as trainer Sam Hildreth liked without any news of the colt's progress reaching outsiders. That meant that the early form of the Rancocas trainees remained completely dark to the press and the railbirds until the beginning of April, when Hildreth announced that Mad Play and another colt named Stanwix would be his most likely starters for the Louisville classic.[21] Even then, there was little concrete information to be had until Hildreth brought his Derby hopefuls to Havre de Grace during the second week of April, and Mad Play was still not being pushed along despite the fact that the Derby was only a month away.

In fact, none of Black Gold's potential rivals seemed to be at all hurried in their Derby preparations, even though most had not raced since the previous November at the latest. For the most part, they were following the training patterns that had been dominant since the Kentucky Derby began, which had in turn been passed down from time-honored ways of preparing three-year-olds for the Derby Stakes back in England: working off winter softness on the gallops after the weather began warming, a combination of two or three private trials and preliminary races within the four to six weeks before the target event to hone fitness and speed, and then the big race. What no one seemed to remember was that the Derby Stakes traditionally took place during the first week of June rather than the middle of May—a crucial difference of two to three weeks of training time for horses beginning their preparations in mid-March—and that the reason the English hopefuls did not race earlier was simply that none of the major English venues conducted racing in the mid- to late winter.

Webb was never highly regarded as a horseman, and he probably knew little and cared less about the history behind the traditions of preparing Derby candidates as trainers in Kentucky and along the Eastern Seaboard had always done. Nonetheless, his grasp of the potential importance of using the winter months and winter racing to lay a foundation of strength, stamina, and mental maturity ahead of the spring's great challenges for three-year-olds was ahead of its time. It was probably no coincidence that it was his younger contemporary Ben Jones, likewise a graduate of racing on the western circuit, who followed suit with Lawrin fourteen years later, using a winter preparation in Florida to win the Kentucky Derby with a dead-fit and battle-tested colt. Jones went on to win the Derby five more times, all with horses that had started their three-year-old campaigns during winter racing in either Florida or California, and from his time onward, winter racing of Derby candidates has been the norm rather than the exception.

24

Waiting Game

Webb continued his cautious handling of Black Gold all through April. The colt continued to be playful and full of energy but was not given any fast work until April 3, when he was allowed to go three furlongs in 0:37⅕ and a half mile in 0:51⅖. Kept under restraint, he obviously wanted more, but he would have to wait for that. In spite of Black Gold's insistent demands to be allowed to really run, Webb kept him to long gallops until April 9. Even then, the timed work was not very fast; over a sloppy track, the colt covered six furlongs in 1:21⅕ and was geared down at the finish. Three days later, Black Gold, still not being allowed to do much, galloped a mile in 1:47⅕.

Black Gold continued to receive mostly slow work, only being allowed to stretch his legs for a half-mile breeze a couple of times during the last part of April. The caution was paying off; there were no further reports of soreness, and the colt was eager to train, to the extent that C. J. Savage commented, "When he [Akers] brings him back to the stable, he displays more fatigue than his mount."[1] Akers himself was openly enthusiastic, with Savage quoting him as proclaiming Black Gold to be "the fastest horse he [Akers] ever threw a leg over."[2]

Visitors to Black Gold's stall were coming away with increasing praise for the colt's looks and fitness, but the railbirds had a different opinion. They wanted to see how his speed was shaping up alongside what the other Derby candidates were doing, and some started questioning openly as to whether Black Gold might be going stale. Others, sportswriter French Lane among them, thought the colt was being coddled. In his May 2 column, Lane wrote,

"If being treated strictly as a parlor pet and allowed to work as he pleases fits a horse for such a race, Black Gold stands out as a possible Derby winner."[3]

Other writers and trainers looked at the colt and came away with a different impression. While *Louisville Courier-Journal* writer M. D. Fulcher was an avowed admirer of Wise Counsellor and found his spring work more impressive than Black Gold's, he admitted that Black Gold appeared "mighty fit" while getting "enough work to keep him on edge."[4] Likewise, the correspondent for the *Cincinnati Enquirer* reported: "Every report coming from the work of the Oklahoma horse, Black Gold, is a good one. The reason you do not see a lot in the papers about this fellow is because the Indian woman who owns him, Mrs. Hoots, has no press agent. All she has is a good trainer in Mr. Webb and a husky exercise boy."[5] The bookies were apparently beginning to agree, for by early May, most of them had dropped their quoted odds on Black Gold to 10–1 or lower.

Webb kept Rosa Hoots advised as to Black Gold's condition and, secure in her backing, ignored critics and supporters alike and stuck to his own methods. He knew Black Gold far better than any of the people who were savaging his training of the colt, and he was certain that with the foundation Black Gold already had, one or two sharp works would be all the colt needed to have him crying to run. Drilling Black Gold for speed too soon would bring him to the peak that Webb wanted to reserve for the Derby too early, and doing too much would also risk a return of the foot problems the colt had experienced earlier. So, Webb and Akers played their waiting game, cajoling Black Gold into conserving his resources until the time to spend everything came.

J. D. Mooney had traveled up to Churchill Downs along with Black Gold, but there was no particular reason besides his fondness for the colt for him to stay there. Akers was more than capable of handling both Black Gold's exercise and the role of Webb's assistant, and there would be no racing in Kentucky until the spring Lexington meeting opened on April 26.

Ordinarily, Mooney might have remained in New Orleans or gone up to Canada to visit his wife's family, but his circumstances had changed in the wake of his ride on Black Gold in the Louisiana Derby. For the first time in his life, he was in demand, able to pick and choose his riding assignments. It was heady stuff for a man still not out of his early twenties.

It was also an opportunity that might not come again, for a jockey's career was as fragile as a Thoroughbred's legs. Mooney had no fear now that Webb would replace him aboard Black Gold, but whatever the nature of the two men's understanding, it was tempered by the unspoken knowledge that one bad step for Black Gold or one spill for Mooney would change everything in the fraction of a second that it took for flesh to tear and bones to shatter. Neither man could afford to put all his eggs in one basket; Mooney could not stake his entire riding career on a single horse, no matter how good, and necessity demanded that Webb keep other jockeys in mind as possibilities in case Mooney went down.

Although Mooney was not going to put his riding on the shelf while Black Gold was in maintenance training, he had no intention of taking every mount available; that was too risky. Nonetheless, he still needed an income, and he also needed to ride enough to keep his skills sharp and his body fit. So, when wealthy sportsman and entrepreneur Baron Long made him an offer of five thousand dollars plus expenses to travel to Tijuana and ride Long's new acquisition Cherry Tree in the Coffroth Handicap on March 30, Mooney had no hesitation about snapping up the deal and packing his bags.[6] The fee—equal to over two years' wages for an average American man—was guaranteed regardless of where Cherry Tree finished, and at the least, it was an opportunity to ride one of the favorites in a $40,000-added race. If he won, even better; it would keep his name fresh in the minds of owners and trainers when hunting for a rider for their own stable stars, and it would also net him a $1,500 prize offered to the winning rider by the Tijuana Jockey Club. Besides, an all-expenses-paid trip to Tijuana had its own attractions, although not all of them were of the sort Mooney was likely to patronize.

Tijuana today is a modern city, forming the southern end of a megalopolis that sprawls across the American border through San Diego up to Los Angeles. Within it lies the Agua Caliente district. Named for its natural hot springs, it features luxury hotels, upscale shopping, athletic centers, and other draws to tourists and well-off locals alike.

Agua Caliente in 1924 was both quieter and rowdier, depending on what one was seeking. The respectable draws were the springs, then surrounded by small hotels and cabins for the benefit of those wishing to "take the waters" for their health; it would be another four years before Baron Long, Wirt Bowman, James Coffroth, and Abelardo Rodriguez built a luxury resort and casino there that became a place to see and be seen for Hollywood elites and hopefuls. The not-so-respectable attractions of Tijuana were drinking, gambling, and prostitution, all illicit and sternly policed in Southern California and therefore irresistible to Americans seeking the excitement of forbidden fruit in an environment where arrest and disgrace were unlikely.

It was perhaps symbolic that the city's largest brothel, the Molino Rojo, occupied a hill overlooking the Tijuana racetrack, which straddled the border between the respectable and the disreputable. The plant was a place with a star-crossed history; opened in 1916, it was taken out by a massive flood only a week after throwing its doors open, then fell prey to fire after it was rebuilt and reopened just months later in April. But the Tijuana Jockey Club was determined that there was going to be racing in Tijuana, and racing there was after San Diego hotel owner John Spreckels provided the money to build the facilities a third time. That apparently was the charm, for the plant reopened in 1917, and racing went roaring on there for another decade before another flood washed out the railroad leading to the track and inundated the betting ring and the clubhouse. Even then, racing started right back up within days and continued until the new, opulent Agua Caliente track—built by Long and his associates on higher ground near their grand hotel and casino—replaced it in December 1928.

The Coffroth Handicap reflected the freewheeling atmosphere of the place. Named for boxing promoter James Coffroth, who had originally put up the money to build the Tijuana track, and first run in 1920, the Coffroth was the richest race of its time for the North American handicap division. The money attracted a large and lively field ranging from established stars under heavy weights to long shots under skeleton rigs, and the race had the kind of anything-can-happen atmosphere that made it both a popular medium for heavy betting and an occasion at which cinematic personalities, boxing champions, and big plungers accustomed to the high life rubbed elbows with men for whom the races were a prelude to a night's carousing at saloons and seedy gambling halls, with or without the company of ladies of negotiable virtue.

Mooney was not a likely patron of Tijuana's seamier attractions. By the time he traveled there, he was probably already aware that he and Marjorie were expecting their first child (a boy, John, would arrive in September), and neither late nights nor serious drinking were going to be conducive to his riding Cherry Tree to the best of his ability. He arrived in Mexico with his mind on business, determined to make sure that his employer got value for his money.

Mooney delivered on his princely fee in the Coffroth, though it was not quite enough to get Cherry Tree the win. Letting his mount settle into stride in unhurried fashion, Mooney was content to sit as far back as fifteenth out of the eighteen runners in the early going. After a half mile, he and Cherry Tree began working their way forward. They reached fourth as they hit the mile, and as they straightened away in the stretch, Mooney asked Cherry Tree for everything. The horse responded instantly. Ahead of him, front-running Runstar was game but leg-weary; Osprey was creeping up on his outside, and behind Cherry Tree, gallant old Exterminator, now past his best form but still formidable, had launched one of his own long, relentless drives. As Cherry Tree came up on the leaders' heels, they drifted apart just enough for Mooney to make a split-second decision and drive his mount into the narrow gap between them. A fainthearted horse would have slackened stride; Cherry Tree never faltered, hurling himself forward fastest of all in the final desperate yards. Straining to their limits, the three horses flew past the finish line as one.

Without the benefit of a photo finish camera, the placing judges held a tense conference while the top finishers walked about, awaiting the ruling. A few minutes crawled by, and then a roar went up from the crowd as the results were hung out. As the judges saw it, Runstar had won by the narrowest of noses with Osprey second; Cherry Tree, another nose back, was third. Exterminator was fourth, another length and a half back.

The next day's newspapers had nothing but praise for Cherry Tree's and Mooney's efforts in defeat, and some of the photos suggested that Cherry Tree might even have finished second rather than third. Nobody disputed that Runstar had won, but Long felt his horse was an unlucky loser and was keen on a rematch with Runstar and Osprey. After discussion with some of the other owners involved, the track agreed to host the Coffroth Consolation Handicap on April 7, and Mooney remained in town to ride Cherry Tree again. As it turned out, Runstar had to pass on the race, but five others from the Coffroth showed up for the ten-furlong event.

Cherry Tree was favored, but once again Mooney's talents were not quite enough to get him to the line first. This time it was Little Chief, one of the best handicap horses from 1923, who got out to an uncontested lead after extricating himself from a jam on the first turn. Though Cherry Tree made a good stretch run, he faltered in the final seventy yards in spite of a strong ride by Mooney and finished second, a length behind Little Chief and barely ahead of the lightly weighted Lady Astor. To his credit, Cherry Tree had pushed Little Chief to a new track record, and he bounced back three days later to take an overnight handicap over the same mile and one-quarter distance, again with Mooney handling the reins.

Mooney's final ride aboard Cherry Tree was in the two-mile Tijuana Cup on April 13, and once again the pair competed creditably without winning. As before, Little Chief was Cherry Tree's bane; racing in the top form of his career, the son of Wrack took the lead from the outset and ended up coasting in by four lengths, smashing the existing track record by four and one-fifth seconds into the bargain. Cherry Tree, getting a seven-pound break in the weights from his rival, ran well but never had a chance to catch Little Chief, settling for second.

Although Mooney lost his whip during the stretch run of the Tijuana Cup, it probably made no difference; Cherry Tree had simply met a better horse, a fact made abundantly clear in the Au Revoir Handicap on April 20. Under 132 pounds, Little Chief ran down The Araucanian in the final stride to win the one and one-sixteenth mile event by a nose. Cherry Tree, carrying sixteen pounds less than Little Chief and with a change of jockeys, ended up third.

By that time, Mooney was back in Kentucky, and he could look back on his stint at Tijuana with reasonable satisfaction. If he had not done what was hoped for with Cherry Tree, neither had he or the horse been disgraced against some tough competition. The pair had finished in the money every time, and Mooney had consistently drawn good reviews for his riding. Even more important, his ride in the Coffroth had refreshed the skills needed for riding in a huge field—skills he would need to ride Black Gold in the Kentucky Derby, now only a month away.

25

Falling Dominoes

While Black Gold and Mooney were preparing for the Derby along their separate paths, the colt's prospective rivals were not idle. Wise Counsellor was probably the one who concerned Webb most, and he was certainly the nearest at hand. All through April he progressed through increasingly fast works, seemingly without effort. By the time that he sailed through a mile in 1:44 on April 8, hundreds of people were turning out every morning to see him exercise, convinced they were watching the Derby winner. The bookmakers were equally impressed, dropping Wise Counsellor's odds to 4–1 and moving him into the role of Derby favorite ahead of Sarazen. Subsequent works over the next two weeks only added to the public's impression that he was coming along as well as anyone could ask for, and Ward announced plans to enter his colt in the Preakness Stakes as well as the Derby.

Some experienced horsemen were not quite so enthused about Wise Counsellor's progress. To their eyes, Wise Counsellor was not being worked "as much as his condition warrants."[1] He was carrying more weight than they liked, and by late April, there was open talk that the colt was being "babied."[2] There were also rumors that all was not well with his feet, especially the right hind. Supposedly the quarter crack that had troubled him the previous fall had healed, but the bar shoes he wore for work in early April told a different tale—yet one ignored by his fans and many of the pundits, who were apparently satisfied by Ward's explanation that the shoes were merely for "protection."[3]

Another question regarding Wise Counsellor was Ward's shifting about with regard to the colt's Derby jockey. Although it had been assumed early on that Earle Pool would ride the colt in the Derby after going four-for-four with him in 1923, Ward changed his mind in early March and started trying to gain first call on a leading rider for the colt. He soon announced that Mack Garner would have the mount, but that announcement was premature. For one thing, Garner was not free to take a riding commitment without the leave of Pete Coyne, who held his riding contract and had two Derby hopefuls of his own in King Gorin II and Bourbon Boy. For another, although Garner liked Wise Counsellor's chances, he did not like Ward and was not willing to jeopardize his relationship with his first-call trainer to press for the mount.

Ultimately, it was up to Coyne, and Coyne was playing his cards close to his chest. Because of the way Garner's contract was written, Coyne could release his services to the trainer of his choice, leaving Ward in the running to secure Garner for Wise Counsellor, but he was in no great hurry to make a decision until he saw how his own colts were shaping up. That meant that with the Derby less than a month away, the matter of Wise Counsellor's jockey was by no means settled. Eventually, Coyne gave his leave for Garner to ride Wise Counsellor in the Preakness, but no commitment was made beyond that, leaving the issue hanging.

Even by the standards of the 1920s, Ward's plans for Wise Counsellor's final preparations were ambitious. After some sniping back and forth between Churchill Downs and Pimlico over race dates, Pimlico had announced on March 16 that the Preakness would be scheduled for May 12. That was just five days before the Derby, but it still left enough time for a colt to compete in the Preakness and then ship to Churchill Downs for the Derby.[4] Ward's plan was to give his colt an easy initial outing in a sprint, then stretch Wise Counsellor out for a trial of his stamina in the nine-furlong Preakness. Bookmakers clearly thought that this might be a bit much, offering odds as high as 40–1 against Wise Counsellor's completing a Preakness-Derby double, but enough people were willing to take those odds that the bookies collectively stood to lose as much as a million dollars if the colt pulled it off. By late April, reports began circulating of a plot to dope or injure Wise Counsellor so that he could not compete in both events. Ward, hearing the rumors, brought in three guards and two watchdogs to safeguard his colt until he could complete the rail journey to Pimlico, where beefed-up track security would augment Ward's precautions.

Wise Counsellor tossed one final bouquet to his fans before leaving for Pimlico. On April 25, the Mentor colt worked a mile in 1:41⅗, the fastest mile that any of the Derby candidates had turned in to that point and considered excellent time over a track that was not in its best condition. He finished blowing and tired, but Ward assured the watchers this was only because the colt had gone through only moderate work over the last two weeks and needed a strong work that would tire him a bit.[5] The experts among the audience were more concerned, but they were heavily outnumbered by the people willing to accept any explanation Ward gave so long as it supported their belief that Wise Counsellor was the horse to beat for the Derby.

Ward seemed vindicated the next morning as Wise Counsellor, apparently in excellent health and spirits, boarded a horse car to Pimlico. As his train pulled out, he left Black Gold as the only leading Kentucky Derby candidate still in residence at Churchill Downs. The Mentor colt's fans saw him off before going back to their day's pursuits, most of them unaware that the same morning, Black Gold had stepped off a "sweet" half mile in 0:49⅖ while "hard held," a pace fast enough to suggest that he could have equaled or bettered Wise Counsellor's mile had Webb chosen to push him a bit.[6] But Webb had no interest in seeing which colt could turn in the fastest work. Only the fastest time in the Derby mattered, and so he sent his eager colt back to the barn still fresh and wanting to do more as the railbirds drifted off, once again unsatisfied.

While Wise Counsellor was impressing many Kentuckians as a sure Derby winner, the eastern colts were also moving ahead in their training. The most impressive among them was St. James, who was reportedly playful and in excellent condition. By the end of the first week in April, Phil McCann opined, "There is not a 3-year-old at the Metropolitan [New York] tracks that has improved as much as the son of Ambassador IV, Bobolink II."[7] Joyner continued to bring his charge along patiently, and the colt did not have his first speed drill until April 16, when he ran a half-mile in 0:46⅖.

St. James continued to train and work well until a spate of rain moved through the New York area, forcing Joyner to go easier on his charge than he might have liked. The colt continued to look magnificent, but a few observers were beginning to comment that he was carrying a trifle too much weight with the spring classics now looming closer.[8] Still, Joyner was sufficiently satisfied with St. James's condition that by April 26, he felt the colt was ready for competition and could go in Jamaica's six-furlong Paumonok Handicap on April 29.

That Joyner was seriously considering the Paumonok as St. James's season opener said volumes, for the potential competition was formidable. Zev, who could sprint with any man's horse, was also targeting the race, which he had won the year before as the kickoff to his championship three-year-old season; the good four-year-old Dunlin was another likely entry. Adding to the potential challenge, the speculation was hot that Sarazen might enter the Paumonok after an influenza outbreak in his stable derailed possible starts in the six-furlong Harford Handicap or the mile and one-sixteenth Philadelphia Handicap, both at Havre de Grace. Thanks to his season-ending victory against older males in the second of the 1923 Pimlico Serial Weight-for-Age races, Sarazen's reputation in Maryland was such that some thought he might even make his seasonal bow in the Dixie Handicap at Pimlico, but that was probably never under serious consideration as Sarazen had never raced a mile and three-sixteenths before and would have been facing good older horses to boot.

Sarazen himself had reportedly avoided the infection that affected his stablemates, but he still had not shed his winter coat and had gained little if any flesh on his slight frame, to the point that *Collyer's Eye* columnist E. G. Hendry called him "scrawny-looking."[9] Further, there were indications that he was not improving on the form he had shown in training earlier in the month and might even be regressing. After the gelding worked an unimpressive six furlongs at Belmont in 1:14⅖ on the 26th, Hirsch was openly uncertain as to whether his charge would start in the Paumonok, in which he would have to carry 115 pounds against 112 on St. James, 130 on Zev, and 119 on Dunlin. (With age adjustments taken into account, Sarazen would have received a one-pound weight advantage from Zev but would have had to concede fourteen pounds to Dunlin.) In the end, Hirsch kept Sarazen in his stall and watched from the stands as St. James seized the lead early and trounced Zev by three lengths, running the distance in 1:11⅗. His time was just two-fifths of a second slower than the track record. Four days later, Zev was out again for the King's County Handicap over a mile and one-sixteenth and won easily by two lengths over Mad Play. This result was an ambivalent reading on Mad Play's form, for although the time was a fast 1:44 and the three-year-old was not pushed to catch his older stablemate, Mad Play was getting an age-adjusted weight concession from the older colt similar to what St. James had received and had never looked like winning the race.

On the other hand, St. James's victory in the Paumonok only looked that much better for Zev's performance in the King's County, and it made him the darling of New York's sportswriters and bettors. A few cooler heads pointed out that the colt had still never raced beyond six furlongs and had less than three weeks to get ready for a distance a half mile beyond that, but they were drowned out by those who touted the superiority of the colt's bloodlines to those of any of his potential rivals. Pure English blood, they said, would doubtless take the measure of plebeians such as Wise Counsellor, Sarazen, and Black Gold over any distance, and St. James's admirers also made much of the colt's size and beauty compared to smaller, less impressive rivals. Regardless of the disagreements, St. James's seasonal debut could hardly have been more impressive, and Joyner indicated the colt's next target would be the Preakness Stakes. His performance there, it was said, would determine whether or not he would proceed to the Kentucky Derby.

Sarazen was not faring as well. After bypassing the Paumonok, Hirsch was probably hoping for an easier spot when he put Sarazen in Jamaica's Lynbrook Handicap on May 2. Instead, he got stung with the first defeat of Sarazen's career. Getting eight pounds from the High Time gelding, which had 115 pounds aboard, Bracadale outran Sarazen by a length and a half while completing the six furlongs in 1:12, substantially slower time than St. James had made in the Paumonok. Following the race, Sarazen's Derby odds jumped to 12–1, and rumors began flying that he might not make the Derby at all.

Although journalists were quick to blame a poor ride by Clarence Kummer for Sarazen's defeat, Hirsch thought otherwise and offered no excuses.[10] He was reassured by the fact that Sarazen cleaned up his next day's feed as usual and seemed none the worse for wear, but he wanted to see the gelding tried in another race before he made a decision about shipping to Churchill Downs. Jamaica's Spring Handicap on May 7 was penciled in as a suitable spot, but when the horses paraded to the post for the race, Sarazen was not among them. Hirsch had not seen what he had hoped for in his horse's work, and that same day announced that, with the consent of Mrs. Vanderbilt, Sarazen would be withdrawn from consideration for the Kentucky Derby.[11]

The news sent shock waves through racing circles and especially through the bookmaking community. On the surface, it was good news for the bookies, for Sarazen had been well played and they would now keep all the money wagered on him. Nonetheless, the bookmakers were uneasy. Sarazen had been considered a major obstacle for Black Gold, who had even more money wagered on him and at longer odds; in fact, the Hoots colt may have been the most heavily played horse in Derby winter book history up to that time.[12] With Sarazen out, Black Gold's Derby chances improved, but his shortened odds meant that it would take more money bet on him to hedge against a massive payout in the event that he won—and that was assuming that the bookies who wanted to make such hedge bets could find anyone willing to take their wagers, for many in the profession had already closed their books against more large bets on the colt, and some were not taking any more bets on him at all. One St. Louis bookie commented glumly, "If Black Gold wins, the biggest blow in a long time will be dealt bookmakers everywhere."[13]

Adding to the bookies' uneasiness, Widener and Joyner continued to be ambivalent about running St. James in the Derby in spite of his new status as a 3–1 favorite, and many believed that St. James would come to Churchill Downs only if he was a hard-luck loser in the Preakness.[14] On May 8, the point became moot. After St. James worked nine furlongs at Jamaica in 1:57 that morning, Joyner put in an urgent call to Widener. "There has been an accident," he said.[15] Within hours, the news was out: St. James was out of the Derby.

Once again, the bookies reaped an immediate harvest, but they were not rejoicing. St. James had not been as heavily played as Sarazen, and his defection made Black Gold look even more likely as a possible Derby winner, especially after Zev threw more clouds on Mad Play's form by losing his next outing on May 10. Now, only Wise Counsellor stood between the black colt and Derby favoritism, and reports from Pimlico gave the bookmakers reason to fear that the last domino might be ready to fall.

26

And Then There Were None

Whatever Webb thought of the news regarding the New York colts during the first week of May, he continued the slow pace of Black Gold's training with little obvious change. Most likely, it was Wise Counsellor who was still in the forefront of his mind, especially after word came in from Pimlico that Ward's trainee had zipped a half mile on April 30 in 0:46 flat, the fastest work over the distance at any of the major tracks that spring.

Several Derby contenders came out and worked brisk miles on May 3, but Webb continued to hold his hand. It was not until May 6 that Black Gold was asked for a touch of speed, going three furlongs in 0:36⅕ and galloping out another furlong to complete a half mile in 0:49⅗. The following day, it was back to galloping, and a slow gallop at that, leaving witnesses wondering just what was going on with the Hoots colt on a day when Pete Coyne's pair of Derby candidates, Bourbon Boy and King Gorin II, worked a "sensational" mile in 1:40⅕.[1]

Neither Webb nor Akers were inclined to talk, and that afternoon the pre-Derby drama took another twist when Colonel Bradley's main hope, Beau Butler, dropped a head decision to Altawood in the Blue Grass Stakes at Lexington after having beaten him soundly in both colts' season opener. Altawood had previously been considered an off-track specialist, and his come-from-behind win in fast time over a dry track served to cloud the Derby picture further, especially after it was announced that Lawrence McDermott—considered one of the best of the local riders—would have the mount in the Derby. Then rumors of Sarazen's defection began flying around the backstretch.

The next morning's papers confirmed that Sarazen was out and brought other news as well: Wise Counsellor had been withdrawn from the May 7 race at Pimlico that Ward had intended to use as the colt's prep for the Preakness Stakes. The Mentor colt was still expected to start in the Preakness on May 12, but though Ward would say only that the horse had "a slight ailment," rumors that all was not well with him received new life; some newspapers flatly stated that Wise Counsellor had come out of his last prerace workout lame.[2] The next day, the *Brooklyn Daily Eagle's* W. C. Vreeland gave an ominous possible reason: Wise Counsellor was reported to have "spread a hoof,"[3] possibly pointing to a recurrence of his quarter crack. Equally ominous, the colt seemed increasingly unhappy and nervous with each passing day.

Wise Counsellor had a brief work that morning anyway, going three furlongs in 0:39 over a muddy track. The time was not impressive, but Ward, who denied that the colt had anything wrong with him other than his nervousness, was reported to be optimistic that Wise Counsellor could still start in the Preakness.[4] But the next day, May 9, gave no grounds for optimism and plenty more for concern. Over a track described as "holding but not heavy," Wise Counsellor turned in a work suggesting he had regressed badly, getting to the mile in 1:44⅗ and then losing his action. He was driven hard to finish the nine-furlong Preakness distance in 1:59⅗, time beaten easily by two other Preakness candidates that also worked that morning.[5] Ward sent for Garner to come to Pimlico anyway, assuring the media that Wise Counsellor was "going fine."[6] Nonetheless, other observers were not convinced. By day's end Mad Play, coming in off a win in a May 8 allowance race, had been installed as the Preakness favorite.

In the meantime, Black Gold continued to look healthy and energetic, and on May 8, Mooney ended speculation that he might take another Derby mount from one of several owners vying for his services by publicly committing to Black Gold. The next morning, the colt finally got his first serious drill since his arrival from Louisiana. With Mooney replacing Akers in the saddle for the workout, Webb instructed the jockey to send his mount through a mile in 1:45. Black Gold had other ideas. Over a "somewhat slow" track, Mooney had all he could do to throttle him down to a mile in 1:41⅖, and the colt galloped out another furlong under hard restraint to finish in 1:58 flat.[7] After that, there was a brief flurry of rumor that Black Gold was lame, but the talk was quickly quashed by Webb, who gruffly asserted that his colt was fine and "ready to run."[8] His claim was supported by the colt's appearance during a slow gallop on May 11, which according to J. L. Dempsey drew "the usual favorable comment,"[9] and Webb let it be known that he planned to start Black Gold in a one-mile allowance race on May 13 as the colt's public trial for the Derby.

Other Derby candidates were also getting serious trials or prep races, and with one week to go before the Derby, no colt was making a more rapid leap up in the public's estimation than Chilhowee. The speedy son of Ballot had been dismissed by many as "just a sprinter" and a likely nonstarter for the Derby after leading early and then fading to be badly beaten in the same April 30 race at Lexington that had featured the seasonal debuts of Beau Butler and Altawood. The label of "sprinter" appeared firmly affixed when the Gallaher Brothers pulled their colt out of the Blue Grass Stakes, but that may have been misdirection aimed at a betting coup, for on May 10, Chilhowee went to the post in the nine-furlong Clark Handicap as the 3–1 second choice against older horses. Carrying a skeletal 100 pounds over a heavy track, the colt waited off the early pace for six furlongs and then sprinted to the lead. Favored Chacolet, fresh from a win in the Dixie Handicap, gave chase from well back, but the six-year-old mare was still a length and a half short at the wire. Another Derby hopeful, King Gorin II, also moved up his Derby stock that day, easily winning the one-mile Falls City Purse over his fellow three-year-olds.

Heavy rains hit Kentucky on May 11, and the only Derby horse of any standing to turn in a timed work at Churchill Downs that day was Beau Butler, who went a mile in 1:43. For most horsemen and racing fans, the focus of attention was now at Pimlico, where the Preakness would be run the following day. With St. James out and Wise Counsellor looking vulnerable, the race appeared wide open, and this was reflected in the nineteen colts and one filly who were named as entries. Sam Hildreth had put in both Mad Play and Bracadale from the Rancocas Stable; Mrs. Walter Jeffords's Diogenes was on the list; and other Derby hopefuls among the entrants included Klondyke, Senator Norris, and Transmute. The lone filly, Nellie Morse, was not eligible to the Derby but was coming in off a win in the Pimlico Oaks on May 8.

Pimlico had already been a sodden mess when the entries were dropped in the box, and more rain fell on the morning of the Preakness, May 12, creating track conditions so poor that some horsemen thought the race should be called off and rescheduled.[10] For John Ward, it was the final blow to his hope of keeping Wise Counsellor in the race. He had already been pressured to withdraw the colt by his partner, Burton, who had broken his silence the day before by saying that Wise Counselor was not fit to run in either the Preakness or the Kentucky Derby.[11] The trainer had resisted the inevitable as long as he dared, but about an hour before post time, Ward reluctantly made it official: Wise Counsellor was scratched and would not contest the Preakness.

After Diogenes, Klondyke, and Senator Norris all pulled out as well, the Rancocas entry of Mad Play and Bracadale was left as the post-time favorite. Then the race itself brought another shock. Sent to the lead after five furlongs, Nellie Morse took command and ended up winning by a length and a half over Transmute, with Mad Play another length and a half back in third. Bracadale, unable to get to the lead as he preferred, ended up thirteenth, beaten over twenty-five lengths.

That evening, the *Louisville Herald* reported receiving a telephone message from Burton. Wise Counsellor, underweight and anxious, was being shipped from Pimlico to Aqueduct, not Churchill Downs. His Derby quest was over.[12] And six hundred miles away from Pimlico, a slow, relieved smile spread across Hanley Webb's face when he heard the news.[13]

27

Derby Trial

After days of heavier rains, May 13 brought intermittent sun and showers to Churchill Downs. In spite of the unsettled weather, a larger than average Tuesday crowd came in, drawn by the feature race on the card. Grandly named the "Derby Trial," the one-mile purse race was shaping up as exactly that. Six colts and two fillies were entered, and all except Kentucky Oaks hopeful Princess Doreen were considered likely entrants for the Kentucky Derby, now just four days away. Black Gold was favored at 0.70–1, with Mrs. Payne Whitney's Wild Aster the next choice at 4–1. More than a few observers were looking over the Whitney runner with considerable interest, for he had an intriguing form line coming into the race; on May 7, the gelding had trimmed Bracadale by a half length in the Spring Handicap at Jamaica, five days after Bracadale had beaten Sarazen in the Lynbrook Handicap over the same track and distance. Granted, Wild Aster had been getting a seventeen-pound weight concession from Bracadale, but he had run the fastest six-furlong time of the Jamaica meeting to win, getting the distance in 1:11⅕.

Black Gold was fresh and lively as he went through the rituals of being saddled and having Mooney boosted into the saddle, and the crowd cheered appreciatively as he made his appearance in the post parade. Although the chart caller noted that he seemed "slightly sore" during the post parade, he was clearly eager to run and was away smartly, to settle just off Wild Aster in the early going.[1]

Considering the track conditions, which were playing "about a second slow" by C. J. Savage's estimation, Wild Aster was cutting out a strong pace, getting the first quarter in 0:23 flat and the half in 0:46 flat—the quickest splits of the day.[2] They were not enough to shake Black Gold. Never more than a half length behind, the little black colt shadowed his rival effortlessly with Mooney keeping him under wraps. Another furlong ticked by; then the six-furlong pole loomed up, and Mooney gave his mount his head. That quickly, Black Gold was a neck in front, hitting three-quarters of a mile in 1:11⅖.

From there on out it was not a horse race; it was an exhibition. Wild Aster kept going gamely and easily held off King Gorin II for second, but Black Gold drew away despite all the Whitney gelding could do. Mooney took his colt in hand again when it was clear that the race was won, and Black Gold was coasting eight lengths in front when he hit the wire in 1:37⅘, a "sensational" time for the mile given the conditions.[3] Continuing on under restraint, the colt galloped out another furlong, getting a mile and one-eighth that was unofficially timed as fast as 1:51⅗—nearly two seconds faster than older horses ran the same distance two races later on the same card. He was pulled down to "a common canter" to finish out a mile and a quarter in 2:08⅖ before coming back to the winner's circle, where he was greeted by wildly enthusiastic cheers from the crowd.[4] After dismounting, Mooney summed up his mount's performance when he told reporters, "As soon as I clucked at Black Gold, it was all over but how much I would win by."[5]

Far away in Oklahoma, Rosa Hoots smiled to herself when she heard the news, and she went out to run one last errand before packing her bags. Soon afterward, a crowd of friends and well-wishers saw her off on a train headed north and east, accompanied by her son and daughter-in-law.

In spite of her colt's stature as the likely Derby favorite, Mrs. Hoots maintained a public demeanor of calm indifference regarding Black Gold's chances. "I am not caring so much whether he wins or loses," she said before she departed.[6] If her private feelings differed from the persona she presented to the press, that was something she shared only with her immediate family and with the memory of her husband. No one noticed the small addition tucked into her luggage: a little box, wrapped in old rose and white and perhaps in the emotions she could not otherwise show.

The next day, Black Gold's triumph was splashed across sports pages in newspapers all over North America. Western racing fans were jubilant, and even those who had been hoping Wise Counsellor would be Kentucky's champion against the eastern elites were quick to hail Black Gold as their own—and to bet on him. By evening on May 13, odds of 5–1 were the most generous that anyone would offer on the colt. By the next morning, Black Gold was the 3–1 Derby favorite, and more and more bookmakers were refusing to take any further bets on him. A few still nursed slim hopes that Wise Counsellor might make a turnabout and join the Derby field when John Ward entered his colt in the Stuyvesant Handicap at Jamaica the day after Black Gold's runaway win, but by the end of that day their faces were longer than ever: Wise Counsellor was out of the money and finally, irrevocably, out of the Derby. As with St. James and Sarazen, the bookies had won only to lose, and collectively, the major bookies were on the hook for at least $2.5 million in winter book losses (the equivalent of more than $40 million in 2022) in the event of a Black Gold victory. That did not take into account losses on bets held by fly-by-night operators who were unlikely to pay up in any event. Only accident, illness, or a major upset befalling the Hoots colt stood between most of the bookmakers and ruin.

Hanley Webb was elated after Black Gold's big win, but he was no fool; he knew as much about the gambling community as any other trainer, and with so much money on the line, it was inevitable that there would be men willing to take risks to "get at" the colt. As soon as Black Gold had cooled out from the Derby Trial and gone back to his barn, Webb, Akers, and Teddy the terrier went on round-the-clock alert. There would be no more casual visitors to Black Gold's stall, and as soon as some of Webb's cronies from Oklahoma arrived at Churchill Downs, they were recruited to join the watch on the colt.

Mooney, too, was cautious. He could not be bought; later, Lally Collyer would report that the jockey turned down a thirty-thousand-dollar bribe to "pull" Black Gold in the Derby.[7] But he knew that others could be, and he was taking no chances with either foul play or misfortune. Pleading an injured foot, he took himself off all his mounts for May 14, and his absence from the jockeys' room continued through May 15 and 16.

With Black Gold heavily guarded and Mooney staying out of easy reach, the bookies' final hopes rested on the rivals streaming into Churchill Downs. Even with Black Gold's stock having risen so spectacularly, many owners and trainers felt that the defections of Wise Counsellor, Sarazen, and St. James gave their horses at least a chance. By the afternoon of May 15, twenty-two Derby hopefuls besides Black Gold were on the grounds, though R. J. Boylan of the *St. Louis Daily Globe-Democrat* wryly commented that "western owners . . . feel that the jet-hued racehorse has the same effect on their chances as if a black cat had crossed their path."[8]

The eastern owners were more sanguine, and among their entries, none were considered to have a better chance than the Rancocas Stable colts, Mad Play and Bracadale. Sam Hildreth's assistant, Willie Brennan, had come down with them from Pimlico, and on May 15, he sent them out for a morning trial. With Laverne Fator on Mad Play and Earl Sande on Bracadale, the two turned in a solid mile in 1:41⅕ and completed nine furlongs in 1:54⅖ over a dull surface still being moistened by occasional showers. Several other colts went faster miles on the same day, but Brennan was satisfied: Both his charges were fit, and he was confident that he had a winner in Mad Play.

While Brennan was overseeing his colts' cooling-out, Fator and Sande decided to do a little scouting of their own and walked over to Black Gold's stable, hoping to get a look at the opposition. Perhaps to their disappointment, Mooney wasn't there, but Akers was. He greeted them affably enough, and the Rancocas jockeys were soon pumping him for anything and everything he could tell them about Black Gold's race in the Derby Trial—how he had gotten away at the break, how he had been placed during the race, when he had gone to the front.

Akers was wise to this game, of course; he'd been playing it before either of them had even been born. He answered their questions patiently and truthfully, but it was soon obvious that he wasn't spilling more than any competent observer of the race could have deduced for himself. In the end, the Rancocas jockeys went off with the polite comment that if Black Gold ran in the Derby as he had in the Derby Trial, he would be "a hard horse to beat"—which was probably about as much information as they had possessed before.[9]

Anticipating the rush of eastern invaders, the trainers of several of the West's top hopefuls gave their colts their last serious workouts on May 14. Those locals seeking a Derby bet at longer odds than Black Gold's watched closely as Beau Butler, Chilhowee, and Altawood went through their paces. In sharp contrast to modern practices, all three went the full Derby distance with the Derby just three days away, even though track conditions remained heavy and tiring. Working with his stablemate Bob Tail, Beau Butler was timed in 2:10, leading C. J. Savage to comment that his trial was "very meritorious."[10] Beau Butler's time was matched by Chilhowee; Altawood went the distance in 2:12. All three were considered sharp and ready to go, with at least an outside chance of pulling an upset. Still, it was generally conceded that, on recent form, Black Gold was Kentucky's best hope—and the bookmakers' worst nightmare.

Those hoping that Black Gold might not have come out of the Derby Trial well had those hopes dashed on May 16, when the Hoots colt emerged from his stall for a work on the track. He was clearly out for the air and a little light exercise rather that a serious speed drill, but he was shining and full of himself. Akers had his hands full as he galloped his mount an easy mile in 1:48⅘, and then the black colt returned to his stable and his ever-present guardians.

Black Gold's obvious health and vigor were not good signs for the book-making fraternity, but the bookies could at least draw some comfort from the weather forecast, which called for clearing weather at last. Black Gold would face his rivals without the help of his favorite surface, mud. And at the post position draw that afternoon, the bookies caught one last wink from Lady Luck. Black Gold drew post position 1, the worst possible position for any horse but a pure speedster and a doubly bad place for an undersized colt who had the reputation of being timid when racing inside or when bumped about.

Webb took the results of the draw stoically; there was nothing he could do about it anyway. But around the stables and in lodgings near the track, other trainers and their jockeys smiled just a little, and began laying plans.

All through May 15 and 16 and into the early-morning hours of May 17, people were pouring into Louisville, creating the largest pre-Derby crowd the River City had ever seen. As many as ten thousand came from Chicago alone, and thousands upon thousands more traveled from New York, St. Louis, New Orleans, and other major cities throughout the East, Midwest, and South. Some came by automobile or river traffic, but most came on the trains that provided the majority of interstate travel in the 1920s. One could tell the social class of the passengers by where they rode: the farther back of the engine and its belches of smoke and cinders, the more expensive the coaches and the higher the status. (The exceptions were the southern trains' "Jim Crow" cars for Blacks, which were always first in line after the engine, mail cars, and baggage cars; segregationist laws and regulations did not permit Black passengers to ride elsewhere, no matter how wealthy they might be.) The elites of society did not even trouble with the coaches; their private Pullman cars rode in comfort at the back end of the regular trains or as part of one of the numerous special trains that converged on Louisville, with passengers' needs and wishes attended to by Pullman porters. Once a private car had been parked at the rail yard, its residents could relax or entertain guests as they pleased, enjoying as many of the luxuries of their class as could be packed into the limited space available—unlike travelers of lesser status, who might be sharing a single hotel room with as many as seven other guests.

Rosa Hoots traveled modestly, by passenger coach, but she did not have to worry about finding hotel space thanks to the arrangements she had made months earlier. On arrival she immediately went from the train station to the house near the racetrack where she had rented rooms. She granted no interviews, and anyone considering following her to her lodgings thought better of it after a glowering look from Alfred Hoots, a tall, strong man and as fierce a guardian of his mother's privacy as Webb was of Black Gold's safety.

On the evening of May 16, Mrs. Hoots made the short trip to the stables at Churchill Downs. Webb brought Black Gold out of his stall for her, and she spent a few minutes stroking the animal's sleek black neck and whispering in his ear. Perhaps she spoke words of encouragement or admiration; perhaps she was telling her colt of the hopes Al Hoots had placed on him before he was ever conceived, and the hopes she now held that he would fulfill her husband's dream. Only Black Gold heard; no one else knew what she said, or would ever know.

Black Gold flicked his ears as she finished. Rosa Hoots straightened and stepped back, her gaze taking everything in: the gleaming, dappled black coat; the strong muscles, hard as steel; the look of poised confidence in the colt's eyes and bearing. She looked at Webb, perhaps remembering the old days when Al Hoots was alive and it was Useeit standing there between them. Webb met her eyes, seeing the unspoken question there, and one of his rare, slow smiles crossed his face.

"Black Gold is ready to do his best," he drawled, "and I believe that best will be to win the Derby."[11]

28

Golden Jubilee

Derby Day dawned with slowly breaking clouds. A few stray shafts of morning sun glanced over the enlarged grandstand and newly refurbished clubhouse, freshly painted in white with green trim. The light touched on the red and gold flowers that spelled out "1875" and "1924" to either side of the paddock and slid across the track to reveal the full of the wide first turn, guaranteed by Matt Winn to be able to manage up to thirty-five horses if so many ever showed up to contest the Derby. The space would not be needed now; only twenty names had been on the entry list on Derby Eve, and there would soon be one fewer as the filly Glide bowed out, her connections electing to reserve her for the Kentucky Oaks on May 31. But Winn had been prepared; it was just one of many details that he had arranged over the years to make sure that the great race and the festivities surrounding it went off as smoothly as human skill and planning could arrange. If there was anything he had overlooked, it was the judges' stand, which was properly placed right on the finish line but just a little too low to have a clear view of the rail horse in a close finish—especially if three or more runners were involved.

It was deceptively quiet in the last hour before the gates opened. Winn was already up, overseeing the final preparations for the facilities. The trainers had been up even earlier than Winn, seeing to it that their charges got their final pre-Derby exercise. Some had sent their colts through short, sharp "pipe-openers," usually three furlongs, meant to put the final edge on speed. Some had their animals merely trot or gallop, limbering their muscles with easy work. They were all back at the barns now, cooling their charges out. Once the horses were made comfortable, trainers and grooms would be settling in to pass the time as best they could, trying not to communicate any nerves to their animals. The horses, too, would be waiting, signaled by the light feed that morning that they would be running soon. Some would doze, hip-shot; some would watch the movements around them with varying degrees of interest; some would shift about restlessly, sensing the building excitement in spite of their humans' best efforts.

Shortly after 7:00 a.m., the track gates opened and the sea of humanity began flooding in. Thousands and then tens of thousands surged into the stands, dressed for a holiday: the men dapper in suits and the flat-topped straw hats commonly called "boaters," the ladies showing off their best dresses and millinery. Many had brought baskets for picnic parties, making use of some four thousand benches that Winn had ordered set out near the old paddock area and the lawns beyond the clubhouse. People of every class packed around the paddock and swarmed the betting windows; even with a hundred pari-mutuel machines in service, the lines were so densely packed that those in them could scarcely draw a deep breath, and the *Chicago Tribune*'s French Lane anticipated that up to $1.5 million or more might be wagered on-track that day.[1] Policemen on foot worked their way through the throngs of bettors, playing a cat-and-mouse game with pickpockets. Mounted officers patrolled along the fence lines, keeping the human mass off the track and out of the infield. More guards waited on the approaches to the stabling area, keeping back anyone who managed to slip past the police patrol from getting access to the stables. On the roofs and rails along the backstretch, the stable workers and their cronies clung and clambered over every available space. Those privileged to be seated in the owners' boxes and the clubhouse formed their own glittering knots, taking for granted the gaze of society writers who would fill columns with their descriptions of the dress and finery of the elite.

Those chronicling the activities of the upper crust had their pick of subjects. The political class was represented by six state governors, Senator Richard Ernst of Kentucky, and Baltimore mayor Howard Bradley as well as Black Gold's would-be owner, Kansas City political boss T. J. Pendergast, who had put $1,500 down on Black Gold in the winter books at 40–1. The eastern racing establishment was there in force, with even those with no direct connection to one of the entrants putting in an appearance; among them were Matt Winn's old friend James Butler, Joseph Widener, George Widener, Walter Salmon, and Major August Belmont II, breeder of Man o' War.

Special interest naturally focused on the owners' boxes, where the popular Harry Payne Whitney held court among his peers. He was enjoying himself even though his entry of Transmute and Klondyke was accorded only a modest chance of pulling off an upset. Nearby, Harry Sinclair alternately chatted with friends and chewed nervously on a cigar, waiting for his Derby horses to make their appearance; his Rancocas Stable entry was second choice in the wagering. Colonel Bradley, erect and dignified as always, was also there, along with his wife and friends. He hoped to win, certainly, and his three-horse entry of Beau Butler, Baffling, and Bob Tail was conceded to have a decent chance. Nonetheless, no one thought that he would be put out if Black Gold won, even though it would not be in his colors. Rumor had it that he had made an offer of forty thousand dollars for Black Gold within the last months before the Kentucky Derby and had been refused, but the colt was still a son of his Black Toney, and the stallion's reputation could only be enhanced by a Black Gold win. Further, Bradley had a horse-and-horse bet going with Sam Hildreth, wagering five thousand dollars that Black Gold would outfinish both Bracadale and Mad Play. He was confident enough to offer to up the wager to ten thousand dollars, and probably would have been even more confident had he known that someone had broken into Hildreth's hotel room the night before and stolen both the trainer's spare clothing and a valise said to contain "medicine" that Hildreth allegedly used to put Mad Play "in a running mood."[2] Hildreth, of course, was not going to disclose any such information; even though enforcement of medication standards in the 1920s was much looser than is the case today, a trainer's open admission that he was "hopping" a horse would have cost him his license. Nonetheless, he clearly had his doubts as to whether his entry could best Black Gold, as he politely declined Bradley's offer to double the bet.

One owner was conspicuous by her absence. Rosa Hoots was nowhere to be seen among the connections of the Derby horses, and she apparently had not even troubled to reserve a box for herself and her party.[3] She had managed to lose herself in the crowd, and no one from the media would see her until much later.

By 1:00 p.m., every bit of usable space in Churchill Downs's stands and lawns had been filled, and still more people were inching toward the gates in automobiles, on bicycles, and on foot through streets as congested as the stands at the track. Newspapers would breathlessly estimate the crowd at one hundred thousand or more; with years of experience at sizing up Derby crowds,

Churchill Downs's resident manager, Colonel Andrew Vennie, provided a more restrained figure of eighty thousand.[4] Above the crowd, the dirigible *TC-3* flew in slow, graceful circles, adding to the spectacle. On board, members of the Louisville Film Company were filming aerial footage on behalf of the *Louisville Courier-Journal,* while others captured the action at track level; their compiled efforts would become the first-ever Kentucky Derby movie.[5] To be released the day after the race for viewings at Louisville's Alamo Theater, it was a forerunner of the newsreel coverage that would become wildly popular a few years later.

Racing got underway at 1:48 p.m. with a $1,500 claiming event, followed by a race for maiden juveniles that proved to be the most lopsided contest of the day. Of the beaten field, only sixth-place George de Mar would ever achieve anything noteworthy, and that was from sheer durability; racing through age fourteen, he would make a total of 333 starts and win sixty races. The front-running winner, on the other hand, turned out to be as good as his seven-length margin made him look. He was Flying Ebony, who would win the Kentucky Derby a year later.

The next two races on the card were both stakes events, and keenly watched by those who were looking for clues as to how the track was playing. Both were won by horses racing on or near the front end and in time suggesting that the surface was fast indeed in spite of an official rating of "good" at the start of the day. In the Brown Hotel Handicap, Actuary clipped off a mile in 1:36⅗, leaving behind a field that included Princess Doreen. He was followed by the juvenile filly Kitty Pat, who laid second early and ran out a one-length winner in the Debutante Stakes in 0:53⅖ for the 4½ furlongs.

The tension in the air had eased just a little in the wake of the Debutante's conclusion, but as the crowd spotted the first of the blanketed Derby runners being led from the backstretch, the excitement surged back. The nineteen horses felt it too; their feet took shorter, quicker steps and their heads tossed. A few jigged hard against the restraint of their grooms, threatening to bolt or rear. As they filed around the clubhouse turn and headed toward the alleyway leading to the paddock, the crowd burst its bounds and spilled across the track into the infield, actually cutting through the string of Derby horses. From the top of the stretch to well past the finish line, people crammed into every inch of space along the inner rail. Among them, unrecognized by their fellow spectators, were Rosa Hoots and her daughter-in-law, Ada Allen Hoots, who had walked across the infield and had found a place just across from the judges' stand.[6]

The horses continued on to the paddock, there to be saddled under the gaze of the throng swarming the walkway around the enclosure. The animals were nervous, seeing, hearing, and smelling far more humans even in this limited space than many would ever see again at one time in their lives. Chilhowee suddenly plunged and reared as his nerves broke, and he had to be half-wrestled, half-soothed back into cooperation with his handlers.

All the spectators' eyes rested on Black Gold, who was alert and eager but obedient, letting Webb and Akers get his tack on without undue fuss. At a shade under fifteen and a half hands, he was the smallest of the Derby entrants but was nonetheless the very picture of a perfectly prepared runner, gleaming with health and hard with muscle. Money continued to pour in on him through the pari-mutuels; his odds would stand at 1.75–1 by post time. (Later, Churchill Downs staff would later determine that on-track attendees had bet $618,536 on the Kentucky Derby alone, with $166,138 of that total having been bet on Black Gold.)

While the horses were being saddled, nineteen short, slight men were finishing their own preparations in the jockeys' room. Some were chatting among themselves; some sat quietly, perhaps playing out in their minds how they might run the race, perhaps praying. Mooney pulled the Hoots silks on, settling the old rose colors with the white cross sashes and sleeve bars over his white undershirt. Earl Sande turned toward Mooney, a half-grin on his face above the green-and-white silks of the Rancocas Stable. "Mad Play will win, you know," he predicted—perhaps a bit ruefully, as it had been announced only the day before that he would ride Bracadale rather than Mad Play as originally planned.[7] That meant that his assignment was to make the pace, trying to soften the field up for a winning charge from Laverne Fator and Mad Play; if he could get Black Gold caught up in an early speed duel or a traffic jam, so much the better.

Mooney knew perfectly well what Sande intended—he'd have done much the same had their situations been reversed—but he merely smiled back. "Earl, you are going to see a right fair horse run today when Black Gold goes in the Derby," he said.[8]

A few moments later, the summons they had awaited came and the jockeys emerged to join the trainers and owners in the paddock, nodding solemnly or sharply as they got their riding orders. At 4:35 p.m., the bugler blew "First Call," and the riders were boosted up into the waiting saddles. Ordinarily, the file-out from the paddock is in order of post position, and Black Gold as number one should have led. Instead, Chilhowee's antics caused the marshal of the Churchill Downs outriders, Joe Moran, to make a quick revision. From astride his pony, he took a firm hold of Chilhowee's bridle and steered the fractious colt toward the track, leaving the other runners to fall in line behind him.

The crowd cheered as Chilhowee stepped out onto the track, though he may or may not have been serenaded with "My Old Kentucky Home." (The popular song was first played at the Derby in 1921—possibly after the conclusion of the race—but no records associate it specifically with the post parade until 1930.)[9] With Moran still in attendance, Chilhowee turned to lead the parade past the clubhouse. Then Black Gold stepped out, and the cheering became more full-throated as the crowd greeted the favorite. One by one, the nineteen horses came out and passed the length of the clubhouse before looping back to jog or canter to the starting line at the other end of the stretch. One, the high-strung Diogenes, was joined by a lead pony as he balked at the noise from both sides; the rest continued on with more or less composure. From the stands and infield, spectators yelled out the names of their favorites or called to the jockeys.

As he guided Black Gold through the post parade and a brief warmup, Mooney slipped into the focus of an experienced jockey—hyperaware of his rivals, their mounts, and his sense of the track's feel under Black Gold's hoofs, and filtering out everything irrelevant to his work. He knew the track. He knew what he could expect in a huge Derby field. And he knew Black Gold and the trust they had built up together; knew as much as any man could know about what kind of speed and acceleration and stamina he had to call on when decisions had to be made in the blink of an eye. It was up to him to make that knowledge count and deliver the ride of a lifetime.

An expectant hush settled over the crowd as the Derby horses lined up behind the starting line and the webbing dropped into place. It was 4:45 p.m. Almost immediately, the usual cries of "No chance, sir!" broke out as the riders starting maneuvering for advantage, some more blatantly than others; Sande, the worst offender, would later find himself slapped with a ten-day suspension for disobeying starter William Snyder's instructions. Black Gold, perhaps made nervous by his proximity to the rail, kept swinging to his right, crowding Transmute into Klondyke. No sooner had Mooney brought his mount back to his proper position than the keyed-up Diogenes plunged through the barrier. In the milling confusion while an assistant starter helped get Diogenes under control and back in his place, Black Gold managed to get five places over from where he should have been; another assistant starter was dispatched to get him back into line. And then Snyder saw his chance: nineteen horses in the right places, with noses all pointed up the track.

"Come on!"

The barrier sprang skyward. To the roar of the crowd, nineteen horses leaped forward.

Mooney pushed forward with Black Gold's initial lunge, his arms and back pumping. The pair shot forward, angling away from the rail. Then a shock slammed through Black Gold and the colt ricocheted back to the left, nearly to the fence. The aggressor was Bracadale, muscling his way through under Sande to grab the early lead; Baffling and Wild Aster were on his heels. Mooney steadied his mount, letting his colt recover his rhythm, but for the moment he was shuffled back to sixth with nowhere to go.

The field poured around the first turn, straightening away into the backstretch. Black Gold wasn't happy with his inside position; his head was a little high, his stride choppy. Mooney held him together, keeping his focus, waiting for a chance—

Now! For the first time since he had gotten the mount on Black Gold, Mooney unlimbered his whip, giving the colt three quick slaps. Black Gold shot forward, skimming to the right, where a hole had opened up. He slipped through, easing off just a fraction as Mooney's hands and weight signaled him: *Enough.* Horses still pounded along furiously to the colt's left, but to his right there was nothing but space, beautiful open space. That was what Mooney wanted. Better to stay on the outside of the onrushing pack, even if he would lose ground, than to go inside again and risk being cut off or letting his mount get intimidated. Chilhowee moved with him, running on by; Mooney and Black Gold waited, biding their time.

Everything is timing in a horse race: the timing to escape a box, the timing to launch a bid. True to his nickname, Mooney sat still, waiting, as the field entered the final turn. Baffling and Wild Aster were long since spent, cooked by Bracadale's opening half-mile in 0:47⅗, and Bracadale himself was feeling the effects of the pace he had set. After a mile in 1:39⅕, the Rancocas colt was still leading but with Chilhowee at his throat. Transmute was struggling to keep up.

The horses surged into the home straight with Black Gold carried out nearly to midtrack by his own momentum, and suddenly Mooney was sitting still no more. *Now! Go!* his weight said, shifting forward as he clucked to his mount and gave the colt his head. The roar of the wind past the jockey's ears was matched by the roaring of the crowd on either side, creating a tunnel of sound that Black Gold ran through without flinching; *I trust you,* his driving muscles and pounding hooves answered back. The stands whipped by Mooney in a blur, given the illusion of motion by the horse flying beneath him. Transmute, still trying but exhausted, dropped back. With a hundred yards to go, Black Gold was gaining with every stride—he was lapped on Chilhowee, who had just thrust his head in front of Bracadale—

From the grandstand side, Mooney caught a flash of motion: photographers, spilling out of the stands near the finish to grab shots as the horses raced toward the line. Black Gold saw them too; startled, he slackened stride. Mooney yelled and his whip lashed down—once, just once. Stung, the colt surged back into the bridle; Mooney tucked his bat away and drove his mount forward with hands and heels, using every ounce of his strength. With a final burst of speed, Black Gold thrust his nose, then his neck, then his withers in front of Chilhowee, and that was where he was when he passed the winning post.

Some moments crystallize perfectly in memory, standing outside time. For Mooney, this was his moment; he had ridden Pegasus and touched the heavens. Black Gold, still in flight, was soaring back through the first turn and into the backstretch. Around and behind him, to left and right, the other Derby horses were slowing as their jockeys pulled them up, preparing to dismount and unsaddle by the rail, but for Mooney there was only himself and his colt. Gently but firmly, he rose in the stirrups and pulled Black Gold back to a canter, then to a walk before looping around to jog back past eighteen merely mortal horses.

People had spilled all across the track in spite of the best efforts of the police, and Black Gold had to weave his way through the crowd as track personnel tried to clear his path. As the colt neared the circle chalked on the track in front of the judges' stand, Mooney finally spotted Rosa Hoots. She faced her colt as the spectators cheered, and then she bowed: not to him and not to the crowd, Mooney knew, but to Black Gold, the horse that had made Al Hoots's dream—and hers—come true.[10]

Finally reaching the winner's circle, Mooney pulled Black Gold to a stop at last, and Webb reached up and took hold of the colt's bridle. Black Gold's nostrils flared red as he sucked in great heaving breaths; a tracery of distended veins stood out on his face and neck, mute testimony to the effort he had just expended. A Churchill Downs staff member came up and threw the victor's blanket of American Beauty roses across the colt's sweaty withers. Black Gold took that calmly enough but then started at the sight of the huge bouquet of pink roses someone else tried to hand to Mooney and skittered backward before a friend came to Webb's assistance and steadied the colt, allowing Mooney to receive the floral tribute. Photographs were taken before Mooney dismounted to weigh out, leaving Black Gold to be blanketed and led back to his barn for cooling out, rest, and a well-earned feed.

With the departure of the idol of the moment, attention turned back to the judges' stand, where, escorted by her son and her daughter-in-law, Rosa Hoots had made her way up the stairs to be greeted by Colonel Winn, Colonel Vennie, and Colonel H. T. Whitehead of the American Remount Service. Wearing a simple gray dress figured with old rose, a scarf in her stable colors, and a black straw hat pulled low over her head, she bore herself with quiet dignity. She made no show of emotion as she received the congratulations of the waiting gentlemen, but after Colonel Whitehead delivered his speech of presentation, she made a short acceptance speech with an easy, pleasant poise that stood out in Matt Winn's mind years later.[11] Whitehead then handed Rosa Hoots the Derby trophy to the cheers of the audience below.

It was beautiful: a simple, classical urn of polished gold, embellished with a horseshoe on its front and topped with a golden horse and jockey. It was also heavy, and Mrs. Hoots needed both her hands to steady it as she turned to display it to the crowd. Mooney had mounted to the judges' stand while she was receiving the trophy, and now it was his turn; as the spectators applauded, he was given a velvet-lined box containing golden spurs in honor of his winning ride. Then Webb was all but pushed up the stairs by his friends to join them, his weathered face cracking into a toothless, almost unbelieving smile as he was presented with a solid gold stopwatch. More photographers' shutters clicked as Mooney and Webb lined up along the front rail of the stand with Mrs. Hoots, each displaying a golden emblem of victory as the onlookers roared their approval; then, one by one, the trio descended back to the track to be engulfed by hundreds of well-wishers. Pushing through the throng, dozens of newspapermen closed in on owner, trainer, and jockey, looking for statements.

"It was a fine race," Mooney said hurriedly as he edged away from the eager reporters. "Black Gold is the best ever. I never rode a better horse, or one like him. Now let me through! I have another race to ride!"[12] And with that, he sprinted for the jockeys' room, only to find himself blocked by the throngs of people at the clubhouse gate. Desperate to get by, he shoved his way to the fence and went up and over, yelling back to friends, "I'll see you tonight. Come back to my room and come early if you wish to hear about it."[13]

Perhaps his head was still reeling with the afterglow of his Derby triumph. More likely, he was just riding a horse that had no real interest in running. In the seventh and final race of the card, a $1,500 claiming event, Mooney came back to earth with a thud; trailing near the back throughout, he finished dead last aboard The Archer, beaten by better than twelve lengths.

Webb, pleading the care of his colt, also made a quick escape. Left to cope with the media, Rosa Hoots bore the attentions of the crowd stoically. Even in the wake of victory, she surprised many by her lack of expression and apparent enthusiasm; when asked about how she felt about Black Gold, she answered, "I guess he has just proved himself a horse."[14] Her one flash of open sentiment was in expressing regret that Al Hoots could not have lived to see the triumph of the son of his beloved Useeit, an emotion echoed by her son. "My father always wanted to own a racehorse that could have a chance at the big race meetings," Alfred Hoots said. "It is too bad he could not live to see Black Gold fight his way to the front this afternoon."[15]

Rosa's relief was palpable when she was able to slip away at last to the relative quiet of her colt's stable. There she could sit with Marjorie Mooney, chatting quietly as Black Gold was walked up and down, up and down under his cooling sheet. There were still a few reporters about, but most had gone to seek more glittering company elsewhere.

One of those who still persisted was from the *Louisville Courier-Journal*. Sensing that she would not get any peace until she made some sort of postrace statement, Mrs. Hoots bowed to necessity. "The Golden Anniversary Derby was a great thing to win," she told him. "Anyone would have been glad to win it. The gold cup should never go out of my family. I guess I shall give it to my grandchildren for them always to keep."[16] Later in the interview, when asked what she had thought regarding Black Gold, her reply was simple.

"I thought he would win."[17]

Not long afterward, Agnes Hoots Freeman waited for a train carrying a special package sent by her mother. It arrived, and the young woman reverently took the package in her arms. With her husband, Waldo, she went to a cemetery near Skiatook—the Captain Cemetery, where members of her family had been buried for nearly half a century. When she left, her arms were empty. Behind her, Black Gold's Derby wreath lay on Al Hoots's grave.[18]

29

Derby Aftermath

The day after the Kentucky Derby was quiet, a return to relative normalcy after the excitement of the previous day. At Churchill Downs, Hanley Webb brought Black Gold out for a morning jog that was witnessed by "thousands."[1] Although Derby historian Peter Chew reported many years later that Black Gold had been lame and in pain the evening after the Derby, contemporary newspaper accounts make no mention of this and indicate that, at least by the next morning, the colt seemed none the worse for his exertions.[2] In the words of C. J. Savage, he "came out of the Derby in fine shape and was . . . as playful as a kitten."[3] Visitors kept crowding to his stable after he had been cooled out, hoping for a closer look; as proud as any doting parent, Webb obliged them, leading Black Gold out repeatedly to be shown to his admirers. J. D. Mooney, said to be the richer by a ten-thousand-dollar riding fee, came by to see his mount, enjoying his own share of the attention.[4] A few days later, the jockey would be the guest on a radio broadcast from Louisville station WHAS, airing a description of his Derby-winning ride.[5]

From Matt Winn's point of view, the Golden Jubilee Derby could not have gone better—a record crowd, record receipts for the gate and betting handle, and a winner with a wonderful story behind him. He was still basking in the afterglow when a tap on his door announced the arrival of a messenger. The fellow handed Winn a small package wrapped in old rose and white—sent from Mrs. Hoots, he said. Intrigued, Winn waited only until the door had closed again before carefully opening the box. It held cigars—ten-cent cigars,

172

good quality by the standards of the time. In Osage fashion, Rosa Hoots had returned a gift for a gift.

He never smoked them. Years later, he still kept the box on a shelf, in memory of a gracious woman and an unexpected act of appreciation that had touched his heart. Other Derby owners came and went, many of them wealthy and socially prominent, but in all the years that Winn presided over the Derby, Rosa Hoots was the only one who ever sent anything after the race to say "thank you."[6]

In her rented rooms, Mrs. Hoots resumed her cherished privacy, receiving only those few visitors who were close enough to her to have been told her whereabouts; she would leave for Tulsa the following Wednesday, taking with her the Derby trophy.[7] She also took Black Gold's Derby purse—according to some accounts, in cash after refusing to accept a check.[8] Most of the eastern elites and their retinues had already departed, bound back to New York on the morning trains along with their defeated runners. Those drawn to Louisville from Chicago, St. Louis, Nashville, and New Orleans were also leaving, emptying the hotels, the rental flats, and relatives' homes as the city deflated back to its normal population.

Among the emptied rooms were ones where odds chalked on a board or written on discarded papers gave mute testimony to another, more furtive exodus. Almost before the dust had settled from the running of the Derby, bookmakers had been slinking out, some just ahead of the customers they could not pay; as Derby historian Jim Bolus later observed, "When Black Gold stopped running in the Derby, some bookmakers started."[9] So many fled from Chicago, St. Louis, and other cities as well as Louisville that observers of the betting scene called it "The Great Runout." Many probably had no intention of paying up regardless of the outcome; one unscrupulous Chicago bookie who was heading out of town before Black Gold even crossed the finish line was said to have owed his customers (who included a number of Chicago politicians) over $6.6 million all told.[10] Other bookmakers, either more honest or more fiscally solvent, stayed in business but took a terrible bath over the results of "Black Saturday"; Tom Kearney, for one, lost seventy-four-thousand dollars and had to use all the cash he had on hand plus the proceeds from cashing fifty-five thousand dollars in Liberty Bonds in order to pay off his customers.[11] He, at least, had the means to pay and later recouped his losses on the strength of the reputation his honesty had won him; there were others who did likewise. But for years afterward, Black Gold's Derby would remain a cautionary tale among moralists and professional gamblers alike about the dangers of "investing" in the winter books, especially with "fly-by-night" operators.

A Kentucky Derby would probably not be a Kentucky Derby without some degree of controversy, and the Golden Jubilee was no exception to that rule. In most years, the controversy would involve no more than a few jockeys or trainers claiming how their horse "shoulda won" were it not for some mishap or the winner's good luck. There were a few opinions of that nature voiced after the 1924 Derby, but not with much heat behind them; Black Gold had clearly won, and his victory had been very popular even with those not holding winning bets on him. It was what had happened in his wake that came into hot dispute, adding another twist to what was already a legendary running of the Derby.

As Mooney posed Black Gold in the Derby winner's circle, most of his defeated rivals were making their way back to the jockeys' room with varying degrees of chagrin or acceptance, already thinking ahead to the next mount, the next day. Not Earl Sande. He was staring at the posted results in disbelief. He knew he hadn't won, but he *knew* he had finished at least third, maybe even gotten one final surge from Bracadale to take second back from Chilhowee. Instead, Bracadale wasn't even placed fourth; he was officially fifth. In third place, where Bracadale should have been, Beau Butler's number had been posted. Colonel Bradley and his party, seated up in the boxes, were equally shocked. They had seen Beau Butler get caught in the webbing at the start, and they knew he had run a good race just to finish in midpack; there was no way that he could have been third. Another stunned party was J. L. Dempsey, serving as the chart caller for the *Daily Racing Form,* who had to make a hasty revision of the Derby chart to conform to the ruling of the placing judges after he himself had placed Bracadale third, with Beau Butler far back.[12] His revised chart showed Bracadale as fifth, beaten a half length, a nose, and two heads for the higher placings. The next day, several sportswriters' post-Derby columns talked of Beau Butler's "great run" to be third—a feat that probably never happened but that testifies to the malleability of human memory when confronted with contradictory information.

The Rancocas people complained bitterly for long days afterward about the error, but in vain; there were no photo-finish cameras or overhead films to resolve the issue immediately after the finish, and the first journalists' photographs of the finish were not posted in print until the following day, too late to affect the placing judges' ruling. Given the angles at which the photos were taken, none constituted definitive evidence of the exact order of finish, but they did show two things: first, that there were only four horses involved in the blanket finish, not five; and second, that as seen from the outer rail—where the judges' stand was—Bracadale, hemmed in on the inner rail, was almost completely obscured by his rivals.

More than likely, the mistake was a completely honest one. Both the Bradley silks and those of Rancocas Stable were white with green trim, though in different patterns, and unlike the Bradley and Sinclair parties, the placing judges were not concentrating on following their particular horses around the track; they were focused on the finish line, identifying each horse as it crossed. In the heat of the wild finish and with a poor view of the inmost horse involved, it would have been easy for a judge's quick glimpse of the Rancocas silks to be mistakenly taken as a sighting of Bradley's colors, and that is apparently what happened. Regardless of the cause, the Bracadale–Beau Butler placing mix-up remains part of the lore and legend surrounding the fiftieth Kentucky Derby.

30

The Final Mile

Black Gold had been a popular runner from his two-year-old days on; even those who felt there were better colts around had kept a warm place in their hearts for the "hard-luck" little black colt who never quit trying. Following the Kentucky Derby, that popularity exploded all out of proportion. Whether it was the romance of the colt's origins, sectional pride, or the populist appeal of seeing the millionaires and the fancy outfits upstaged by a "one-horse stable," Rosa Hoots and Hanley Webb found themselves deluged with requests for the colt's appearance. Seemingly every track from Canada to Mexico and from Kentucky westward wanted Black Gold to come for a race or, if he could not race, to be paraded or worked between races so that fans might come and see him.

In truth, Black Gold probably needed a prolonged rest. He had lost weight following his hard run in the Derby, suggesting that he had burned through his physical reserves and needed recovery time, but that was not the most serious concern. All through the winter and spring, his old soreness had kept recurring whenever he was kept in hard training or racing for more than a few weeks at a time. With the aid of Brown and Akers, Webb had done a remarkable job in getting Black Gold to the level of fitness he wanted and then maintaining it while keeping the colt sound enough to run when it counted, but the balancing act could not be maintained forever. Unless the underlying issue causing the pain could be resolved, the only possible means of managing Black Gold's condition was rest before soreness became full-blown lameness; yet too much rest would mean loss of fitness and a long interval before the colt could be readied to race again, with the risk that the problem would reemerge during the process of getting him racing fit.

Perhaps another trainer, more experienced in dealing with both public pressure and his own pride in a star horse, might have been better able to keep his own emotions and the expectations of others from influencing his judgment as to when his colt should race and when he should rest. But for Webb, this was all new, and he was caught between promises he had already made, public demand, and his natural desire to show that his "baby" was the best horse in the country. As for Rosa Hoots, though she was an experienced horsewoman, she, too, had no experience with the circumstances in which she found herself, and she had to depend on Webb for day-to-day knowledge of how Black Gold was faring.

Western pride wanted to see Black Gold go east and humble the best of the eastern colts on their own turf, but as the colt had no engagements in any of the major stakes events at Belmont or Saratoga, that plan was never under serious consideration by his connections. In the end, Mrs. Hoots and Webb mapped out two goals for the Derby winner. The first was to try to win more "Derby" races on the midwestern circuit. Like the Louisiana Derby and the Kentucky Derby, each track's "Derby" was usually its most prestigious and lucrative event for three-year-olds. Victories in several of these races would not only push Black Gold past one hundred thousand dollars in earnings—a notable milestone in the 1920s—but would break the record of four "Derby" wins set by Ornament in 1897 and tied by Claude in 1903. The other goal was to prepare Black Gold to race against the French champion Epinard. In one of the great sporting gestures of racing history, Epinard's owner, Pierre Wertheimer, had agreed to send his fine horse across the Atlantic to face the best American runners of all ages in a series of three races at different tracks and distances. The last one was to be contested at the fall Latonia meeting over a mile and a quarter, and this was the race that Mrs. Hoots and Webb hoped would be the crown to Black Gold's season.

Black Gold's post-Derby campaign began on May 24 in the Ohio State Derby at Maple Heights, just a week after the Kentucky Derby. Facing only weak opposition, the colt won easily. He then got a break until June 23 at Latonia, when, to the shock of experts and fans alike, he refused to extend himself and finished last in his prep race for the Latonia Derby on June 28.

The Kentucky Derby winner's poor showing was widely blamed on Webb's having babied the colt too much in the weeks since the Ohio State Derby, but in retrospect, it probably had more to do with the notoriously hard Latonia surface and the colt's chronic foot problems. As he had when Black Gold seemed sore after arrival at Churchill Downs, Webb blamed the colt's shoes. He had them changed prior to the Latonia Derby, hoping that would ease his colt's discomfort, and on June 26 was able to send Black Gold through a slow mile-and-a-quarter gallop with no problems being reported afterward.[1] Nonetheless, Webb made another equipment change that suggested all was still not well: he substituted a more severe wire bit for the colt's regular snaffle bit, apparently in the hope of keeping Black Gold from bearing in toward the rail.[2] Given that the colt had if anything been averse to running along the rail in the past, especially with rivals to his outside, the emergence of this behavior was an ominous sign, suggesting that the colt was attempting to move away from pain.

Those horsemen and sportswriters who suspected that Webb's actions had not resolved Black Gold's issues were proved right in the Latonia Derby. In spite of his poor prep race and race conditions that required him to carry eight more pounds than any of the other entrants, Black Gold went off as the second choice behind Chilhowee, but it was soon obvious that he had more to overcome than his rivals. Showing an unwillingness to race that he had never displayed before, Black Gold was increasingly difficult as he approached the barrier and kept trying to swerve away.[3] Mooney managed to get him in line with the others, but even his skills and his rapport with Black Gold could not get the colt to break smartly or to show speed early. Not until the horses entered the stretch did Black Gold's competitive instincts overcome his reluctance to run, and by that time, he had too much ground to make up. He closed well but had to settle for third behind Chilhowee and Giblon, a nose and four lengths back of the winner.

Mooney felt that part of Black Gold's refusal to extend himself in the early going might have been due to pain from the wire bit.[4] Nonetheless, it was obvious to experienced observers that Black Gold was not the same colt that had won the Kentucky Derby; he needed a lengthy rest if he was to compete in the fall.[5] Unfortunately, he would not get that rest. Rosa Hoots and Hanley Webb were continuing to feel the pressure of the demands for the colt's appearance, and both were perhaps overconfident in Black Gold's ability to rebound from problems as he had before. Further, Webb had an obligation hanging over his head from early in the spring, having promised Joseph Murphy back when he was still at the Fair Grounds that Black Gold would race in the Chicago Derby.[6]

Accordingly, Black Gold was shipped to Hawthorne, where Murphy was the general manager and where the Chicago Derby was to be contested on July 12.

Hawthorne was a softer, more forgiving track than Latonia, and Black Gold seemed to appreciate the change. He showed more enthusiasm for his work and won his prep race by eight lengths on July 10. Even so, in the Chicago Derby he again seemed disinclined to race and dropped well back in the early going before coming on in the stretch to charge home a six-length winner over Giblon with August Belmont II's good colt Ladkin—a winner of five New York stakes in 1924, including the second International Special over Epinard—among the also-rans. It was Black Gold's fourth "Derby" win, and it would be his last major victory. One week later he was in action again, this time at the new Raceland track near Ashland, Kentucky, and came out visibly sore from a third-place finish in the Raceland Derby behind Bob Tail, who had run dead last in the Kentucky Derby, and Altawood, fourth at Louisville.

Tired, worn, and hurting, Black Gold was clearly not the colt he had been in May, and he was finally given a break from training and racing. Still, Mrs. Hoots and Webb hoped that Black Gold could be made fit to appear in the third International Special to face Epinard on October 11, and after several weeks of rest, the colt seemed more comfortable and had gained fifty pounds.[7] By early September, he had returned to light training at Latonia, where his old friend Chief Johnson took over the exercise riding chores from Charley Akers.[8]

Initially, Black Gold showed no evidence of soreness as he went back to work, and Webb was reportedly optimistic regarding Black Gold's chances of running in and winning the Special.[9] The optimism did not last. As the colt's training progressed, he showed signs of a deteriorating temperament, developing a "playful" habit of "tearing clothes off visitors."[10] He was also plagued by increasingly obvious physical problems and was able to run only twice more before his worsening lameness forced his connections to bow to reality. After running unplaced on September 24, Black Gold scored the last victory of his career in a one-mile purse race at Latonia on September 27, 1924. Eleven days later, on October 8, he pulled up lame from a slow work and was declared out of the International Special and out of training for the rest of the year.[11]

Sometime after that, Webb finally diagnosed Black Gold's problem as "a blind quartercrack," a narrow, difficult-to-spot crack in a rear quarter of the hoof wall.[12] Usually developing from top to bottom, such cracks were once attributed to poor farrier work but are now believed to arise from a combination of environmental stressors and genetics. In Black Gold's case, the precipitating factors may have been the nail injury he had suffered as a two-year-old, having his feet improperly trimmed early in his three-year-old year, and overwork, combined with the inherent weakness that had probably been passed down from Domino.

Webb was neither the first nor the last horseman to miss such a crack for months or more. Years later, the top trainer Horatio Luro—a member of the Racing Hall of Fame in both the United States and Canada—apparently failed to spot a similar crack afflicting E. P. Taylor's fine colt Nearctic, leading to a chain of events that compromised the horse for better than a year. Nearctic, though, was more fortunate than Black Gold; when he finally got the rest he needed and a chance for the injury in the hoof wall to grow out and be replaced by healthy horn, he proved to have escaped other musculoskeletal injuries caused by his instinctive attempts to redistribute stress away from his painful foot. He was able to race soundly for most of his four-year-old season, becoming the 1958 Canadian Horse of the Year, and was later an important sire. Black Gold, less lucky, had been compromised by the delay in diagnosis and treatment, apparently sustaining some degree of chronic damage to the joints and tendons of his forelegs that remained even after the quarter crack grew out. After a winter's rest, Webb made repeated attempts to get the colt sound enough to race again as a four-year-old, but they failed. In October 1925, Black Gold was retired to stud at Jack Howard's Rookwood Farm near Lexington, where he was advertised for the 1926 breeding season at a fee of five hundred dollars in cash at time of service.

In spite of the disappointments attending the last part of his racing career, it seemed that Black Gold had finally found his way to a happy ending, but Lady Luck was about to show her crueler side. By the end of Black Gold's first season at stud, it had become apparent that the young stallion was infertile. He mated readily with his mares, but they did not become pregnant. He remained at stud for a second season, but his reproductive woes continued, and the veterinary science of the time was not able to resolve them. Only one colt ever resulted from his two years' efforts as a stallion, and in a cruel stroke of fate, that colt was killed by lightning before it was ever named or raced.[13]

Rosa Hoots was also facing harder times, for Osage oil production and revenues were beginning to decline, and her income was also affected by a sharp drop in prices for agricultural products. She had another racehorse in training with Webb, Black Gold's full brother Beggar Boy, but although he had seemed very promising in his early training, it soon became apparent that he lacked his famous brother's talent. Useeit had died several months after Beggar Boy's birth, so there would be no more good racers to follow from her. And Black Gold, now obviously a bust as a stallion, was generating only expenses, not income. So it was that Waldo Freeman, now acting as his mother-in-law's racing manager, contacted Webb in June 1927 and told him to put Black Gold back in training.[14]

Black Gold was not the only top horse of his time to be put back into training after a long time away from the races. Old Rosebud had been widely acclaimed as the best American racehorse of 1917 after being laid off for nearly three years following his win in the 1914 Kentucky Derby, and more recently, the 1921 champion three-year-old Grey Lag had returned to training after proving sterile at stud and had won some races. But viewed objectively, Black Gold was not a good candidate for a comeback. He had never been sound for more than a year before his retirement, and he had grown taller and thicker during his two years of stallion duty; his increased weight was an extra handicap in trying to get him racing fit without overstressing his legs. None-theless, Webb worked with Black Gold through the summer and fall and by mid-October was optimistic enough to state that he thought the horse could win the New Orleans Handicap in February.[15] Others were not so optimistic, among them J. D. Mooney. Semi-retired from the saddle and helping to train a few horses, he was contacted about coming back to ride Black Gold. Having heard elsewhere that the horse was still lame, he refused and urged that Black Gold not be raced.[16]

Black Gold ran three times in December 1927 at Jefferson Park without finishing in the money, and his lameness—now persistent rather than inter-mittent—was painfully evident after each race and each workout, to the point that horsemen and sportswriters were openly wondering why the stewards were not refusing his entries.[17] Further, the horse's mental state was deteriorating. He had always been strong-willed and sometimes fractious when asked to do something he did not care for, and he had a history of aggression toward visitors he did not know from the latter part of his three-year-old season onward. Now he was becoming dangerous even toward Webb, who had been the recipient of as much affection as Black Gold had to give any human. On one particularly bad day in January, the horse lashed out with his hooves and knocked Webb out for a good fifteen minutes.[18] Yet Webb seemed unable to see or acknowledge the change in his beloved pet; after coming to, he was quoted as saying, "He's so playful. He's just like a baby boy."[19] As for Black Gold's persistent soreness,

Webb kept insisting that it would work itself out as it had during the horse's glory days, and that he was fine on the mornings after he ran or worked. Any private doubts the trainer entertained may have been drowned in alcohol as his drinking problem worsened; stories passed around the tracks years later tell of his taking Black Gold from his stall at night and riding him down to a local saloon, there to stand hitched to a post or tree like a common cow pony while Webb drank himself drunk.[20]

On January 18, 1928, the last of Black Gold's luck ran out. Entered in the one-mile Salome Purse, he showed speed through the first six furlongs before starting to give way . . . and then his right foreleg broke with a snap audible all over the Fair Grounds. Spectators gasped in horror or hid their eyes as Black Gold kept trying to run on his remaining three legs, the fourth dangling grotesquely. Finally, Dave Emery managed to get his mount pulled up and slid from his back. A few minutes later, Black Gold hobbled his final few steps to the paddock, where a lethal injection ended his suffering.

Black Gold was buried in the Fair Grounds infield the following day, not far from the grave of Pan Zareta; Hanley Webb wept openly and inconsolably. Two weeks later, when Justice F. won the New Orleans Handicap, winning jockey Anthony Pascuma took the victor's sheaf of roses and laid them on Black Gold's grave.

Epilogue

For years after Black Gold's death, the ill luck that had bedeviled the Derby winner seemed to cling to those associated with him. None felt its sting more than Rosa Hoots. In 1929, her son Alfred died after an illness of several months. His death left her unable to continue managing the ranch where she and Al Hoots had lived in their youth, and by the mid-1930s, the property—now known as the "Black Gold Ranch"—had passed to the ownership of William and Sarah Jordan. Today, the Black Gold Ranch still remains in the Jordan family.

Rosa Hoots remained involved in racing for a few years after Black Gold's death, but whatever attachment she retained for the sport could not survive the economic and personal pressures she was facing as Osage oil revenues continued declining and the Great Depression deepened. After the manner of her mother, she had been fostering a number of orphaned children as well as helping to care for her grandchildren, and she was also contributing to the care of her disabled older brother, Peter Augustus Captain. Thus, in early 1933, Mrs. Hoots announced plans to sell off her small stable and retire her racing colors.[1] Among the horses she sold was Useeit's last foal, Beggar Boy, who followed his brother to Rookwood Farm for a time before going west to stand at the Black Gold Ranch. Used as a sire of both Thoroughbreds and American Quarter Horses, he died in 1945, leaving behind twelve foals that won sanctioned races for Thoroughbreds, but none remotely close to what Black Gold had been.

The only horse Mrs. Hoots retained was Miss Tulsa, who, next to Black Gold, was the best horse she would ever breed. A daughter of Tuscola by the champion two-year-old Tryster, she won fifteen races and placed in two small stakes races. She would be responsible for producing the last Thoroughbred bred by Rosa Hoots, a 1936 colt by Kilkerry. Named Heinous, he failed to win or place in eleven starts, providing an ignominious aftermath to the dream brought to such brilliant fruition by Black Gold.

Even Rosa's hopes of passing her Kentucky Derby trophy on to her three grandchildren would not survive. She and her family were attending the races in 1933 when someone broke into her house in Tulsa and stole both Black Gold's golden trophy and the collection of racing memorabilia that went with it. Aside from the trophy for the Chicago Derby, most of the stolen items were never recovered.[2]

Although Rosa Hoots's descendants believe that a trophy already in the Kentucky Derby Museum's collection—one initially misidentified as the 1937 trophy awarded to War Admiral—may be the one awarded to Black Gold, this trophy's identity is still under investigation by the Kentucky Derby Museum.[3] The Black Gold trophy currently identified as such in the Museum's collection is a replica commissioned by family members with the permission of Churchill Downs; this trophy was given to Rosa Hoots's grandson Richard Freeman in a surprise ceremony in 2000 before being donated to the Museum in 2004.

Rosa Hoots died on April 24, 1938, two years after losing her last surviving child, her daughter Agnes. After services at Christ the King Catholic Church, she was buried in the Captain Cemetery, joining her husband and her children. Her legacy has been carried on by Agnes's descendants, who continue to maintain the memory of Black Gold and of the woman whose love for her husband and determination to see his last wishes carried out created the horse's legend.

Hanley Webb's fate was, if anything, still more tragic than Rosa Hoots's final years. Widely vilified as responsible for Black Gold's death, he continued to train Beggar Boy for a little while but was soon displaced as the trainer of the Hoots horses by Waldo Freeman. Afterward, Webb slid into a gray existence at the fringes of the Thoroughbred world. He trained a few cheap horses here and there during the 1930s, but never again would anyone trust him with a horse of any potential or standing. As if wishing to forget that he ever existed, none of the major Thoroughbred publications made mention of his death, and all that is left to testify to the end of his life is an obituary from the Cook

County, Illinois, town of Bremen, stating that Hanley Webb, janitor, had died on January 7, 1940, at the age of sixty-nine.[4]

The year of Black Gold's triumphs was the highwater mark for J. D. Mooney, who recalled making about thirty-seven thousand dollars in 1924 (the equivalent of close to six hundred thousand dollars in 2022) between riding fees, bonuses, and bets placed through the trainers he rode for.[5] Although he was not as prosperous in 1925 and 1926, the reputation he had built riding Black Gold stayed with him, getting him mounts on horses like Chilhowee, the good handicap horse General Thatcher, and a difficult juvenile named Display who later won the 1926 Preakness Stakes and other top races for other riders.

By 1927, continuous, strenuous reducing was taking too great a toll on Mooney's health to be ignored, and he walked away from riding in 1928. He had one more moment of glory in the saddle; persuaded to try a comeback by George Davies, he got his jockey's license reinstated in Canada in 1929, just two weeks before piloting Davies's horse Shorelint to victory in Canada's premier race, the King's Plate. A year and a half later, Mooney rode his final winner, Uncle Matt, in an eight-hundred-dollar claiming race at Jefferson Park on December 1, 1930. He continued to ride occasionally after that until March 21, 1931, when he donned silks for the last time to ride Bardalid in the third race at Jefferson Park. In an anticlimactic finish, he ended up tenth of twelve.

For the next thirty-five years, Mooney continued to make his living around Thoroughbreds, training a small string of horses while the money he had earned during his riding days slipped away. When times were hard, he did other racetrack jobs to keep his family fed and housed, sometimes becoming an agent for other jockeys' books, sometimes serving as a valet in the jockeys' room. He remained kind, honest, and uncomplaining. From time to time, some newsman would recognize the slim, dark-haired man with the increasingly weathered face as Black Gold's former jockey, and then the raconteur in Mooney would come alive with stories of racing in a bygone era.

Mooney got one last kiss from Lady Luck in 1962 when he claimed a horse named Crafty Lace and developed him into that year's Canadian Horse of the Year. Four years later, he died of a heart attack on November 16, 1966, at the age of sixty-five, survived by Marjorie and their four children. He lived to see all three of his sons involved in the racing world that he loved so well, and two would achieve a measure of fame in their own right: John, whose career as a racing executive eventually led to his induction into the "Builders" category of the Canadian Horse Racing Hall of Fame, and Paul, who leapfrogged from horse racing to hockey and became the president of the National Hockey League's Boston Bruins.

J. D. Mooney was not a great rider as measured by number of victories, percentage of winning mounts, or career earnings, and while Black Gold was inducted into the National Museum of Racing Hall of Fame in 1989, Mooney has never received serious consideration for this honor. Nonetheless, his achievements have not gone without notice. In 1975, J. D. Mooney became the first representative of the sport of horse racing to be inducted into the Louisiana Sports Hall of Fame, a fitting legacy for a New Orleans man who never gained more than a brief brush with greatness, yet gave himself wholeheartedly to the sport, the people, and the horse that he loved.

The years have come and gone since Black Gold raced into triumph and tragedy, and the world of a century ago has changed almost beyond recognition. Jefferson Park and the old Lexington Association and Latonia tracks are only memories now, and in Oklahoma, the oil boom of the 1920s is likewise long gone.

Still, some things remain. At Churchill Downs, the twin spires still stand, silent witnesses to the Golden Jubilee, and the sun glints off the golden lettering of Black Gold's name among the list of Derby champions. There are also the memories and traditions preserved among Rosa Hoots's descendants, who often can be seen visiting the Fair Grounds for the Louisiana Derby or coming to Remington Park in Oklahoma, where a local stakes race pays tribute to the fleet Useeit.

One other legacy remains. Early in each year, the Black Gold Stakes appears on the Fair Grounds racing card. It is not a particularly important race; at one time a prep for the Louisiana Derby, it is now a minor turf stakes for three-year-olds. But it is not its competitors that make it memorable. It is what happens afterward, when the winning jockey dismounts and a floral wreath is placed in his arms. Alone or accompanied by members of Rosa Hoots's family, the rider walks with solemn dignity into the infield, to where a white obelisk stands as a silent sentinel over the grave of a fallen hero. There, the jockey gently places the flowers around the monument, which bears a simple plaque that says all that need be said regarding the recipient of this tribute.

It reads, "BLACK GOLD."

Acknowledgments

Books may have a single "parent," but like babies, they need an extended family to bring them to maturity. Many of the contributors to Black Gold's story died before I was ever born, and without the memories they left behind them in the form of newspaper articles, racing charts, and other records, this book would not have been possible; they are, if you will, the ancestors of *Dream Derby*. I also owe a debt of gratitude to the silent work of archivists in preserving these memories and making them available through the modern internet, a blessing beyond price at a time when restrictions related to the COVID-19 pandemic greatly reduced physical access to libraries and research centers. Among these keepers of knowledge, Chris Goodlett, Director of Curatorial and Educational Affairs at the Kentucky Derby Museum, and Kelly Coffman, Research Services Librarian at the Keeneland Library, provided invaluable assistance with specific requests and could not have been kinder or more prompt with their responses, while noted authors Laura Hillenbrand, Dorothy Ours, and Mary Simon generously shared their time and thoughts to provide me with valuable tips on conducting research.

My thanks go out to Thoroughbred historian Dale Wyatt, who not only reviewed my initial drafts but recruited friends as additional readers; without their feedback, this book would be far weaker. I also received valuable input from editor and content manager Scot Gillies, a former colleague at *The Blood-Horse* whose encouragement meant as much as his suggestions. Others whose support has meant much to me during the long hours of sitting at a desk and sifting through thousands of pieces of background material include my fellow racing enthusiasts at the "Thoroughbred Fanatics" discussion board and the followers of my "American Classic Pedigrees" page on Facebook. I couldn't have done it without all of you!

Many thanks go out to fellow author Jennifer Kelly, who has been a wonderful cheerleader and helped get me a hearing from the University Press of Kentucky, and acquisitions editor Patrick O'Dowd, who got me on board and since then has patiently discussed ideas and answered questions. And behind everything I have ever achieved as a writer is my best friend and beloved husband, Tab, who has been in my corner ever since I began putting words to paper and has provided the space in which my writing career could grow and flourish.

Finally, no list of acknowledgments would be complete without giving praise to God for His many gifts and His abundant love. To Him be the glory!

—Avalyn Hunter

Notes

1. A Man and a Mare

1. T. T. Johnson Jr., "Useeit and Her Little Black Colt." *Daily Oklahoman* (Oklahoma City), May 5, 1935, Newspapers.com.

2. In legend, this was the match race that led to Useeit's purchase by Al Hoots. Accounts of the race agree that she was narrowly defeated by a mare owned and trained by Ben Jones, but they are conflicting as to details, and contemporary newspapers provide no information. Peter Chew (*The Kentucky Derby: The First 100 Years* [Boston: Houghton Mifflin, 1974]) states that the match took place in Chickasha when Useeit was still a two-year-old and names Useeit's conqueror as Belle Thompson. Joe Hirsch and Gene Plowden (*In the Winner's Circle: The Jones Boys of Calumet Farm* [New York: Mason & Lipscomb, 1974], 8–9) state that the race took place at a meeting at Oklahoma City the following year and that the victor of the match was Parnell Girl.

3. Dick Maher, "'Black Gold' Champion Two-Year-Old Star, Is Owned Here," *Tulsa (OK) Tribune,* April 8, 1923, Newspapers.com.

4. "Jack Witt Proves Pounds the Best," *Daily Oklahoman* (Oklahoma City), June 26, 1910, Newspapers.com.

5. Maher, "'Black Gold' Champion Two-Year-Old Star, Is Owned Here."

6. Jack O'Donnell, "The Romance of Black Gold," *American Legion Weekly* 6, no. 38 (September 19, 1924): 7, 13–14, Archive.legion.org.

7. "A Western Flyer," *Fairview (OK) Republican,* July 1, 1910, Newspapers.com.

8. Morris-Yates Abstract Co., "Real Estate Transfers," *Pawhuska (OK) Capital,* September 1, 1910, Newspapers.com.

2. Useeit's Odyssey

1. Dick Maher, "'Black Gold' Champion Two-Year-Old Star, Is Owned Here," *Tulsa Tribune*, April 8, 1923, Newspapers.com.

2. Ibid.

3. The first Florida racetrack able to attract "name" horses and their owners from the Northeast, Moncrief Park opened in 1909 and closed following its 1911 meeting.

4. "Racing Form," *Cincinnati Enquirer*, February 28, 1911, Newspapers.com.

5. T. T. Johnson Jr., "Useeit and Her Little Black Colt." *Daily Oklahoman* (Oklahoma City), May 5, 1935, Newspapers.com.

6. "Missourians Arrested in Topeka, " *Lawrence (KS) Daily Gazette*, April 13, 1893, Newspapers.com.

7. Although some accounts state that Webb was a US marshal, he is not listed on the Marshal Service's rolls.

8. A less charitable explanation for Webb's nickname is that it came from his habit of asking that his whiskey glasses be filled to three fingers' depth (David P. Schultz, "Legend of Racing's Black Gold," *Scranton [PA] Tribune*, July 26, 1972, Newspapers .com).

9. "Noted Stable Arrives Here," *Louisville Courier-Journal*, September 10, 1913, Newspapers.com.

3. The Queen of Juarez

1. "Racing Form," *Cincinnati Enquirer,* August 1, 1914, Newspapers.com.

2. "Pan Zareta Reigns Queen of the Turf," *New York Times,* August 1, 1917, Newspapers.com.

4. A Month in New Orleans

1. According to a chart published in the *El Paso Morning Times* of December 19, 1915, Useeit raced twenty-three times in 1914, with three wins and five seconds. For her efforts, she earned $1,190.

2. Now defunct, Palmetto Park conducted winter racing meets in 1912–1915.

3. "Winter Race Meeting of New Orleans Opens Jan. 1," *Montgomery (AL) Advertiser,* December 20, 1914, Newspapers.com.

4. Traditionally, Colonel Bradley and Al Hoots have been believed to have become acquainted while at the Fair Grounds, which would only have been possible while Useeit was racing there in 1915; at that time, Bradley was said to have expressed interest in Useeit's future breeding career and even to have offered Hoots a season to one of his stallions. Although the exact timing of such a conversation is uncertain, a circumstantial case can be made for its having taken place following Useeit's January 27 race. According to the "Heard About Town" column in the *Lexington (KY) Leader* of December 21, 1914, Bradley and his wife were wintering at Palm Beach, Florida

(as was their custom), but Bradley was known to make side trips to his Palmetto Club in New Orleans and to the Fair Grounds when he had horses running there. As it happened, Brick and Mortar was his only starter at the Fair Grounds in 1915, and the January 27 race was the only one in which the Bradley horse and Useeit crossed paths.

5. "Useeit Smashes Track Record by Running the Six-Furlong Distance in 1:12," *Cincinnati Enquirer,* January 30, 1915, Newspapers.com.

5. Ruled Off

1. J. K. Stringfield, "Col. Winn Sees Early Business Revival in Mexico; Texans Eagerly Await Running Texas Futurity," *El Paso Morning Times,* December 19, 1915, Newspapers.com.

2. "Gabby Gabe Says," *Cincinnati Post,* September 11, 1915, Newspapers.com.

3. "Reflections of the Week in Sport World," *Cincinnati Enquirer,* May 25, 1924, Newspapers.com.

4. "Camden's One Step Is Douglas Park Winner: Captures the Feature Race at Louisville from Hanover and Fleetabelle," *Lexington (KY) Herald,* September 25, 1915, Newspapers.com.

5. "Reflections of the Week in Sport World."

6. Stringfield, "Col. Winn Sees Early Business Revival in Mexico."

7. "Horse Special Reaches Goal," *Louisville Courier-Journal,* November 6, 1915, Newspapers.com.

8. "Trainer Kay Spence and Jockey Acton Handle Two Winners Each: Riders and Horses Caught in Webbing at Start in Fifth," *El Paso Morning Times,* February 13, 1916, Newspapers.com.

9. "Ormes Loses Stirrup and Kootenay Lands Unplaced in Feature," *El Paso Morning Times,* February 23, 1916, Newspapers.com.

10. Walter H. Pearce, "Live Turf Gossip from across the Rio Grande," *Louisville Courier-Journal,* February 29, 1916, Newspapers.com.

11. Ibid.

12. Walter H. Pearce, "Dead Heat at Juarez Course," *Louisville Courier-Journal,* February 24, 1916, Newspapers.com.

13. Pearce, "Live Turf Gossip from across the Rio Grande."

14. "May W First Baby Winner of New Year; Cost Owner Weir Only $500 at Latonia," *El Paso Morning Times,* January 23, 1916, Newspapers.com.

15. Jim Bolus, *Derby Magic* (Gretna, LA: Pelican, 1997), 203.

16. Frank J. Teahan, "Refuses to Surrender Mare Bid up in Race; Indian Chief Ruled Off," *Windsor (Ontario) Star,* February 25, 1916, Newspapers.com.

17. United Press, "Hoots Used Guns to Keep Black Gold's Mammy," *Cincinnati Post,* May 20, 1924, Newspapers.com.

18. "Lola and Billy Culberson Dead Heat in Third Race—Olga Star Wins," *El Paso Morning Times,* February 24, 1916, Newspapers.com.

19. "Memories of Black Gold," *The Blood-Horse,* April 30, 1983. From the Jim Bolus Collection at the Kentucky Derby Museum, courtesy of Chris Goodlett, Director of Curatorial and Educational Affairs, Kentucky Derby Museum.

20. J. K. Stringfield, "Waremore Purchased Cheap; Proves Good Bargain for Weber," *El Paso Morning Times,* March 5, 1916, Newspapers.com.

21. "Bump Does Not Stop Utelus, For He Goes and Defeats the Favorite, Joe Blair," *Cincinnati Enquirer,* January 15, 1917, Newspapers.com.

22. Untitled column on local citizens' activities, *Skiatook (OK) News,* November 15, 1917, Newspapers.com.

23. French Lane, "Widow Hoots Overwhelmed with Success: Tells How Her Late Husband Predicted Winner," *Pittsburgh Daily Post,* May 18, 1924, Newspapers.com.

6. A Woman of Two Worlds

1. Sarah L. Lockwood, "'Aunt Jane' Appleby Dies Near Skiatook: Triumphed over Poverty, Disease, Illiteracy, Near-Primitive Habits and Became Wealthy," *Tulsa Democrat,* November 19, 1917, Newspapers.com.

2. A. T. Dickerman, "The Queen of the Osages: Some Early Day Incidents among Southern Kansas Indians," *Pittsburgh Headlight,* January 14, 1909, Newspapers.com.

3. "'Shoot the Half-Breed Renegade' Was the Advice of Governor S. J. Crawford," *Erie (KS) Record,* February 18, 1910, Newspapers.com.

4. "Has Saved Osages over $1,000,000: 'Aunt Jane' Appleby's Knowledge of Tribal Relations Prevented Frauds—'Oklahoma's Most Remarkable Woman'—More Than 70 Years with the Indians—Now Past 80 and Wealthy—An Expert with the Pistol—Romantic Early Life and Later Thrilling Experiences," *St. Louis Post-Dispatch,* February 26, 1911, Newspapers.com.

5. Ibid.

6. Kelly Dennis Park, "Genealogy Report: Descendants of Jean Baptiste Gresa Dit Capitaine," February 24, 2011, www.genealogy.com/ftm/p/a/r/Kelly-D-Park/GENE75-0003.html.

7. "Has Saved Osages Over $1,000,000."

8. Ibid.

9. Jim North, "Osage Tribe," Gaylord College of Journalism and Mass Communications, University of Oklahoma, undated, www.ou.edu/gaylord/exiled-to-indian-country/content/osage.

10. Beulah Eaton Pender, interview by Effie S. Jackson, Tulsa, Oklahoma, October 4, 1937, transcript, https://digital.libraries.ou.edu/utils/getfile/collection/indianpp/id/1262/filename/2128.pdf.

11. Ibid.

12. "Goes after the Money: C. N. Walker Considers His Wife's Love Worth $15,000," *Tulsa Democrat,* April 17, 1903, Newspapers.com.

7. Bradley's Luck

1. The "deathbed vision" story appears to have originated with J. E. Crown, who published his account of Black Gold's origins in the *New Orleans States* of February 25, 1923. This story was widely circulated in the weeks following its original appearance without reference to its author's byline and was later reprinted in the *Louisville Courier-Journal* of May 18, 1924, under the heading of "Old Indian's Faith in Little Pony, Useeit, Justified by Derby."

2. Dick Maher, "'Black Gold' Champion Two-Year-Old Star, Is Owned Here," *Tulsa Tribune,* April 8, 1923, Newspapers.com.

3. Harry Grayson (Newspaper Enterprise Association), "Bradley Puts Self in Training, Prepares for Bimelech's Derby," *Lexington (KY) Leader,* December 16, 1939, Newspapers.com.

4. Jim Bolus, *Run for the Roses* (New York: Hawthorn 1974), 36.

5. "Bradley, Noted Turfman, Dies: Fabulous Career of Race King, 86, Ends in Kentucky," *Miami Herald,* August 15, 1946, Newspapers.com.

6. "Baker-Gentry and Other Sales," *Louisville Courier-Journal,* July 21, 1898, Newspapers.com.

7. "Kentucky Colonel Wins: Takes the Junior Stakes at Harlem without Trouble," *Chicago Tribune,* July 28, 1898, Newspapers.com.

8. Henry V. King, "'Dynamite Jack' Helped to Make Bradley Wealthy: As Partners They Won Fortune in 1898 on Plater Called Friar John," *New York Herald,* December 30, 1922, Newspapers.com.

9. A Kentucky tradition since 1813, Kentucky Colonels receive an honorary commission in the state militia from the governor of the Commonwealth of Kentucky in recognition of noteworthy accomplishments and exceptional community service. The appointment is for life and is the highest honor that can be accorded by the governor of Kentucky.

10. Bruce Dudley, "90,000 See Black Gold Win: Golden Jubilee Second Woman's Victory in Derby History," *Louisville Courier-Journal,* May 19, 1924, Newspapers.com.

11. Ed Bowen, *Legends of the Turf: A Century of Great Thoroughbred Breeders,* vol. 1 (Lexington, KY: Eclipse, 2003), 110.

12. "Career of Black Gold, 1924 Derby Winner, Recalled," *Owensboro (KY) Messenger,* January 18, 1931, Newspapers.com.

8. Gold and Turmoil

1. "Frosted Grass Fatal," *Lexington (KY) Leader,* October 26, 1923, Newspapers.com.

2. Dick Maher, "'Black Gold' Champion Two-Year-Old Star, Is Owned Here," *Tulsa Tribune,* April 8, 1923, Newspapers.com.

3. "1921 Tulsa Race Massacre," Tulsa Historical Society and Museum, 2022, https://www.tulsahistory.org/exhibit/1921-tulsa-race-massacre/.

4. Buck Colbert Franklin, "The Tulsa Race Riot and Three of Its Victims," unpublished manuscript, cited in Allison Keys, "A Long-Lost Manuscript Contains a Searing Account of the Tulsa Race Massacre of 1921," May 27, 2016, Smithsonianmag.com.

5. Maher, "'Black Gold' Champion Two-Year-Old Star, Is Owned Here."

9. Three Fingers and a Chief

1. J. L. Dempsey, "Credit Given Black Gold for Overcoming Double Case of Interference," *Cincinnati Enquirer,* May 19, 1924, Newspapers.com.

2. "Black Gold's Dam, Useeit, Was Great Favorite in Bygone Years," *St. Louis Globe-Democrat,* April 14, 1924, Newspapers.com.

3. "Black Gold Is Being Prepared for Stake at Coney Island Sept. 7," *St. Louis Post-Dispatch,* July 19, 1925, Newspapers.com.

4. Marion Porter, "Derby Week Cinderella," *Louisville Courier-Journal,* May 7, 1938, Newspapers.com.

5. "63 and Still Riding Speedsters," *Collyer's Eye and Baseball World,* June 30, 1934, Newspapers.com.

6. Charles A. Bergin, "'Chief' Johnson, Old-Time Jockey, Only One Who Ever Talked Back to Cassidy and Got Away with It," *Indianapolis Star,* January 13, 1918, Newspapers.com.

7. "Johnson Gets Back and Rides," *Tulsa Daily Democrat,* September 11, 1913, Newspapers.com.

8. Ibid.

9. "63 and Still Riding Speedsters."

10. Johnson was sometimes prone to padding his age to support his claim of being North America's oldest living jockey, but the best available records indicate that he was born on May 2, 1871.

11. Melvin D. Fulcher, "After the Derby," *Louisville Courier-Journal,* May 18, 1924, Newspapers.com.

12. Jack O'Donnell, "The Romance of Black Gold," *American Legion Weekly* 6, no. 38 (September 19, 1924): 7, 13–14, Archive.legion.org.

13. C. J. Savage, "Big Handicap to Start Meet on Last Lap," *Louisville Courier-Journal,* December 25, 1922, Newspapers.com.

10. Baby Steps

1. "Special Notice," *Skiatook (OK) News,* December 28, 1922, Newspapers.com.

2. For racing purposes, all Thoroughbreds in the Northern Hemisphere are considered to be born on January 1, regardless of the actual foaling date.

3. "The Homestretch," *Baltimore Evening Sun,* January 1, 1923, Newspapers.com.

4. C. J. Savage, "New Year's Handicap to Open Winter Meeting at Fair Grounds Oval Today," *Louisville Courier-Journal,* January 1, 1923, Newspapers.com.

5. J. L. Dempsey, "Form Disappears in Clouds: Wet Track Blamed for Fair Grounds Reversals," *Cincinnati Enquirer,* January 8, 1922, Newspapers.com.

6. James Brown, "No Juvenile Star Yet Shown at New Orleans," *Collyer's Eye,* January 20, 1923, Newspapers.com.

7. Jimmy Brown, cited in "Expect Black Gold to Make Great Racer," *Buffalo (NY) Courier,* January 24, 1923, Newspapers.com.

8. "Racing Form," *Cincinnati Enquirer,* January 27, 1923, Newspapers.com.

9. C. J. Savage, "Favorite Players Have Disastrous Day at Fair Grounds Track: Louis A. Noses Out Favored Wynnewood in Claiming Handicap," *Louisville Courier-Journal,* January 27, 1923, Newspapers.com.

10. The account of a nail in Black Gold's foot appears to have first seen print when J. E. Crown published his account of Black Gold's origins in the *New Orleans States* of February 25, 1923, a story later reprinted in the *Louisville Courier-Journal* of May 18, 1924, under the heading "Old Indian's Faith in Little Pony, Useeit, Justified by Derby." In April 1924, Hanley Webb confirmed that Black Gold had suffered such an injury as a two-year-old, though he did not specify exactly when it occurred.

11. Horace Wade, "Black Gold's Unlucky Star," *San Francisco Examiner,* March 16, 1947, Newspapers.com.

12. Even if Hoots had still been alive, he could not have seen a comet on the night of Black Gold's birth. There were no comet sightings visible to the naked eye in the spring of 1921, though in May of that year, solar flares caused a major geomagnetic storm that triggered electrical fires and aurora borealis (Northern Lights) displays as far south as Texas.

11. Hot Property

1. "Black Gold Thrown out of Training," *Collyer's Eye,* April 5, 1924, Newspapers .com.

2. Preston M. Burch, *Training Thoroughbred Horses,* 4th ed. (Lexington, KY: The Blood-Horse, 1976), 108.

3. As recounted by Peter Chew in his *The Kentucky Derby: The First 100 Years* (Boston: Houghton Mifflin, 1974), Gentry stated that he recalled Black Gold's having run a nail into his right forefoot while in training at Churchill Downs in 1924. There is no independent confirmation of such an injury in 1924 news accounts, and it seems likely that Gentry may have inadvertently conflated an earlier memory regarding Black Gold's 1923 injury at the Fair Grounds with his recall more than four decades later of the colt's being intermittently sore during the lead-up to the Kentucky Derby.

4. "Racing Form," *Cincinnati Enquirer,* February 13, 1923, Newspapers.com.

5. "Crack Colt Black Gold in New York Stakes," *Brooklyn Daily Times,* February 26, 1923, Newspapers.com.

6. Ibid.

7. C. J. Savage, "Black Gold Lowers Track Record in Opening Dash At New Orleans," *Louisville Courier-Journal,* February 20, 1923, Newspapers.com.

8. C. J. Savage, "Lexington Turfman's Thoroughbred Wins New Orleans Handicap," *Louisville Courier-Journal,* February 21, 1923, Newspapers.com.

9. "Love of Indian for His Mare Responsible for Black Gold," *Collyer's Eye*, March 3, 1923, Newspapers.com.

10. Dick Maher, "'Black Gold' Champion Two Year Old Turf Star, Is Owned Here," *Tulsa Tribune*, April 8, 1923, Newspapers.com.

11. "Love of Indian for His Mare Responsible for Black Gold."

12. One Man's Dream

1. Peter Chew, *The Kentucky Derby: The First 100 Years* (Boston: Houghton Mifflin, 1974), 30.

2. "Kentucky Derby History," Louisville City Guide, February 10, 2021, www.brixlouisville.com/kentucky-derby-history/.

3. Jim Bolus, *Kentucky Derby Stories* (Gretna, LA: Pelican, 1993), 59.

13. Mr. Derby

1. Matt Winn, *Down the Stretch: The Story of Colonel Matt J. Winn, as Told to Frank G. Menke* (New York: Smith and Durrell, 1945), 1.

2. Jim Bolus, *Kentucky Derby Stories* (Gretna, LA: Pelican, 1993), 65.

3. Ibid., 66.

4. Regret was the first filly to win the Kentucky Derby, and since then only two other fillies—Genuine Risk in 1980 and Winning Colors in 1988—have emulated her feat.

5. "Track Gossip," *Cincinnati Enquirer*, May 9, 1915, Newspapers.com.

6. Jim Bolus, *Run for the Roses: 100 Years at the Kentucky Derby* (New York: Hawthorne, 1974), 27.

7. Added money in a stakes race is the amount guaranteed to be put up by the track in addition to the pooled nomination, eligibility, entry, and starting fees of the competitors.

8. Riddle finally relented in 1937, when he sent Man o' War's son War Admiral to the Kentucky Derby. War Admiral won and followed up by sweeping the American Triple Crown.

14. Kentucky Trial

1. Phil McCann, "Block's Aspiration Steps Mile in 1:41⅕; Other Horses in Fast Moves," *Lexington (KY) Herald*, April 27, 1923, Newspapers.com.

2. James Kerr, "Racing Notes," *Lexington (KY) Leader*, March 29, 1923, Newspapers.com.

3. "Racing Form," *Cincinnati Enquirer*, April 29, 1923, Newspapers.com.

4. Ibid.

5. James M. Kerr, "Racing Notes," *Lexington (KY) Leader*, May 7, 1923, Newspapers.com.

6. Ibid.

7. John Belski, "Belski's Blog—Anniversary of Kentucky's Biggest May Snow," May 20, 2020, WLKY.com.

8. Connelly would ride a third Kentucky Oaks winner in 1927, when he brought Mary Jane home first. The second man to ride as many as three Oaks winners (the first was the noted Black jockey John Stovall), he died of tuberculosis in 1931.

9. "Lexington Form Chart," *Louisville Courier-Journal*, May 8, 1923, Newspapers .com.

10. Simes, *Black Gold*, photograph in the *Louisville Courier-Journal*, May 15, 1923, 9.

11. Horses from the same stable normally run as a single entry in races, so that bettors on the entry are paid off regardless of which horse from the entry wins, places, or shows. In the 1923 Derby, the two-horse H. P. Whitney entry was declared to be coupled with Greentree Stable's horses because Greentree was owned by Whitney's brother and sister-in-law, removing any suspicion that the two stables might be in collusion at bettors' expense.

12. Jim Bolus, *Run for the Roses: 100 Years at the Kentucky Derby* (New York: Hawthorn, 1974), 39.

13. Ibid.

14. "Great Throngs Roll into Louisville to See 24 Thoroughbreds Start in Blue Ribbon Event of Turf Season," *Dayton (OH) Herald*, May 19, 1923, Newspapers.com.

15. John E. Wray, "Victory of Zev in the Kentucky Derby Stuns Great Crowd," *St. Louis Post-Dispatch*, May 20, 1923, Newspapers.com.

16. "Downs Form Chart," *Louisville Courier-Journal*, May 20, 1923, Newspapers.com.

17. The source of the offer was later identified by *Collyer's Eye* as trainer Thomas J. Healy, acting on behalf of Richard T. Wilson Jr.

18. Stuart T. Morse, "Eastern Oklahoma and Texas," *Oklahoma Farmer*, July 10, 1923, Newspapers.com.

15. Summer of Futility

1. C. J. Savage, "Placing Thoroughbreds Crowns at Downs Is Not Difficult Task: Zev Undisputed King of 3-Year-Olds; Baby Honors to Ruddy Light," *Louisville Courier-Journal*, June 4, 1923, Newspapers.com.

2. "Crack Juveniles Meet Saturday," *Lexington (KY) Leader*, June 18, 1923, Newspapers.com.

3. C. J. Savage, "Ruddy Light and Ten Lec Capture Feature Races at Latonia: Juvenile Is Made Big Choice but Handicap Winner Is Overlooked," *Louisville Courier-Journal*, June 10, 1923, Newspapers.com.

4. In fact, Ruddy Light and Black Gold never met. After the Clipsetta, the filly won her next outing, but that was the last race of her season and her career.

5. Abram R. Hewitt, *The Great Breeders and Their Methods* (Lexington, KY: Thoroughbred Publishers, 1982), 102.

6. Gerald Griffin, "Foal of $100 Mare Won $115,740," *Louisville Courier-Journal*, March 26, 1939, Newspapers.com.

7. Ben Dahlman, "Wise Counsellor Now Ranks with Leaders," *Cincinnati Post,* June 25, 1923, Newspapers.com.

8. C. J. Savage, "Wise Counsellor and Whiskaway Equal Latonia Track Marks: T. C. Bradley's Racer Wins Easily, but Clark Colt Is Hard Pushed," *Louisville Courier-Journal,* June 24, 1923, Newspapers.com.

9. "Latonia Form Chart," *Louisville Courier-Journal,* June 21, 1923, Newspapers .com.

10. "Wise Counsellor Wins Harold Stakes," *Thoroughbred Record,* June 6, 1923, Babel.hathitrust.org.

11. "Racing Form," *Cincinnati Enquirer,* June 27, 1923, Newspapers.com.

12. Bob Saxton, "The Clown Is First in Derby," *Cincinnati Enquirer,* July 1, 1923, Newspapers.com.

13. Tom Ainslie, *Ainslie's Complete Guide to Thoroughbred Racing* (New York: Simon and Schuster, 1968), 221.

14. Estimates of one horse's superiority to another are commonly expressed in terms of the amount of extra weight the better animal would supposedly need to carry in order to have the inferior horse finish on even terms with it. Thus, stating that Swiftfoot is ten pounds better than Just Okay is expressing the opinion that, all other conditions being equal, Swiftfoot would have to carry ten pounds more than Just Okay for the two to finish a race at the same time.

15. "Fair Phantom Wins Clifton: Audley Farm Entry Shows Way to In Memoriam and Triumph—Whitney Fillies Arrive from East," *Lexington (KY) Herald,* July 6, 1923, Newspapers.com.

16. J. L. Dempsey, "Actuary Defeats Lady Madcap," *Cincinnati Enquirer,* July 12, 1923, Newspapers.com.

16. J. D. Mooney

1. Betty Trahan, "Furlongs and Finish Lines," *Lafayette (LA) Daily Advertiser,* May 9, 1975, Newspapers.com.

2. According to the *Lexington (KY) Herald* of April 21, 1922 ("Mooney Changes Stable: Brother of "Set Still" to Ride for California Man"), this nickname was originally borne by Mooney's brother Joe.

3. Will McDonough, "Saga of Jaydee and Black Gold," *Boston Globe,* April 30, 1982.

4. "Jockey Hayes Expires in Saddle," *Thoroughbred Record,* June 9, 1923, Babel .hathitrust.org.

5. Murray Olderman, "Between You 'n' Me," *Tallahassee Democrat,* April 17, 1961, Newspapers.com.

6. Jim Coleman, "Late Jockey Mooney Had Way with Horses," *Edmonton (Alberta) Journal,* November 18, 1966, Newspapers.com.

7. Ibid.

8. Lally Collyer, "Jockey Mooney Too Honest to Suit Some Tricky Horsemen," *Collyer's Eye,* July 19, 1924, Newspapers.com.

9. "Jockey Is Ruled off for Life in Latonia Scandal," *St. Louis Post-Dispatch*, November 4, 1925, Newspapers.com.

10. Frank Graham, "Graham's Corner," *Ottawa (Ontario) Journal*, March 5, 1951, Newspapers.com.

11. Barney Oldfield was the best-known American automobile racer of the early twentieth century.

12. Graham, "Graham's Corner."

17. Converging Paths

1. "Black Gold to Ashland," *Collyer's Eye*, July 28, 1923, Newspapers.com.

2. "Best Recent Workouts," *Collyer's Eye*, September 15, 1923, Newspapers.com.

3. C. J. Savage, "Rocky Mountain First in Lexington Feature with Chacolet Second," *Louisville Courier-Journal*, September 16, 1923, Newspapers.com.

4. According to McDermott's own testimony in an unpublished interview of June 30, 1974, with Jim Bolus (now part of the Jim Bolus Collection at the Kentucky Derby Museum), "it wasn't kosher to claim foul against another—regardless of the—how much he interfered with you or not. You left that up to the stewards."

5. "Lexington Form Chart," *Louisville Courier-Journal*, September 16, 1923, Newspapers.com.

6. Ibid.

7. Savage, "Rocky Mountain First in Lexington Feature with Chacolet Second."

8. "Black Gold Shows He Is Much Better Colt Than Worthmore," *Cincinnati Enquirer*, September 22, 1923, Newspapers.com.

9. Ibid.

10. Norris Royden, "Worthmore, Owned by Fayette Man, Captures $16,200 Breeders' Futurity as Fall Race Meet Comes to Close," *Lexington (KY) Herald*, September 27, 1923, Newspapers.com.

11. "Worthmore Is Victor in Rich Breeders' Futurity Event: Suspension Is Handed Owner for Reversal of Form Shown by Winner," *Cincinnati Enquirer*. September 27, 1923, Newspapers.com.

12. "One Bad Ride Is Coming to All the Jockeys?," *Collyer's Eye*, September 29, 1923, Newspapers.com.

13. "Racing Form," *Cincinnati Enquirer*, September 22, 1923, Newspapers.com.

14. "Black Gold Shows He Is Much Better Colt Than Worthmore."

15. "Worthmore Is Victor in Rich Breeders' Futurity Event."

16. Ibid.

17. Though Webb may have been looked at briefly in connection with the late money that came in on Black Gold in the Orchard Hall Handicap, he was no heavy gambler—according to the October 6, 1923, edition of *Collyer's Eye* ("Keep Close Eye on Actions of Jockey Heupel"), Webb seldom bet more than a hundred dollars on the outcome of any race, and there was no reason to suspect that he had any foreknowledge that Worthmore would run a subpar race. Worthington, on the other hand, was

known to bet heavily, accounting for the stewards' suspicions. He and Kelsay were later reinstated after the Kentucky State Racing Commission had it proven to their satisfaction in a hearing on April 25, 1924, that Worthington had had nothing to do with the last-minute bets, but by that time Worthington had dispersed his stable.

18. "Worthmore Is Victor in Rich Breeders' Futurity Event."

19. C. J. Savage, "Black Gold Outclasses Field of Juveniles in Feature," *Louisville Courier-Journal,* November 14, 1923, Newspapers.com.

18. Slim Chance

1. Frank Graham, "Graham's Corner," *Ottawa (Ontario) Journal,* March 5, 1951, Newspapers.com.

2. Ibid.

19. Season's End

1. "Track Notes," *Cincinnati Enquirer,* October 13, 1923, Newspapers.com.

2. "$10,000 Queen City Handicap Goes to Wise Counsellor," *Brooklyn Standard-Union,* October 28, 1923, Newspapers.com.

3. C. J. Savage, "Wise Counsellor Has No Difficulty Winning Queen City Handicap," *Louisville Courier-Journal,* October 28, 1923, Newspapers.com.

4. "Wise Counsellor Is Well-Trained Horse: Trainer John Ward Lavish in Praise of His Star Colt," *Miami Herald,* April 15, 1924, Newspapers.com.

5. Ibid.

6. R. T. Boylan, "Racing Notes," *St. Louis Globe-Democrat,* November 10, 1923, Newspapers.com.

20. The Road Less Traveled

1. Joe Palmer, "From Roamer to Whirlaway," in *The Blood-Horse Silver Anniversary Edition: A Quarter Century of American Racing and Breeding,* 3rd ed., ed. Ray Paulick (1941; Lexington, KY: The Blood-Horse, 1941, 2000), 56–154.

2. C. J. Savage, "Ginger, at Short Odds, Last in Field of Four," *Louisville Courier-Journal,* May 11, 1921, Newspapers.com.

3. "An Indian Woman Has Entry in Big Kentucky Derby: Mrs. R. M. Hoots Will Send to Post Black Gold, a Colt by Black Toney," *St. Louis Star,* January 23, 1924, Newspapers.com.

4. "Black Gold Has Hard Training," *Winnipeg (Manitoba) Evening Tribune,* April 18, 1924, Newspapers.com.

5. Frank Graham, "Graham's Corner," *Ottawa (Ontario) Journal,* March 5, 1951.

6. "Call Black Gold 'Iron Horse of the Turf,'" *Collyer's Eye,* March 22, 1924, Newspapers.com.

7. "Word of Warning by the Chief Clocker," *Collyer's Eye*, January 19, 1924, Newspapers.com.

8. "Webb Working Diligently to Have Black Gold Ready for Louisiana Derby Race," *Louisville Courier-Journal*, January 14, 1924, Newspapers.com.

9. "Filly Is Derby Dark Horse," *Collyer's Eye*, February 16, 1924, Newspapers.com.

10. Otis Hulleberg, "Take It from Pinky Brown . . . Ky. Pioneer May Graduate at Garden Memorial Day," *Camden (NJ) Courier-Post*, May 26, 1964, Newspapers.com.

11. French Lane, "Black Gold's History Human Interest Yarn," *Sioux Falls (SD) Daily Argus-Leader*, May 31, 1924, Newspapers.com.

12. Ibid.

13. "Call Black Gold 'Iron Horse of the Turf.'"

14. Ibid.

15. "Sport Improving at Fair Grounds for Track Folks," *Miami News-Metropolis*, February 8, 1924, Newspapers.com.

16. Lally Collyer, "'Luckiest Guy on the Turf' Has Derby Purse Cinched?," *Collyer's Eye*, March 1, 1924, Newspapers.com.

17. "Prices Shows Which Way Wind Blows," *Collyer's Eye*, March 1, 1924.

18. Walter Pearce, "Varidosa Hailed Champion Juvenile in South," *Collyer's Eye*, March 1, 1924, Newspapers.com.

19. "Black Gold Looms as Derby 'Dark Horse,'" *Collyer's Eye*, February 9, 1924, Newspapers.com.

20. J. L. Dempsey, "Edward Gray, in Spirited Stretch Duel, Defeats Sympathy," *Cincinnati Enquirer*, March 1, 1924, Newspapers.com.

21. J. L. Dempsey, "Poor Ride Cause of Defeat," *Cincinnati Enquirer*, March 2, 1924, Newspapers.com.

22. "Black Gold Does Sensational Work-Out," *Collyer's Eye*, March 8, 1924, Newspapers.com.

23. Ibid.

24. J. L. Dempsey, "Flintstone Clinches Title as Leading Horse at New Orleans," *Cincinnati Enquirer*, March 5, 1924, Newspapers.com.

21. Laissez Les Bon Temps Rouler

1. J. L. Dempsey, "Black Gold Smothers All Opposition in Derby Trial," *Cincinnati Enquirer*, March 7, 1924, Newspapers.com.

2. Sam E. Whitmire (Universal Service), "Indian Woman's Race Horse Is Backed to Win Big Derby," *Pomona (CA) Bulletin*, March 29, 1924, Newspapers.com.

3. "Black Gold Wins Sarazen Purse at N. O. with Consummate Ease, " *Louisville Courier-Journal*, March 7, 1924, Newspapers.com.

4. Dempsey, "Black Gold Smothers All Opposition in Derby Trial."

5. J. L. Dempsey, "Black Gold Scores, But Victory Is Far from Impressive," *Cincinnati Enquirer*, March 11, 1924, Newspapers.com.

6. Ibid.

7. "Black Gold, Favorite for Louisiana Derby, Will Be Given Route Test Today," *Louisville Courier-Journal,* March 10, 1924, Newspapers.com.

8. Walter Pearce, "Monday Derby Offers a Real Turf Problem," *Collyer's Eye,* March 15, 1924, Newspapers.com.

9. "Black Gold Has No Trouble Taking Feature at Jefferson Park," *Louisville Courier-Journal,* March 11, 1924, Newspapers.com.

10. Dempsey, "Black Gold Scores, But Victory Is Far from Impressive."

11. Tuscola ended up next to last.

12. "Black Gold Is Easy Winner in Louisiana Derby," *Chicago Tribune,* March 18, 1924, Newspapers.com.

22. Kentucky Bound

1. J. L. Dempsey, "Black Gold Romps to Easy Victory in Louisiana Derby," *Cincinnati Enquirer,* March 18, 1924, Newspapers.com.

2. "Black Gold Beats Crack Field in Louisiana Derby," *Buffalo (NY) Courier,* March 18, 1924, Newspapers.com.

3. "Local Turf Operators Not Impressed with Victory of Black Gold," *St. Louis Post-Dispatch,* March 18, 1924, Newspapers.com.

4. William McG. Keefe, "Viewing the News," *New Orleans Times-Picayune,* May 19, 1924, Nola.newsbank.com.

5. "Horsemen Start Hegira from Southern Tracks for Spring Races Here," *Louisville Courier-Journal,* March 23, 1924, Newspapers.com.

6. "Black Gold Arrives: Reaches Churchill Downs after Three Days' Journey," *Daily Racing Form,* March 25, 1924, www.drf.ky.edu.

7. "Black Gold to Louisville," *Daily Racing Form,* March 8, 1924, www.drf.ky.edu.

8. "Black Gold Arrives."

9. Sam E. Whitmire (Universal Service), "Black Gold Louisiana Derby Winner, Favorite in Kentuck," *Akron (OH) Beacon-Journal,* March 24, 1924.

10. "Black Gold Arrives."

11. "An Indian Woman Has Entry in Big Kentucky Derby: Mrs. R. M. Hoots Will Send to Post Black Gold, a Colt by Black Toney," *St. Louis Star,* January 23, 1924, Newspapers.com.

23. Preparations

1. Sam E. Whitmire (Universal Service), "Black Gold Louisiana Derby Winner, Favorite in Kentuck," *Akron (OH) Beacon-Journal,* March 24, 1924, Newspapers.com.

2. R. J. Boylan, "Rancocas Jockeys after Information on Black Gold," *St. Louis Daily Globe-Democrat,* May 16, 1924, Newspapers.com.

3. "Black Gold Arrives: Reaches Louisville after Three Days' Journey," *Daily Racing Form,* March 25, 1924, www.drf.ky.edu.

4. Sam E. Whitmire (Universal Service), "Black Gold at Louisville for Kentucky Derby: Winner of Louisiana Derby Takes Fast Workout at Churchill Downs Sunday," *Fort Worth (TX) Record,* March 25, 1924, Newspapers.com.

5. Ibid.

6. "Ward Candidates Showing up Well on Churchill Downs Gallops," *Miami News-Metropolis,* April 4, 1924, Newspapers.com.

7. R. T. Boylan, "Racing Notes," *St. Louis Daily Globe-Democrat,* April 3, 1924, Newspapers.com.

8. "Black Gold Arrives at Louisville; Not to Run at Lexington," *Lexington (KY) Leader,* March 25, 1924, Newspapers.com.

9. C. J. Savage, "Turfmen Still Discuss Abilities of Different Colts in 50th Classic," *Louisville Courier-Journal,* May 19, 1924, Newspapers.com.

10. C. J. Savage, "Cold Weather Checks Activities at Downs and Douglas Park," *Louisville Courier-Journal,* March 31, 1924, Newspapers.com.

11. G. F. T. Ryall, "Sarazen, Favorite in Winter Books on the Kentucky Derby, Works Daily Despite Lameness," *St. Louis Post-Dispatch,* March 30, 1924, Newspapers.com.

12. "35 Horses Saved in Downs Blaze," *Louisville Courier-Journal,* January 7, 1924, Newspapers.com.

13. Charles A. Reinhart, "Derby Horses Are Getting into Open: Chinn Buys Candidate; In Memoriam's Owner Wants Brush with Zev," *Salt Lake (UT) Tribune,* February 10, 1924, Newspapers.com.

14. "Wise Counsellor Not Sure to Start in Derby," *Collyer's Eye,* March 22, 1924, Newspapers.com.

15. Ibid.

16. O'Neil Sevier, "One Year Should Be Enough to Permit Bookies to Retire with Riches," *Cincinnati Enquirer,* March 23, 1924, Newspapers.com.

17. "Famous Horse to Run in New York," *Spokane (WA) Spokesman-Review,* March 2, 1924, Newspapers.com.

18. Reinhart, "Derby Horses Are Getting into Open."

19. W. C. Vreeland, "St. James, Best Looking 3-Year-Old in Training, Preparing for Classics," *Brooklyn Daily Eagle,* March 9, 1924, Newspapers.com.

20. Sevier, "One Year Should Be Enough to Permit Bookies to Retire with Riches."

21. "Sarazen Favored to Win Kentucky Derby," *Houston Post,* April 2, 1924, Newspapers.com.

24. Waiting Game

1. C. J. Savage, "Soft Track Will Not Stop Wise Counsellor in Derby or Preakness," *Louisville Courier-Journal,* April 16, 1924, Newspapers.com.

2. C. J. Savage, "Wise Counsellor Again Evinces Worth in Trial at Downs Oval," *Louisville Courier-Journal,* April 12, 1924, Newspapers.com.

3. French Lane, "Kentucky Eyes Black Gold as Derby Mystery," *Chicago Tribune,* May 3, 1924, Newspapers.com.

4. M. D. Fulcher, "Wise Counsellor Takes Last Workout before Leaving for East," *Louisville Courier-Journal*, April 26, 1924, Newspapers.com.

5. "Work by Wise Counsellor Off, According to Reports Coming from Maryland Track," *Cincinnati Enquirer*, May 5, 1924, Newspapers.com.

6. United Press. "Famous Horses Will Start in Tiajuana Race," *Visalia (CA) Daily Times*, March 26, 1924, Newspapers.com.

25. Falling Dominoes

1. "Black Gold's Price Drops to 15–1 in Future Books; East Partial to Sarazen," *Louisville Courier-Journal*, March 31, 1924, Newspapers.com.

2. "Wise Counsellor in Fine Workout; Critics Routed," *St. Louis Post-Dispatch*, April 23, 1924, Newspapers.com.

3. "Wise Counsellor Has Good Work," *Brooklyn Daily Times*, April 1, 1924, Newspapers.com.

4. Prior to 1932, the Preakness sometimes preceded the Kentucky Derby, and in 1917 and 1922, the two races were run on the same day, leading to some ill feeling between the managements of Churchill Downs and Pimlico. Sir Barton, now recognized as the first winner of the American Triple Crown, won the 1919 Preakness just four days after breaking his maiden in the Kentucky Derby, becoming the first horse to win both races.

5. "Favorite Steps Along: Wise Counsellor Travels Mile in 1:41⅗—Pulls up Tired," *Cincinnati Enquirer*, April 26, 1924, Newspapers.com.

6. Charlie Ross, "Chilhowee Gets Big Play in Winter Books to Cop Kentucky Derby," *Nashville Tennessean*, April 27, 1924, Newspapers.com.

7. Phil McCann, "News of Derby Eligibles in East," *Louisville Courier-Journal*, April 8, 1924, Newspapers.com.

8. Phil McCann, "Fast Metropolitan Courses Aid in Speedy Trials of Stake Horses: Zev Takes First Gallop at Jamaica Since Race with British Champion," *Louisville Courier-Journal*, April 25, 1924, Newspapers.com.

9. E. G. Hendy, "Sarazen Does Not Look the Part, Say Experts," *Collyer's Eye*, May 10, 1924, Newspapers.com.

10. "St. James in Preakness: Winner of Paumonok Will Be Shipped to Pimlico," *Gazette* (Montreal), May 5, 1924, Newspapers.com.

11. George Daley, "Max Hirsch Will Not Bring Sarazen Here for Kentucky Derby: Has Failed to Show Form since Defeat," *Louisville Courier-Journal*, May 8, 1924, Newspapers.com.

12. "Black Gold Most Heavily Backed Horse in History," *New Orleans Times-Picayune*, May 19, 1924, Nola.newsbank.com.

13. "Books Get Fine Break When Sarazen Is Withdrawn from Derby: Many Thousands Backed Favorite at Short Price," *St. Louis Post-Dispatch*, May 8, 1924, Newspapers.com.

14. "Sarazen out of Derby: St. James Is Doubtful," *Brooklyn Daily Times,* May 8, 1924, Newspapers.com.

15. United Press, "Out of Derby: St. James, Favorite, Has Accident," *Knoxville (TN) Journal and Tribune,* May 8, 1924, Newspapers.com.

26. And Then There Were None

1. French Lane, "Bradley Derby Colts Beaten in Lexington Stake," *Chicago Tribune,* May 8, 1924, Newspapers.com.

2. Associated Press, "Wise Counsellor Fails to Start and Disappoints," *Lansing (MI) State Journal,* May 8, 1924, Newspapers.com.

3. W. C. Vreeland, "S. C. Hildreth, St. James and Wise Counsellor Stir the Racing Circle," *Brooklyn Daily Eagle,* May 9, 1924, Newspapers.com.

4. Associated Press, "Wise Counsellor May Start in Preakness, According to Message from John S. Ward," *Pittsburgh Gazette Times,* May 10, 1924, Newspapers.com.

5. "Wise Counsellor Not Impressive," *Brooklyn Daily Times,* May 10, 1924, Newspapers.com.

6. Associated Press, "Wise Counsellor May Start in Preakness."

7. J. L. Dempsey, "Laurels Retrieved by Colt: Chilhowee Triumphs in Churchill Feature," *Cincinnati Enquirer,* May 11, 1924, Newspapers.com.

8. Associated Press, "Wise Counsellor May Start in Preakness."

9. J. L. Dempsey, "Invaders Are Due Tuesday: Cochran's Horses Will Be First on Scene," *Cincinnati Enquirer,* May 12, 1924, Newspapers.com.

10. Raymond S. Tompkins, "30,000 Fans See Fisher's Filly Win Preakness: Nellie Morse Leads Field of 14 Rivals Home at Pimlico," *Baltimore Sun,* May 13, 1924, Newspapers.com.

11. Harvey Woodruff, "Wise Counsellor Withdrawn from Preakness and Kentucky Derby," *Pittsburgh Post,* May 12, 1924.

12. *Louisville Herald,* cited by the Associated Press in "Wise Counsellor Not to Run in Kentucky Derby, Burton Says: Famous Colt Follows St. James and Sarazen into Retirement—Black Gold's Stock Goes up as Result of Action—100,000 Persons Expected to Attend Louisville Race Classic," *Pittsburgh Gazette Times,* May 13, 1924, Newspapers.com.

13. Associated Press, "Louisville Hears Wise Counsellor Is Out of Derby," *St. Louis Post-Dispatch,* May 12, 1924.

27. Derby Trial

1. "Racing Form," *Cincinnati Enquirer,* May 14, 1924, Newspapers.com.

2. C. J. Savage, "Black Gold Stampedes Friends to Him in Victory at Downs: Black Colt Goes Mile in 1:37⅘ over Track at Least One Second Slow," *Louisville Courier-Journal,* May 14, 1924, Newspapers.com.

3. Ibid.

4. Ibid.

5. Ibid.

6. "'Black Gold' Touted to Win: Bookies Favor Horse Owned by Tulsa Woman in Tomorrow's Derby," *Bartlesville (OK) Daily Enterprise,* May 16, 1924, Newspapers.com.

7. Lally Collyer, "Jockey Mooney Too Honest to Suit Some Tricky Horsemen," *Collyer's Eye,* July 19, 1924, Newspapers.com.

8. R. J. Boylan, "Rancocas Jockeys after Information on Black Gold: Sande and Fator, Who Will Ride Bracadale and Mad Play in Tomorrow's Derby, Question Trainer on Rival Three-Year-Old," *St. Louis Daily Globe-Democrat,* May 16, 1924, Newspapers.com.

9. Ibid.

10. C. J. Savage, "Great Jaz Beats Barrier and Easily Wins Downs Feature: Last Hope for Ward's Wise Counsellor as Derby Starter Is Lost," *Louisville Courier-Journal,* May 15, 1924, Newspapers.com.

11. Associated Press, "Black Gold Will Carry a Majority of Derby Hopes Today: Black Gold Derby Favorite, but East Pins Hopes to Sinclair Entry," *Nashville Tennessean,* May 17, 1924, Newspapers.com.

28. Golden Jubilee

1. French Lane, "Fortune Will Change Hands on the Derby: Estimated over Million Dollars Will Pass through the Mutuels Today," *Memphis (TN) Commercial Appeal,* May 17, 1924, Newspapers.com.

2. Walter Pearce, "Ky. Derby Aftermath Unpleasant to Many," *Collyer's Eye,* May 24, 1924, Newspapers.com.

3. R. T. Boylan, "Golden Jubilee Best of Recent Kentucky Races, Boylan Says," *Louisville Courier-Journal,* May 18, 1924, Newspapers.com.

4. George Daley, "Derby Viewed by Greatest Racing Crowd," *Pittsburgh Daily Post,* May 18, 1924, Newspapers.com.

5. Reuters—Gamont Graphic Newsreel. "The Kentucky Derby Golden Jubilee," Britishpathe.com. video file, May 17, 1924, https://www.britishpathe.com/video/VLVAEW 6DSRMUH12A463PHZW1ZUU9Z-1924-KENTUCKY-DERBY/query/kentucky +derby.

6. Boylan, "Golden Jubilee Best of Recent Kentucky Races."

7. United Press, "19 Starters at Post in Kentucky Derby: Sky Clear as Crowd Gathers," *Santa Ana (CA) Register,* May 17, 1924.

8. Ibid.

9. "My Old Kentucky Home," KentuckyDerby.com, www.kentuckyderby.com /history/traditions/my-old-kentucky-home.

10. Harry Grayson (Newspaper Enterprise Association), "Carry Back's Story Ordinary Compared to Black Gold Saga," *Warren (PA) Times-Mirror,* April 25, 1961, Newspapers.com.

11. Bill Corum (International News Service), "Only One 'Thank You': Matt Winn Has Soft Spot in Heart for Mrs. Hoots," *Kansas City Star,* January 20, 1949.

12. "Jockey Gives Credit to Horse: Winner's Rider Says Black Gold Is Best Racer He Ever Rode," *Louisville Courier-Journal,* May 19, 1924, Newspapers.com.

13. Ibid.

14. Boylan, "Golden Jubilee Best of Recent Kentucky Races."

15. Marguerite Martyn, "How Rosa M. Hoots 'Squared' Her Husband's Account with the Turf," *St. Louis Post-Dispatch,* May 23, 1924, Newspapers.com.

16. "Old Indian's Faith in Little Pony, Useeit, Justified by Derby," *Louisville Courier-Journal,* May 18, 1924, Newspapers.com.

17. Ibid.

18. "Roses Given Black Gold Are Placed on Hoot's Grave," *Tulsa Tribune,* May 25, 1924, Newspapers.com.

29. Derby Aftermath

1. J. L. Dempsey, "Credit Given Black Gold for Overcoming Double Case of Interference," *Cincinnati Enquirer,* May 19, 1924, Newspapers.com.

2. Peter Chew, *The Kentucky Derby: The First 100 Years* (Boston: Houghton Mifflin, 1974), 45–46.

3. C. J. Savage, "Turfmen Still Discuss Abilities of Different Colts in 50th Classic," *Louisville Courier-Journal,* May 19, 1924, Newspapers.com.

4. George Daley (New York World), "Mooney Gets $10,000 for Riding Black Gold to Victory in Derby," *Louisville Courier-Journal,* May 19, 1924, Newspapers.com.

5. "Driver of Black Gold to Be Heard on Radio Tonight," *Port Huron (MI) Times-Herald,* May 21, 1924, Newspapers.com.

6. Bill Corum (International News Service), "Only One 'Thank You': Matt Winn Has Soft Spot in Heart for Mrs. Hoots," *Kansas City Star,* January 20, 1949.

7. J. L. Dempsey, "Flying Ebony Fairly Oozes through Mud at Churchill Downs: Youngster Beats Good Ones over Heavy Track in Race for Juveniles," *Cincinnati Enquirer,* May 22, 1924, Newspapers.com.

8. "Black Gold: The Dream Colt," November 23, 2020, https://pastthewire.com/black-gold-the-dream-colt/.

9. Jim Bolus, *Derby Magic* (Gretna, LA: Pelican, 1997), 208.

10. Stanley Parsons, "Bookie Decamps with $100,000 on Black Gold," *Collyer's Eye,* May 24, 1924, Newspapers.com.

11. "Tom Kearney, Widely Known Bookmaker, Dies," *St. Louis Post-Dispatch,* February 24, 1936, Newspapers.com.

12. Jim Bolus, *Remembering the Derby* (Gretna, LA: Pelican, 1994), 173.

30. The Final Mile

1. Associated Press, "Fisher's Horse on for Derby," *Paducah (KY) Evening Sun,* June 27, 1924, Newspapers.com.

2. C. J. Savage, "Chilhowee Wins Latonia Derby by Nose from Fast Field," *Louisville Courier-Journal,* June 29, 1924, Newspapers.com.

3. Bob Saxton, "Chilhowee, in Desperate Finish, Captures Latonia Derby," *Cincinnati Enquirer,* June 29, 1924, Newspapers.com.

4. Savage, "Chilhowee Wins Latonia Derby by Nose from Fast Field."

5. "Track Notes," *Cincinnati Enquirer,* June 29, 1924, Newspapers.com.

6. "Murphy Plans Racing Season at Hawthorne: Entry of Black Gold Promised for Chicago Derby, Turf Official Says," *Decatur (IL) Herald,* March 22, 1924, Newspapers.com.

7. Ben Dahlman, "Black Gold Is Heavier Now: Long Rest Brings Increased Weight to Four-Time Derby Winner—Fine Chance in Third Special," *Covington (KY) Post,* September 3, 1924.

8. "65-Year-Old Boy Now Gallops Black Gold," *Covington (KY) Post,* September 3, 1924, Newspapers.com.

9. "Black Gold Back in Form for Fall Races," *Collyer's Eye,* September 13, 1924, Newspapers.com.

10. Associated Press, "Black Gold's Trainers Groom Him for October 11," *Manhattan (KS) Morning Chronicle,* September 24, 1924, Newspapers.com.

11. Ben Dahlman, "Sensational Work of Third International Candidates Keeps Horsemen Guessing: Sarazen Now Is in Limelight," *Covington (KY) Post,* October 9, 1924, Newspapers.com.

12. "Black Gold Ready for Races Again after Stud Stay," *Brooklyn Daily Eagle,* October 16, 1927, Newspapers.com.

13. Jim Bolus, *Derby Magic* (Gretna, LA: Pelican, 1997), 208.

14. Frank Graham, "Graham's Corner," *Ottawa (Ontario) Journal,* March 5, 1951, Newspapers.com.

15. "Black Gold Ready for Races Again after Stud Stay."

16. Bolus, *Derby Magic,* 209.

17. "All Sports," *Cincinnati Enquirer,* January 22, 1928, Newspapers.com.

18. Associated Press, "Black Gold's Death Causes Mourning in N. O. Racing Colony," *Alexandria (LA) Daily Town Talk,* January 21, 1928, Newspapers.com.

19. Ibid.

20. Peter Chew, *The Kentucky Derby: The First 100 Years* (Boston: Houghton Mifflin, 1974), 47.

31. Epilogue

1. "Sloppy Track Mars Day's Program at Fair Grounds Oval as Favorites Are Beaten," *Cincinnati Enquirer,* January 31, 1933, Newspapers.com.

2. John D. Ferguson, "Trophy Recovered." *Tulsa World,* May 1, 2005, https://tulsaworld.com/archive/trophy-recovered/article_05a428d7-52b5-5091-82ee-57e762a07e62.html.

3. Chris Goodlett (Director of Curatorial and Educational Affairs, Kentucky Derby Museum), email to author, July 27, 2021.

4. Illinois Deaths and Stillbirths Index, 1916–1947, Ancestry.com.

5. Frank Graham, "Graham's Corner," *Ottawa Journal,* March 5, 1951, Newspapers.com.

Index

Page numbers in italics refer to illustrations.

211

Horses in History

Series Editor: James C. Nicholson

For thousands of years, humans have utilized horses for transportation, recreation, war, agriculture, and sport. Arguably, no animal has had a greater influence on human history. Horses in History explores this special human-equine relationship, encompassing a broad range of topics, from ancient Chinese polo to modern Thoroughbred racing. From biographies of influential equestrians to studies of horses in literature, television, and film, this series profiles racehorses, warhorses, sport horses, and plow horses in novel and compelling ways.